Beyond the Spanking Stick

Anthony J. Major

iUniverse, Inc.
New York   Bloomington

Beyond the Spanking Stick

iUniverse books may be ordered through booksellers or by contacting:

iUniverse
1663 Liberty Drive
Bloomington, IN 47403
www.iuniverse.com
1-800-Authors (1-800-288-4677)

ISBN: 978-1-4502-5539-4 (sc)
ISBN: 978-1-4502-5540-0 (ebook)

Printed in the United States of America

iUniverse rev. date: 08/30/2010

To my father, who only months before his death inspired me to write. Unfortunately, he never lived long enough to see what all of his children would go on to do with their lives. Long live the memory of him, a man who in my eyes was larger than life.

Our deepest fear is not that we are inadequate. Our deepest fear is that we are powerful beyond measure. It is our light, not our darkness, that most frightens us. We ask ourselves, "Who am I to be brilliant, gorgeous, talented, fabulous?" Actually, who are you not *to be?*

—Marianne Williamson

Preface

Work began on this manuscript in November of 1986 when I found myself alone and bored senseless in an army barracks room in Kitzingen, Germany. Even while overseas and years after all my juvenile mischief had ended, I found myself telling and retelling the true stories of where I grew up. Eventually, someone suggested that I simply put it all into print. I finally accepted the advice and began the work.

The first draft of the book was entirely handwritten throughout the winter of 1986–87. I had miraculously cured my own boredom and laughed out loud the entire time as I wrote. I sipped on German beer for hours at a time and recalled the events of the past with crystal clarity. The second draft had then been typed out shortly thereafter with the use of a cheap, portable typewriter. From there, the pages were hole-punched and placed into a Mead three-ring binder. I began to show off my work. Although I was making progress, I realized that the time had not yet come to publish it.

After nearly ten years of continually revising the manuscript, the third complete draft grew much more advanced, and I ended up actually printing it out in the form of two booklets (Part 1 and Part 2). As an added feature, I placed my own hand-drawn doodles on the front covers. Those drafts had been photocopied at a Staples store in Aberdeen, Washington, and then saddle-stapled with the covers intact. I only distributed them to my immediate family. Unfortunately, most of those copies have been lost since then.

One of the biggest reasons that I had to write this book is simply the fact that truth is stranger than fiction. Few people actually believe that so many wild events could have possibly taken place and so many bizarre characters actually lived. But all of the events are true, and all of the characters are real. And as my own brothers and sisters can attest, I have always told the stories with incredible accuracy, never changing them from decade to decade. There has never been a need to embellish; as I have stated above, truth is stranger than fiction.

I believe that the time has finally come to release the following work. My dear mother is now in her eighties and claims that she will no longer be ashamed of the things her children have done and has given me her full permission to publish this book. Over thirty years have passed, and while the world has changed so much, this story hasn't.

Acknowledgments

I would like to express my sincere thanks to my older brother Chris, "Kit," a fellow writer, who shared his creative expertise with me as I continuously edited and reedited this manuscript. Also, I'd like to thank my younger brother Timothy for critiquing my writing and, in doing so, bringing some very critical points to my attention. Lastly, I'd like to thank Marci Ivic, who arrived at the most crucial time during the completion of this manuscript. With her on my team, she was indeed the one who pushed me through the eye of the needle and was greatly instrumental in making this book a reality.

Table of Contents

Introduction

There once was a mighty silver mine on the south side of Kellogg that lay just on the outskirts of town. Along with the famous mine also stood the once state-of-the-art ore-processing mill and its gargantuan smelter. So efficient and flourishing was the operation that it supported the entire local economy with its wealth. In its day, "Daddy Bunker" was the pride and joy of the Silver Valley, enriching the local residents with jobs, purpose, and prosperity. The heavenly manna that nourished the region appeared not on the ground but under the ground in the form of immensely rich veins of lead, zinc, and silver. And for nearly a hundred years, shiny ingots of these precious metals made their way from the foundry rooms in the local smelter and out into global circulation. (Some say Bunker Hill helped win World War II by producing much of the lead that went into America's bullets.)

Unfortunately, no matter how famous the mine may have been in days gone by, today there isn't much left of the original site. The huge industrial complex no longer exists, and neither do the two seven-hundred-foot smokestacks that had once reached gallantly into the sky like two twin towers of Babel.

Nearly a decade after the death of the company and the dismantling of the plant, the stacks were blown down, and the aging structures on the ground were mercilessly destroyed. Today, at the original location of the near-forgotten Goliath, new homes have been erected, and next to them, a recently developed golf course quiets the distant echo of the past. Down in the valley below, the town of Kellogg crumbles away while the new generation of Kelloggians lives and breathes each day almost oblivious to a proud era that has all but been lost in time.

I was there during the final days before the mining industry (and with it, the town) died. It was in those very streets that I experienced the triumphs of my youth, back in the days when riches flowed through the region, and the gears of the great Bunker Hill machine ground on and on around the clock.

In an ironic twist of fate, I just happened to graduate from the Kellogg High School and left for the military the same year that the fatal blow was struck to the community. By the time I returned late that December, the fateful announcement had already been made; the Bunker Hill mining complex was to be shut down forever, leaving thousands of workers unemployed and causing hundreds of businesses to choke and starve themselves into extinction.

However, in the final years just before the death throes of the great mine had set in, my friends and I experienced the greatest of any childhood years, in the greatest region, in the greatest state, and in the greatest country known on Earth. But, most important of all were the people of the town. This book is a testimony to how so many individual paths were crossed and countless lives were touched and changed forever by the boys who lived on Mission Avenue. It is only now that I realize that by telling their stories, I am actually telling my own.

It has taken many years for the following chapters to be published; they have been delayed because of a fear that I deeply harbored. I felt that after all the years of telling the tales, once they were put into print and shared with the world, I would never tell them again. Fortunately, I have decided to be brave, after all—for all of life is an adventure. And for me, my adventure began on a cold February morning in 1963 when I found myself gasping for air in a tiny hospital room in a small, unpretentious town known as Kellogg, Idaho. Always remember: life is nothing but a story, and this one is mine.

Chapter 1

The Halloween Dummy

It was Halloween 1978, and darkness fell quickly over Kellogg as the sun disappeared behind the mountains. I rushed home from the junior high school, walking as briskly as I could across town. As I burst through our front gate, I stopped and looked up at the October sky, watching for a moment as the thick blanket of clouds swept over the valley and ushered in the night. On this particular evening, a certain kind of darkness fell over me. I was in a race with time and stricken with panic. Hell, I was fifteen years old, and my trick-or-treating days were over. Everyone else was going to participate in the All Saints' Day celebration. What was a gentleman of my age suppose to do?

While the entire town prepared for a night of festivities, I paced the hallway in our small home and prepared for nothing. It was so unlike me. The pressure only grew worse. I had to dream up something new, and I had to do it fast. I would be damned if I was going to just sit around the house and let this once-a-year event pass without making my mark on the town.

This particular October day brought us no snow just like other years in the past—only a crisp, cold evening with a partially clouded sky. As I stepped out into our backyard, sizing up the Halloween setting, the stars were only momentarily visible (and there were no wolves howling), while the dark clouds tumbled across the heavens—eerie, but yet ideal for the perfect caper that waited to be hatched. Despite the tension, I knew deep inside that something would soon materialize. It always did, especially in the midst of the fierce competition that raged throughout our neighborhood. We fought over whom could create the most mischief. With so many hellions continually disrupting the peace up and down our street, no one dared to stand in our way—especially the neighbors.

1

However, there was one entity that did dare stand in our way—the local police. They felt our mischievous presence so strongly that the new officers of the Kellogg Police Department were always given a special briefing before a large map of the town. They were told to beware of a certain section of Sunnyside known as Mission Avenue. That was my street, and they had reason to fear us; we loved to harass them, and we saved up all our treachery for this one very special night. It may have been merely a grudge that we held, but at the time, it was as if they screamed out and begged for our personal attention.

With the minutes passing by, I paced the house racking my brains for specific ideas. I clearly envisioned many possible standoffs with the local law enforcement. During one of my many passes through our dining room, I realized that my baby sister, Allyson, knew exactly what she was doing. She balanced herself against the kitchen table and squeezed herself into a furry, pink and white bunny costume. She was wasting no time at all. Her grade school friends were waiting, and she was determined to go out and get some candy.

My older brother Kit was on a similar wavelength. He devoted serious time to bodybuilding, playing in a rock-and-roll band, and modifying his souped-up Ford Torino Fastback . Kit had the darkest hair and the widest shoulders out of all of us brothers. He idolized Arnold Schwarzenegger and not only built muscles but also groped women. I knew he was probably going to get some candy tonight, too, after seeing some of the beautiful creatures that he had catered to over the summer. He was already gone for the night—probably destined to come home late with his car headlights off, as he would traditionally idle down the street and then pull into the safety of our driveway. Outrunning the police was one of his hobbies as I once experienced while we reached 135 mph on straight stretch on the highway toward Osborn just east of Kellogg (just as a state patrolman aimed his radar gun at us).

This year, our house wasn't as full as it had been in the past. Some of my siblings had already left. My oldest brother, Peter, was already away in Butte struggling through his second year of engineering school at Montana Tech, and I thanked God he was gone. I couldn't handle any more of his lectures on personal responsibility or pep talks about the virtues of being like Clint Eastwood. Pete failed to realize that Dirty Harry was pure fiction. And, at this time, Jeri-anne had also ventured further away to attend college in Pocatello.

As Allyson wiggled her way into her costume, Phil sat just across the table from her in deep concentration as he systematically arranged endless rows of firecrackers and bottle rockets left over from the previous Fourth of July. He also had a plan. Like the rest of us brothers, Phil was built thin and wiry. With his round face and wavy, brown hair, he resembled Peter from *The Brady Bunch*. While an extremely affable nature showed on the outside, a tough, independent streak lurked on the inside, keeping Phil's personal boundaries very clear to everyone around him. He was liked by everyone, but took guff off no one. After being in a fierce fistfight with another neighborhood kid much taller than himself, his opponent pulled out a knife. Phil, seeing this, fled home and returned to the kid's back porch wielding a machete. He would never be outdone by anyone, especially on the wrestling mat. All of the Major brothers steered clear of team sports, yet gravitated toward the individual ones. We all wrestled. Out of all six of us, Phil was the best. I once watched him ward off a takedown attempt by his fellow wrestler. I winced at the way Phil slammed his forearm so hard into the guy's face that it twisted his head violently to the side and flipped him straight onto his back—another victory for my older brother.

While I paced and worried, Phil merely waited for his two protégés to show up—the Tobias brothers. They were so faithful to him and followed him anywhere, anxiously helping execute any of his plans, no matter how risky. If trouble were to arise, Phil would take the heat, as usual, and probably deflect any blame, surfacing unscathed—as usual. But as usual, I was forbidden to join them. Shit, it was time for me to do something unusual—something to top all previous known stunts.

In the midst of all the hustle and bustle in our little home, my younger brother Steve had planted himself on a mushroom stool in front of living room turntable. He had been playing a new 45 record of "Keep It Comin' Love" by KC and the Sunshine Band over and over and over ever since he had gotten home from school. I couldn't stand that song, but I never gave him as much shit about it as he did with me over Nicolette Larson's one hit "Lotta Love" that I had once purchased on 45.

I finally dived into the privacy of my room, one that I shared with several of my brothers. Although our house continuously buzzed with energy, I did manage to carve out my own space despite all the interruptions. My bedroom resembled an army barracks with the two double bunk beds, but as a kid, it really didn't matter to me. Science meant more to me than anything.

Ever since my kindergarten days, that little room grew into a virtual laboratory complete with soldering irons, rocket engines, chemistry sets, homemade radios, and countless, low-quality novelties from the Johnson Smith mail order company. I felt so at home in my room because it was the birthplace of many of my diabolic inventions—the secret transmitters, the nine-foot hot air balloon, the experimental rockets, and even my robot—Buster. Despite the intense emotional pressure that plagued my nerves this evening, I still believed that this night could still somehow end up being my finest hour.

Sometime near six o'clock, just when I was on the verge of conjuring up something wild during an imaginary game of Pictionary that I played with myself (trying to force a creation to materialize), God sent a savior right to my doorstep—and this savior arrived just like room service. It happened to be my best friend Dizzy Dan. Dan magically appeared on our front porch with an overnight bag in his hand and a Lee Marvin-style grin spread across his typically blasé face. He beat on our door with his balled-up fist, dying to share something truly ingenious.

After hearing the booming on the door, I raced over and opened it up. Right there and then, Dizzy strolled into our house just like the Cat in the Hat.

Not wanting to disrupt my train of thought, I motioned to Dan with a hand gesture, and he immediately followed me through the house, snaking around my other siblings and into my bedroom. Dan politely said hello with his deep, baritone voice as he passed Phil and his growing munitions pile. Phil had already begun stringing the firecracker fuses together, while my older sister Kim labored away with her hands in the soapy dishwater. Kim was two years older than I and was the middle sister. She was quite thin with short, dark hair that she always curled in the morning. She was highly energetic but avoided participating in sports. She always followed the current fashions by wearing bell-bottom jeans at every chance, even to church. Being in high school at the time, she and her friends had plans to do something across town, no doubt—probably at a friend's house whose parents weren't home to supervise them.

I slammed the bedroom door behind us, and I immediately blurted out, "What in the heck are we going to do? Phil's got all those firecrackers, and I ain't got nothing."

Dan, being the strong, silent type, stood there thinking of what to say while I began to babble on and on, "We could egg the cops. Or … or … or we could barricade the road or something. Or …"

Dan cut me off midsentence and finished my statement with three simple words. "Hang a dummy?"

I stopped right there and stared right at Dan. We were locked eye to eye. Suddenly, it was like my entire life passed before my very eyes. I instantly saw his entire idea, from start to finish, take place all in fast motion: the dummy, the noose, the swaying body, the maniacal screaming of the witnesses. My vision ended with a photo of our dummy on the front page of the *National Enquirer* tabloid, the one that is available at any grocery store checkout stand.

From that moment on, I became a firm believer in the philosophy that there is genius in simplicity. Dan had proved that on many occasions with his timely suggestions that he had famously illustrated with crudely, pencil-drawn diagrams of scientific apparatus that he had envisioned during many glue-sniffing episodes. He was full of ideas because he had all the time and space in the world to dream them up. Dan was an only child with no father at home to help raise him and a hard-working mother who was not always there for him. I was his friend—his only friend—just like Jenny was to Forrest Gump.

When I first met Dan at summer camp three years earlier, I thought that he was as normal as any other kid out there. But that first impression faded fast as he refused to participate in the popular activities with the rest of the group. Instead being sociable, he only wanted to embark on sneaky adventures. Although the term "slow" may be overly simplistic, Dan was definitely slow. He thought slowly, spoke slowly, and although thin and wiry like me, he moved slowly—that is, until the time I shot him in the eye with a BB gun. He moved fast then. Damned fast! Trying to get a piece of my ass. Dan really didn't have any other friends, and since he didn't have any brothers or sisters, either, our family unofficially adopted him.

Dan had a very deep voice and didn't talk much. Puberty had set in at an exceptionally young age, and because of that, Dan became a model for some of the local kids. He almost topped the bearded guy in my eighth-grade class. The first day of school, I thought that guy was our teacher. That was until I found out that he was just a local inbred and had an IQ of an oyster.

Mentally, Dan also had his quirks. He took plenty of time thinking things through before he answered questions. When he did speak, it was in very short verses, usually sentences with one word in them. Dan didn't waste his English. He wanted to get right to the point. With his curly, blond hair and sober expressions, the girls could have mistaken him for the strong, silent type, but he was almost as terrified of girls as I was. However, Dan did fantasize about getting picked up by older women—the Kellogg high school girls.

He had coaxed me on many occasions to walk around town at night with him. That bored me so much that I pressed Dan for an answer as to why he insisted on doing it. He claimed that he was "looking for action." Looking for action? What kind? I passed that phrase of his onto everyone else. They loved it and had marked Dan with that comment for life.

One night, his fantasy of being picked up by older women nearly came true. Just as we were walking across the bridge near the middle of town, a car whizzed by us but then unexpectedly screeched to a halt. The little compact backed up slowly to where we were and finally stopped. An attractive girl with long, dark hair rolled down the window. She quickly looked back at the other two girls, who were crowded in the front seat with her. The three of them giggled suspiciously. Finally, the girl turned to us and asked, "Are you guys tired of walking?"

Dan froze in his tracks. I could hear his knees knocking and his heart pounding. He humbly looked up into the sky to thank God for this blessing—these three beauties coming to our aid. With butterflies swimming in his stomach and a lump in his throat, he answered in his wavering voice, "Ssssure!"

The threesome timed their response perfectly and in unison yelled out the window, "Well, start running, then!" They burst out in cruel laughter and drove away, leaving Dan a shattered man.

While the thoughts of this dummy were still settling in my mind, Dan solemnly placed his hand on my shoulder with a sincere gesture and made it crystal clear to me that it was a moral imperative—our duty, our destiny—to get back at the local police for spoiling our summer fun.

"Tony. Think about it. The cops. They ruined so damned many kickball games of ours. And they interrupted so many … of our apple-throwing sessions. Come on, Tony!"

No. He was right. We had to give the cops a definite sign of our rebellion. The plan had an air of familiarity to it. Dan had actually mentioned this precise idea to me on several previous occasions, but this time, his voice inflection, his tonality, and his tempo were so precise and effective that it was I who screamed out that we must do it.

"We *have* to hang that dummy off the freeway overpass. We must, we must!" I said as I banged my fist onto to wooden frame of my bunk bed.

Now that both our personal objectives were in total agreement, we each did our part. Dan took his position on my top bunk. He began working on the strategy and the tactics. He began mentally rehearsing the timing procedures for the hanging, while I laid out the materials for the body on my bedroom floor.

I soon left him to his calculations, snuck into our laundry room, and retrieved a large stack of newspapers that Mom always kept under the laundry basket. For all she knew, I was working on a social studies project. It was relatively easy to sneak around our house because there were so many kids coming and going from room to room. I had so many siblings that on some evenings, half the neighborhood joined us for Monopoly, piano playing, or simply a viewing of the latest *Waltons* episode. Who were some of the strange kids that appeared in our house? Even I didn't know.

On my second pass through the house, I made off with a handful of huge safety pins from my mom's sewing kit (no one was in diapers anymore), and then I stumbled across some picture frame wire from the junk drawer. Scrounging the supplies grew into a pure scavenger hunt.

Back in the privacy of my room, Dan and I wadded up the newspapers and began stuffing the faded sweatshirt and ragged jeans with the balled-up clumps of newsprint. It didn't take long for the body to take shape.

I remember during sex education classes how fast a single cell can divide and form into an embryo in no time at all. Well, that was our dummy. We had newspaper pages dividing like cells. I really pumped our friend full of steroids when I reached the colored pages of the Sunday special edition. Soon enough, I began to make random correlations. For example, *The Six Million Dollar Man* just happened to be a popular TV show at the time, and as I saw it, our dummy was The Sixty Cent man (not counting Idaho sales tax, that is). I personally could eat lead and not gain an ounce of weight, so it was actually exciting to see our buddy put on a few pounds with ease.

Although I had thought of creating a dummy in the past, I hadn't spent any real time thinking through the final phases of constructing the perfect human specimen. If his forearms were too big, he'd look like Popeye. If his pects were too big, he'd need a bra. If his gut was too big, he'd look like Uncle Bill. I had only envisioned the end product and had unfortunately seen many versions of *Frankenstein*. So the final shape began to resemble that of a broad-shouldered monster.

We stuffed the pants and shirt until they were bulging, pinned a pair of shoes on him for feet, and then finally attached a pair of gloves on him for hands. But something still seemed to be missing. I was stumped. My hesitation began to plague the assembly line, and we were running out of time before the night's events were in full bloom. I was about ready to reach up and push the red button and call Lee Iacocca down from the office of the Chrysler plant. Once again, time was short, and I had to think fast.

Dan didn't have a clue what I was going to do next. He simply sat on the floor next to the dummy and scratched his head. On one more mission, I stealthily snuck through the house, fighting my way past my mom while she loaded up the washing machine. Damn! She was right in my way. I needed to get past her into the junk cabinet. I froze in place and realized that "the closer to Caesar, the greater the fear."

Luckily, she turned the timer on the dryer and left the room, hardly even noticing me. This time, I got on my hands and knees and started tearing into the laundry cabinet. For some reason, the vision of a bleach bottle kept popping into my head. I don't know why, but it did—probably because of the old substitute teacher that we had at school one day, the one with the squeaky voice. Roland Martell said that she drank a bottle of bleach when she was a little kid. Someone else said she smoked a train car full of cigarettes. Roland's story somehow stuck with me more deeply than the other one—and what a good thing, because it sparked a last-minute idea.

I discovered that one of the bleach bottles was nearly empty. Perfect! I dumped the rest of it down the drain (when I should have saved it for the substitute teacher) and then rinsed the bottle out. Back in the room and with the dummy on the operating table, Dan and I stitched the bottle into the neck of the sweatshirt with the picture frame wire. (Mom would have to rehang that stupid sailboat picture somewhere else. I needed this stuff.) A minute later—and presto! We had a dummy, and his worldly debut was only an hour away.

The entire time that Dan and I constructed the dummy, my youngest brother, Timmy, had been in the next room playing with Legos. He had a vast imagination similar to mine, but his true specialty was his meticulous organizational skills. Even with all the door slamming, newspaper ruffling, and giggling, he hadn't realized what we had been up to. He had been building an entire Lego city on Alpha Centauri.

Timmy also had an impeccable memory. He knew every model of Ford Mustang, ever year of production, every engine package, and every version made. I envied that ability of his just like I envied his ability to attract pretty girls. Just when I thought I had a voluptuous cheerleader eating out of the palm of my hand, she would meet little Timmy and fall in love with him. Gramma used to call him "Blue Eyes." I don't know why because we all had blue eyes. I guess he was just a little more lovable than I.

Eventually, Timmy had his fill of spaceports and lunar rovers, and so he systematically loaded up all his Legos and dumped them directly into a huge toy box. He had had enough of imagination time. His next move was to join us in the "real" world in my bedroom. Tim abruptly opened the door that joined the two bedrooms and unknowingly stumbled into the midst of our operation.

Initially, he gazed at me and then at Dan, and finally he gazed at the dummy. He looked confused at first. But within seconds, a devilish smile developed on his face, and excitement sparkled in his baby blue eyes. "Whatcha up to?" he asked.

I stood the dummy up and felt the firmness of the body, squeezing the midsection with my hand. "Hey, Tim, punch this guy in the stomach a couple of times," I ordered him. Without questioning me, Tim jabbed the dummy in the gut over and over and chuckled as he threw each blow.

"Harder, man! Hit him harder!" I yelled. Tim punched again but wasn't giving it his all. "Punch him harder!" I screamed. "Just pretend this is your teacher. Hey! Better yet, pretend it's Rod Thompson, that fat pig!" Tim jabbed faster and faster like a prizefighter. Finally, I danced the dummy around until Tim missed one wildly thrown punch and almost fell over. The three of us laughed.

The punching effort was actually a test to see how well the body had been constructed. Unfortunately, the stomach sagged. We definitely needed more stuffing to firm up his abs. Dan and I laid him back down and began wadding up more newspaper to stuff in him—that is, until my mom burst through the door with a load of freshly folded clothes.

She stopped still in her tracks and looked dumbfounded at first, just like Tim, and then she realized that we were up to no good. "Oh, no! Oh, no! You'd better not put anything in there with our name on it, or the police will know exactly who made that. Oh, no! Oh, no! You'd better not get caught!"

She hastily flopped the stack of clothes on the top bunk and instantly turned around and slammed our door on her way out of the room. Who said anything about the police? Shit. I was hoping she wasn't going to crack up on us.

Despite her short barrage of negative waves, we continued with our plan and stuffed as much newspaper as we could into our unsuspecting victim. Only one thing was missing—a personality. The dummy had no face except the blank, white bleach bottle head. Just then, another lightbulb turned on in my head.

I climbed up onto my bunk and pulled down my trusty Frankenstein mask that I had worn the year before. I placed the mask over the bleach bottle and snapped the rubber band strap around it. We now had a proud dummy with a unique personality. Ole Frankie was going to have the night of his life.

I was so proud of Dan with the way he had thought his plan out in great detail. Even though his perpetual motion machine and his compressed-air-powered wristwatch designs didn't work, I knew that tonight's project definitely would. The next step of his plan involved my brother Phil. We had to coax him away from the kitchen table.

I slid open our bedroom door and looked out to see if the coast was clear. Phil still sat at the end of the table, tying together the rest of the firecracker fuses to his demolition package. "Pssssst!" I motioned. Phil looked up.

"Pssssst!" I gestured again until he saw my head poking out of my bedroom door. "Come here!" I whispered loudly. "Come here. I've got something to show you."

Phil knew I was serious this time, and so he got up from the table, and I introduced him to Frankie. Phil's eyes lit up, part with envy and part with pride. He immediately pledged his support. In fact, he thought the idea was so great that he volunteered to hang the dummy himself. But hell, we couldn't let him steal the glory. Instead, we simply begged him to drive us across town in our family station wagon just to the bottom of the Hill Street freeway overpass.

When Phil strolled out of my room and up to the window to nonchalantly lift the keys to the family car, my mother had no idea what was to ensue next. "Ma, I gotta run to the store for a second in the car, okay?" Mom always muttered in agreement if she felt no sense of treachery. Phil had pulled off the first step in our trek into the Kellogg Hall of Fame.

Dan and I climbed into the back seat with Frankie between us. It was as if we were two of Al Capone's henchmen bringing in a star witness to prime for a stacked case against the G-men. After the drive several blocks from the house, Phil casually pulled over to the side of the road right below the freeway bridge and waited for all the cars to pass by and go their merry way.

When the traffic was clear, Dan and I each grabbed one of Frankie's arms and leaped out of the back of the car. We hustled up the long, steep cement embankment leading up to the unlit freeway above us. Our footing slipped on several steps from the loose sand and gravel that had spewed down from years of overhead traffic. But with each slip, we scrambled harder to get up the steep cement embankment. Cars whizzed down the interstate, shooting across the bridge without even noticing Dan or me huddling in the darkness with Frankie. Phil had already sped away seconds after we left the car. Good for him. Oh, well—Phil would have never talked if he had been caught.

While Dan and I crouched in the shadows and waited for the traffic to clear on the freeway, we looked down below us and noticed a slow-moving patrol car creeping down the street. I became terror stricken at the prospect being caught, while Dan displayed no concern whatsoever. He and I were so different. In fact, we were kind of like the two partners on *Paint Your Wagon*.

The landing zone at this time was simply too hot, so we glanced at each other and without words agreed that we had to leave Frankie in the ditch between the eastbound and westbound lanes of the interstate.

With one unmistakable cue from Dan, we both took off in dead sprint down the quarter-mile-long stretch leading to the Division Street overpass. We didn't stop running until we reached the other bridge. I feared that the people in the passing cars would surely suspect that we were up to no good by being so out of place—running down the middle of the highway after dark and on none other than Halloween night. By the time we reached the next embankment that led down to the Dave Smith Chevy dealership, my throat hurt. Damn, I had never been so winded. My chest ached while my heart pounded inside. Luckily, the cop that had passed below us a few minutes before was so preoccupied with a jelly doughnut that he didn't spot us. The project was still going according to plan.

Just to make sure things were okay back at Frankie's overpass, Dan and I regained our composure and walked as casually and inconspicuously as we could while we made a loop back around on Cameron Avenue, past Sunnyside Elementary School, and back toward the site of our future hanging.

By this time, it had barely turned seven o'clock, and the Halloween festivities were now in full swing in the residential areas of town. The little kiddies were going door-to-door collecting their rot-gut candy, the high schoolers with vehicles were cruising the town, and the other defiant teenagers like me were combing the back streets armed with eggs looking for targets of opportunity. All this meant that the local police had no other choice but to shift into the highest alert status. They were on such a high alert that they even placed a reserve police officer in the city's small blue utility jeep to help patrol the streets.

This particular nimrod selected to man the jeep just happened to drive past us as he vaguely remembered, between his gulps of Circle K coffee, that he was patrolling for mischievous youths. A flash of brilliance bounced throughout his cranial cavity. *Hot damn*! He suddenly whipped the jeep onto the little side street that we were beginning to cross. Using frantic hand gestures, he motioned for us to stop where we were. We complied by immediately halting. Normally, I would have outrun that tub o' lard, but this time I couldn't compromise the mission.

Dan and I thought for sure that we were nailed for planting Frankie up on the freeway. We waited patiently, almost standing at attention, for the public servant to get out of the vehicle, but he couldn't. He wasn't used to the military-style doors on this little reconditioned World War II relic. I couldn't help but laugh at the idiot fumbling with the door latch—obviously the town's newest rent-a-cop.

Finally, he opened the door and almost rolled out onto the ground. His coffee probably soaked the passenger seat and destroyed the texture of his crumb doughnuts. (Oh, well—the cost of justice being served.) He stood up, straightened his badge-wielding blue jacket, and stepped up to Dan and me. "Okay, boys, do you have any eggs?" I almost burst out laughing. That was like asking a doper if he had any dope or asking Jack the Ripper if he owned a knife. Luckily, we hadn't loaded up on eggs—yet. Frankie was our main concern.

The cop didn't believe our negative response and started to frisk Dan's jacket. Dan obediently stood very still in total (and somewhat sarcastic) submission. The officer came across a bulge in one of the side pockets and abruptly stopped his search. He began to squeeze the bulge in excitement, thinking he had found an egg and was going to make a nice mess for Dan. He strained so hard he almost grunted. After a few seconds, he tore into Dan's pocket and pulled out a group of keys on a miniature football key chain. That ended the cop's efforts. He should have felt stupid—if brains were dynamite, he didn't have enough to blow his nose. Without any eggs to be found, the cop had nothing to report and ended up driving away in disgust.

After wandering back to our neighborhood and meeting up with Tim and his stash of eggs that he had invested in with his paper route money, we bombed a couple of patrol cars from the dark spot in our alley until Dan and I realized that it was time to do the deed. We left Tim to his own fate and ambled up Hill Street to the scene of our future crime. At that period in local history, the "trick or treat" time was scheduled for a full two hours. Dan had planned the hanging for the middle of that period—precisely 7:00 pm—and we were definitely behind schedule.

Once we crossed the main intersection at Cameron Avenue, we briskly walked directly toward the overpass. To our surprise, we noticed two local police cars sitting together at the far end of the IGA parking lot. This was something we hadn't expected, and it could possibly prove to be problematic. These two bozos had to have been having a doughnut-dunking fest— or else they were too terrified to drive down Mission Avenue one more time. There was too much going on for them to simply be sitting there. Their presence put a little strain on our plans—either a little strain or a little more challenge. Luckily, where they were parked, their view of the overpass was blocked by the state-operated liquor store that stood next to the main sidewalk.

Dan, taking charge of the ever-changing situation, told me to stand at the corner of the liquor store building and keep vigil on the police. I stood still as he dashed down the sidewalk and up the embankment for a second time. Up on the freeway, while he prepared the noose and dragged Frankie into position, I was to signal him if they went on the move.

Just below the overpass, there were several bright streetlights illuminating the freeway on-ramp and also the little hamburger stand across the street called the Humdinger. I must have looked pretty conspicuous rubbing my back against the corner of the building like a bear while I glanced up at the overpass and then back around the corner at the police cars. In fact, I did look conspicuous enough to catch the attention of one lone pedestrian who had just walked underneath Dan's location and was heading right toward me.

With my shoulder blades pressed against the cold wall, I felt an infantile sense of guilt come over me. I felt as if I was ready to dump my cereal bowl over the side of my high chair. However, these feelings had never stopped me before. But this time, it was Dan ready to dump the dummy over the side of the bridge.

This slender young man in his midthirties seemed to strut along without a care in the world until he saw me. He noticed that I looked up at the overpass and then back around the corner. Now that I realized that I had attracted suspicion, I wondered what in the world was taking Dan so long.

Finally, after seeing me look up at the overpass several times and then back around the corner into the parking lot, this lone pedestrian began to wonder. This guy wanted to see what I saw. As he walked, he turned his head over at his shoulder for a brief moment and then looked back at me. He looked back and forth a couple of times as he continued walking.

Then it happened. As our intruder turned his head to look back at the overpass one last time, a figure appeared just behind the freeway guardrail. The figure rose into the air and then leaped over the side. It was a body, and it performed a very poor swan dive. The body fell through the air, halfway to the street below, until the rope tightened and yanked the carcass to a dead stop. Frankie hung lifelessly and swung from side to side in the cold air.

The unsuspecting pedestrian witnessed everything. He jumped into the air and screamed. He pointed wildly up at the hanging body. "Did you see that? Did you see that?" This idiot didn't quite make the connection that I was part of the whole act. Why else would I be standing there the entire time, by myself under the streetlights?

A few seconds later, Dan ran down from the dark overpass and past our shocked witness. The guy was speechless. He only stood there pointing at the dummy with his mouth gaping open.

So far, there wasn't any traffic, so Dan and I casually walked back through the intersection toward Mission Avenue. We only wanted to get clear of the hot zone and watch the response from a safe distance.

Still, the police sat in their patrol cars, not moving at all. Ironically, they finally started their cars and returned to patrolling the streets—but they drove off in the other direction! Boneheads.

Finally, cars began driving under the overpass. They swerved out of the way of Frankie. Some honked their horns. Others slowed down to look closer and make sure it wasn't a real person. Somehow, the traffic began to pick up, and soon there were streams of cars driving by to pay their respects like a funeral procession heading to the cemetery.

Within minutes, a tall, beefed-up, four-wheel drive truck pulled underneath Frankie, and a couple of high school kids got out. They climbed onto the roof of the truck. One began to pull and tug on the dummy, but Frankie didn't give. So the kid began to hang on Frankie with his whole body weight. Frankie's pants and sweatshirt began to stretch and stretch.

Frankie was getting longer! Without any luck, the guys finally gave up and drove away.

Somehow, word had eventually gotten to the authorities that a hanging had taken place. By the way the police cars rapidly approached and congregated under the bridge, it was clear that they either thought it was a real hanging, or they were getting the hell beat out of them by the eggings on Mission Avenue and needed to retreat to safer ground. Not only did one car show up … and not even two, but four cars—*and* the dickhead in the little blue jeep.

While the four police cars blocked off Hill Street and flashed all their blue lights, the little blue jeep drove up on the highway on-ramp with its orange warning beacons flashing.

Up above Frankie, in the cold night air, the reserve police officers spent several minutes untying the deadly rope that hung five pounds of the *Kellogg Evening News* and enough attire to make a nice contribution to the Salvation Army.

Like perfect clockwork, the moment the little blue jeep returned back down the on-ramp, all the police cars sped away in a desperate procession toward police headquarters. They were going to interrogate that dummy even if it took all night and ten thermoses of coffee!

Dan and I laughed all the way back to the house. When we got back, Phil was laughing about it, too, since he had driven by the overpass a couple of times himself. Kit, home from college for a few days, had also seen ole Frankie when he was out with a couple of old high school friends driving around egging other rival hot rodders.

When Dan and I explained that the police had taken our dummy away, one of Kit's friends, B. B. Kurtz, a short but very chubby young man who always seemed to wear nothing but plain white T-shirts, grew severely indignant. He shook his head from side to side while his large, framed glasses nearly flew off of his bulbous nose. B. B. wasn't necessarily a close friend of the family, but he was a fellow motorcycle enthusiast who shared the same love of motorbikes as all of us Major brothers. I was actually surprised that B. B. had the nerve to hang around with us after the tragedy he suffered just the previous summer when he showed up at our place with his brand-new, shiny Yamaha TT-550.

It was a big mistake for him because my oldest brother, Pete, who was the wheelie king, asked to ride the new machine. Pete, more overtly than Phil, would never be outdone by anyone. However, Pete always chose oddities in which to display his bravado. Instead of buying a Ford Mustang or Chevy Camaro like everyone else, he selected a 1969 AMC Javelin SST. The car was hot, all right—equipped with chrome wheels, a souped-up 390 CID engine, a four-speed manual transmission, and a white racing stripe. He did the same thing with motorcycles. Instead of a Honda or a Yamaha like everyone else owned, he bought a lime green Kawasaki 350 Bighorn. Although he was very thin and light for his age, he could pop the front wheel up on the heavy but powerful bike and wheelie it all the way up the high school road. All this was okay with me as long as he didn't mention Clint Eastwood again.

With Pete behind the handlebars of B. B.'s new Yamaha, he not only rode it up the street and attempted a wheelie, but he managed to flip it and roll it down the pavement, scratching up himself and the bike. Pete got up unshaken and with a look of shame on his face as if he had eaten a sour grape, simply picked up the bike, and audaciously asked to give it a second try while B. B. held his stomach and tried to keep from vomiting. Second mistake: B. B. did let Pete try it again, only to watch Pete flip the beautiful thing one more time and wreak even more damage to it—a broken clutch lever, a ripped seat, and even a dent in the fuel tank. But this incident was all in the past now, and on this Halloween night, B. B. shared the same disdain for the local police that we did. He ordered Dan and me to jump into his old station wagon. We were going to pay the police a visit.

We drove up Main Street very slowly and eyed City Hall. I noticed something peculiar in the window, and sure enough, I identified the object as Frankie. He was long, stretched out, and hanging in the tall, slightly tinted window of the police headquarters. Unbelievably, Frankie still kept his head. He still donned the Frankenstein mask that I had originally put on him. In total disgust, B. B. drove a block further and whipped the car around in the middle of the next intersection. "I want you guys to bomb those bastards!" he told Dan and me. "Reach behind you. There are a couple of cartons left."

He was right. Dan and I reached back and loaded our hands with eggs. As we drove by, we laid a barrage on the front of the police station. Egg yokes splattered against the tall, thick windows. Eggshells littered the sidewalks, and in the midst of all that glory, no one was even around to witness our crime, let alone pursue us. Regardless, the mission had been accomplished, and my earlier fears of being caught were never realized. Back in the safety of our driveway, Dan and I climbed out the car and stood with our chests puffed out in pride. We looked at each other, simultaneously held out each of our hands, and joined them in a victory shake. Dan displayed one of his rare smiles.

The next morning, I stumbled into my first period English class. I tried to appear as nonchalant as possible, but there was a buzz throughout the classroom. As I sat down at my desk and looked over at a young, thin, beautiful brunette that I had befriended since the beginning of my seventh-grade year, someone yelled out to me from the group in the back of the class, "Hey, Tony, I heard you hung a dummy off the bridge last night!"

Shit! I was just about ready to flirt with this girl when my cover was blown. She smiled at me, and her eyes sparkled with admiration. Back then, I didn't know that girls liked bad boys. I didn't want the credit for the hanging. I didn't want to be known to her as a prankster; I wanted to be known as a macho man instead. For six years, I was infatuated with this beauty, and I don't think she ever had a freakin' clue. I was simply too involved with my childish endeavors to take the chance and let her know how I felt. In the end, she was probably better off without me and would fair much better by marrying an attorney or something.

That same afternoon when I arrived at home just in time to watch *The Brady Bunch*, I stumbled across a small article in the local paper that reported the events of the previous night. It stated that the mischievous activity was minimal. The article went on to dryly say: "However, there was a hanging off the Hill Street Bridge, but the victim found his way to the waste basket at the police station." Just as I have always believed—the local cops and their sense of humor was as dry as day-old doughnuts.

We saved the newspaper, and when Jeri-anne came home for Thanksgiving, she continued her part as the family historian. For posterity's sake, she cut out the article and put it in one of the family scrapbooks. Dan and I were never caught and remained as anonymous heroes (officially, that is) just like the Delta Force teams of the military—all adventure, but no glory.

Chapter 2

Roland Martell and the Miser

About a month after I started the fifth grade, our teacher called the class to order and introduced us to a chubby, freckle-faced kid. She wanted us to give him a nice, warm welcome, for he was joining us from afar. Roland Martell had just moved into town from Missouri with his mom and older sister, and he needed to make new friends.

From the very first day, Roland didn't have any problem making himself feel at home. He strutted around the school like he owned it and instantly mesmerized the class with his stories—some so wild that they bordered on the supernatural. Roland, being a superhuman fifth-grader, was absolutely amazing. He had more brains than any teacher and could whip anybody's butt in any fight. He had been everywhere and done everything. Roland also could make most anyone laugh. In fact, he did such a good job at it that he challenged me for the position of class clown. With both of us in the same class, we realized that the room wasn't big enough for the two of us. Our poor teacher! Her stress level rose immensely with Roland and I teeing off to terrorize the other students.

Roland and I started to get along after a few nerve-racking weeks. In fact, we got along so well that I decided to trust him with a few boyish secrets of mine. (That was a mistake; exposing sensitive information was another one of his great qualities.) Moments after I confided my feelings about a certain girl to Roland, the teacher left the room. As soon as she was out of range, Roland turned to the class and blabbed out loud to everyone what I had said about having a crush on Carey Wilson. With our classmates in an uproar, I turned red in the face and denied everything. The more he pointed his finger at me and claimed it was true, the more I wanted to bite that stubby finger off.

I wasn't the only one he began giving flack to. One poor kid was asked to read a math word problem out loud. The kid began to read: "Jimmy weighs seventy el-bees, and Sally weighs sixty el-bees— " Roland exploded, "El-bees? You idiot! That's pounds! Seventy *pounds*, you idiot! Ha. What a saphead!"

After a few more weeks of his shit, many others began to dislike Roland as much as I did. I only started to truly worry about him when he challenged my reputation as the number one prankster. That was a title that I would defend to the end. One day in class, I thought I was being pretty clever by laying one tack on the teacher's seat when she was out of the room. For some reason, it fell off of her chair, and she never sat on it. The next time the teacher left the room, Roland snuck up to her desk and taped seventeen upside-down tacks to her chair. (He didn't want them falling off like mine did). The surface of her seat looked like a Vietnamese punji stick.

While we waited for the teacher to return, Roland waved his finger at the other classmates and threatened to personally kill anyone who might tip her off to what he had done. No one needed to point it out because it was very obvious—eight strips of tape and seventeen upside-down tacks.

The teacher soon returned only to discover the trap before she had a chance to sit down. She rushed Roland straight down to the office. The trip to Principal Beasley's office didn't bother him because with each stunt he pulled, successful or not, he got to brag about it. Roland reveled in all his stories about the experiences at the principal's office. Too bad he could never tell the truth. Principal Beasley really didn't have a bullwhip or cat o' nine tails. That was simply Roland—a bull-shitter in the worst way. The tales he told were so trashy and far-fetched that I knew they weren't true.

During one of his yarn-spinning sessions, we both discovered a mutual interest—motorcycles. Roland, realizing that, invented his best story for me yet. In this wild tale, he claimed that during the previous summer, he had taken a cross-country trip on his Suzuki 185. That by itself was hard to believe because, with a little bike like that going across country, he wouldn't have a butt left. He went on to tell of how his excursion went afoul the night he stumbled smack into the middle of a devil-worshipper gathering. Roland convincingly claimed that he arrived at the scene precisely when they were performing a human sacrifice. For some reason, he gave away his position, and according to him, he quickly jumped back on his bike and fled the scene. What then ensued was one hell of a chase. The ironic part about the whole story is that, a week later, I went to the Rena Theater and watched a movie with the exact scene that Roland had described. The movie was *Race with the Devil,* starring Peter Fonda.

Finally, after another month of close contact with Roland at school, I felt so friendly toward him despite his irritating habits that I invited the continental adventurer over to our house after school. That guy couldn't help but find sarcasm in everything he encountered. While in front of our TV set, he sang along with the *Flintstones* theme song, swinging his arms and tapping his foot, and he said they would truly have a gay old time! At that age, I wasn't quite sure what a lot of what he said meant, but I knew that I shouldn't dare ask any adults about it. In addition to the *Flintstones*, Roland particularly loved making fun of the peanut butter commercials. For the Jiffy peanut butter commercial, he had a little act that he always performed. He stood up and said, "First you *Jiff,*" and then he would hike his leg up, pass gas, and continue, "—then you whiff!" and then he'd sniff the air. That little joke went right along with a story that he told of how he used to hide in the bushes outside his house and wait for the postman to arrive with the mail. Roland claimed that when the postman came within earshot, he would chant, "Postman, postman, greasy hair, cut the cheese into the air." He chanted over and over as he simultaneously pounded his balled-up first into the palm of his other hand.

When I asked Roland what the chant meant, he simply shrugged his shoulders and said, "Hell, I don't know, but it used to scare the hell out of the postman." I am sure it did—seeing a chubby kid in the bushes doing that would have scared the hell out of me, too. But just like always, I discovered similarities between Roland's stories and certain Hollywood productions. There just happened to be a *Star Trek* episode where deranged children gathered on the bridge of the starship *Enterprise* and chanted a magical chant as they pounded their balled-up fists into their palms just as Roland had described about himself.

Not only was Roland a pathological liar, he was also very filthy minded. He stated that he had once wiped peanut butter on his dog's testicles. I asked him why in the world he would do that. Roland said that his dog always licked his testicles, but this time he'd really have something to lick. Never before and never again would I ever meet someone who was so determined to turn the world upside down.

Although we had learned to throw eggs at police cars on Halloween by ourselves, Roland introduced the activity to us as a year-round sport. He mentioned that eggs cost too much and that, without an allowance or any paper route revenue, eggs were a scarce commodity. In our neighborhood, that was no problem because we found plenty of substitutes. Our entire block had an abundance of apple, plum, pear, and peach trees—ours for the picking!

With Roland now a permanent part of our gang, we regularly gathered up bags of apples or plums and positioned ourselves in the dark places behind a few old ladies' hedges just houses down from ours. Sometimes, when we got too lazy to walk halfway down the block to our favorite hiding spot (or perhaps because we just got a little braver), we would boldly stand in the shadows at the end of our alley. We bombed any car that came by and dared them to chase us.

The thrill and adrenaline rush that came from hurtling a rotten apple at a car, knowing the driver was going to kill you if he caught you, was just too much. If I had done this as an adult, I would have said it was better than sex, but back in those days, I didn't want to catch girl germs. All I knew was that it was better than behaving.

There was one problem that I soon discovered that plagued Roland— he often got caught. When I could run like a deer, scale a fence, crawl under a car, sneak through a narrow passage, and not stop until I was safe, Roland—being overweight—got caught quite frequently. Fortunately, he could sometimes talk his way out of it and successfully blame it on someone else.

On one cold October night, we tried a new location. Despite the mystical powers and evil forces surrounding the Mrs. Welman estate, Roland, Tim, and I decided to venture into her yard with a box of mushy plums. The large popper-berry bush on the edge of her yard, with the bright streetlight shining on it, cast a beautiful shadow for us to hide in. We often played around the huge bush during the day catching bees in glass jars and popping the white berries by squishing them with our fingers. It was as fun as popping the bubbles in a sheet of bubble wrap packaging. On this occasion however, being nighttime, we couldn't risk making any noise. We had other reasons for being there—we were on a mission. With the high-intensity sodium light burning brightly from the light pole and the contrasting shadows, no one could see us lying in the open stretch of grass and preparing for our strike.

After we sat in the cool, moist grass for a couple of minutes, a few cars drove by. We cut loose on each of them with a barrage of plums. Splat! Splat! Splat! The first few drivers slowed down, but none stopped. Shucks! Finally, a Chevy El Camino drove past our line of fire. The rumble of the dual exhaust turned out to be an obvious display of the driver's temperament.

This may have been someone we didn't want to mess with. But adrenaline overruled logic, and we let the plums fly. Two of Roland's and Tim's projectiles hit the driver's side of the car, but my plum grazed the top edge of the half-rolled-down window. It fragmented, spraying juicy particles all over the driver's face. Instead of "*Six Seconds in Dallas*," it was "*Three Plums in Kellogg*." Our crime was committed. The Warren Commission would have found one plum seed, an angry driver, and bubble gum wrappers on the grassy knoll by Mrs. Welman's house, but no witnesses.

This time, we had a live one. I imagined how plum chunks would have felt and how mad this guy must be. This driver, instead of slamming on his brakes, mashed on his accelerator and raced on down to end of the block at record speed. He skidded to a quick halt at the stop sign. By that time, Tim and I had already jumped to our feet, run out of Mrs. Welman's yard, and run through the alley to the safety of our own backyard.

We just barely made it through our back gate when tires squealed and headlights veered around the corner and beamed down the unlit alley. The driver wasted no time in reaching the back of Mrs. Welman's house. He hit Mach 2 in first gear, bashed into garbage cans, flattened a couple of scrapping alley cats, and even turned his car in a racing-style slide in the churchyard gravel. He then nosed his car directly onto the grass of Mrs. Welman's yard. He had instinctively plotted our position by the trajectories of the fired plums.

Tim and I stood on our back patio, safely catching our breath. Where was Roland? Instead of sprinting with us, Roland made an attempt at climbing the fence over into our yard. His lard wouldn't allow it. Roland ended up slithering back down, trapped. He stood there frightened, pinned to the fence by the high beams of our victim's El Camino.

The car door flew open, and a large, bearded man got out and walked toward Roland. Through the cracks in our tall fence boards, all we could see were the blinding headlights and a large, ominous figure with clenched fists slowly approaching Roland.

The man began yelling, swearing, wiping plum juice off his face, and he shook Roland around like a rag doll. Tim and I shuddered, hoping Roland would survive. Luckily, a moment later, we heard the car door slam shut and the car drive away. Moments later, Roland staggered down the alley and through our back gate. He had a crushed spirit. He said he didn't feel good and couldn't throw any more plums with us that night.

Tim and I released Roland from duty for the remainder of the evening and told him that we'd see him at school the next day. By the time we arrived on the playground the following morning, Roland had already been making up all kinds of versions of what happened the night before. In one version of Roland's story, he said that he almost kicked the dude's ass, but when the guy started to cry "uncle," Roland let loose of the death grip he had on the poor driver's throat. Roland apparently had fully recovered from the previous night's incident.

We continued our bombing streak for several years and had chalked up quite a kill ratio. Tim and I went as far as to tape a piece of paper to the wall above our bed and had drawn a figure of an apple (or plum) for every car that we hit. My mom came in a few times to put away our clothes and wondered what the fruit figures meant. We told her it was an experiment in nutrition.

After Roland and I hung around together in those first few months of our friendship, he started to discover all the wonders of our neighborhood. When he got to know some of our bizarre neighbors, he singled out a few of them for specific reasons and began his own crusade to harass them. He called them old coots, geezers, codgers, fogies, veggies, and a bunch of other names that I had never heard before. With Roland and his newly developed people skills helping me identify unique personalities, I began to discover a wealth of lunatics dwelling within walking distance of our house. I uncovered some real gems, especially when I first took over the local paper route.

I had spent my first month delivering the papers without seeing much of my customers. I diligently left the papers where the previous papergirl instructed me to do so. Not until collection time did the real mysteries begin to be exposed and personalities revealed. Some of the people whom I thought might be the nicest at first ended up being the biggest jerks, and some of the biggest weirdoes were the friendliest and gave me the largest tips. These people were just happy to find someone other than a shrink to talk to.

One particular customer lived in a garage. Actually, he owned a large, four-unit garage complex on the street corner near our egg-throwing position. He lived in the cramped quarters located in an addition attached to the back corner of the building. Each of his four garages had large bay doors with small, dusty windows in them. The garages were basically used as storage units—all except the one on the north side. This was the one where this strange little man used his table saw to regularly saw up bloody bones. Each time this weird little character returned home from a jaunt across town, he parked his dark purple Volkswagen Karmann Ghia under a carport in front of the entrance to his tiny hovel.

I remembered seeing him on many occasions drive through town in his dirty old car, and now I was finally going to have a chance to meet him. From the very first day that I had knocked on his door and witnessed the condition of his creepy abode, I became totally fascinated. It was obviously my duty to alert all my friends to this man's presence. After describing him to my mother, she explained to me that his name was Carl Zarkosky. Supposedly, he was very wealthy and owned a lot of property in town. She warned me that he was a very bizarre person with many peculiar tendencies and for me not to get too close to him.

Apparently, by the clutter near his door, Carl loved animals very much. He left countless dishes of tasty food out for them. However, the things he fed them were very questionable.

Once I came by to deliver the paper and noticed that Carl had just laid out a bloody Styrofoam meat tray (it probably had hamburger in it originally). On the tray were several large scoops of chocolate ice cream—a nice treat for the dogs to snack on (just as long as it didn't ruin their dinners). I know Carl was only trying to be thoughtful, but most of the dogs were turned off by the culinary concoction and refused to touch it. After several days, the ice cream had melted down and had cast itself into a semisolid form similar to a Jell-O mix. Although no pooches dared to eat this, the flies sure did. I could see them fly up to the trays every day with huge smiles on the faces and red-checkered bibs around their necks ready for their daily feast.

One day, our dog Oscar came with me to deliver papers. He smelled the ice cream and blood mix and started to lap up the gooey slime in the little tray. I yelled and screamed at him to get away, but he loved it too much. I had to kick him to get him to stop, and he almost bit my foot off for disturbing his snack. Oscar was a very sick-minded pup. He licked all kinds of gross things. Luckily in this case, even with his cast-iron gut, he could only glug down a few mouthfuls before looking for a mud-puddle chaser.

After I got home and quarantined Oscar for a couple of days in our shop, I realized that he wasn't going to die. He didn't as much as throw up. Miraculously, Oscar went on after that unusual snack to live to a ripe old age. It must be a similar phenomenon for the old guys who drink a bottle of whiskey and smoke two packs of cigarettes a day and still live to be one hundred.

My first month of paper delivering went by, and the big day of collection finally came. I got the opportunity to pound on Carl's door and demand my money. I hit the door hard, but since I didn't get an immediate response, I peered through the large, square, cobweb-lined window. I could barely make out some of the features in the tiny room. I could see a small sink against the far wall that was filled with empty dog food cans. A stack of TVs filled one of the corners. The one and only TV operating happened to be an RCA on the very top of the pile. Suddenly, in the midst of my unauthorized examination, a figure appeared in the room under the dim light. It lumbered slowly toward me. I took a couple of steps back away from the door.

When this creepy little man opened the door, a blast of stale, rotten air blew at me. I bent over and gagged. Directly behind Carl's legs, a dog stood panting for oxygen and did a little dance, trying to step around Carl and just get outside (probably for a breath of fresh air). I looked up and found myself standing face-to-face with a vampire-like person.

Carl stood only about five foot two. He was a small, almost dwarflike person, with very pale skin and with two-day-old beard stubble covering his face. Instead of wearing normal clothes, Carl wore a very old, black tuxedo and a white shirt (the style with all the little ruffles on the front). I knew he hadn't just returned from a wedding since the cloth appeared to be extremely soiled from being worn for weeks—if not months—since its last washing. He may have just climbed off of one of Titanic's long-lost lifeboats. In addition to the soiled outfit, flesh-colored makeup had rubbed off his face and onto the collar of his white shirt. Carl's gray, curly hair rose high into the air like Albert Einstein's.

After a moment of us staring at each other, he opened his mouth to speak. Just as he moved his jaw, I saw a greenish brown film caked around his lips and in the corners of his mouth. (Later on, I found out that he habitually chewed Copenhagen snuff.) In addition to the slime around his mouth, Carl's teeth were also severely rotten. I could smell the stink of his breath from his first words.

"Yes, bud?" he asked me. Instead of talking plainly, he spoke with a slight accent. He called everyone "bud," but it wasn't *bud*—it was *bawd*. "What can I do for you, bawd?" he added.

"I'm here to collect for the paper," I responded.

"Which paper, bawd?" Carl asked.

"*The Daily Chronicle*," I replied. This same line of questioning went on every time I came to collect in the future. He'd ask me what paper and then ask how much it was. Each time, I told him two dollars and twenty-five cents, and he'd slowly turn around without saying anything else and head for his money can (an overflowing coffee tin). I'd always wait patiently for him to come back because it gave me a chance to peek inside his place.

As far as I could tell, it was merely a one-room dwelling with a sink, a potbelly stove, and junk stacked everywhere. Other than the TV playing in the corner, a dull, small-wattage bulb hung above the sink by a twisted pair of wires. The filament inside the clear bulb glowed a dull yellow hue and provided the only light for him to see with. The walls of his room were nothing more than moist mounds of crumbling cement.

When Carl left to get his money, he always came back to the door with a handful of tarnished coins. His money-handling technique drove me crazy. Instead of just counting out nine quarters or even a series of dimes and nickels, Carl chose to count out the coins as they happened to appear in his fingers.

"That's twenty-five, bawd, thirty, bawd, thirty-one, bawd, thirty-six, bawd ..." He didn't care in what increments you got your money, just as long as you got it. Before I left each time, Carl and I spent a few minutes talking about life in general. A few of his pet peeves dealt directly with the local authority figures. He made it very clear to me that he no longer had any respect for bureaucrats who "sat in those swivel chairs" at City Hall.

According to my mom, Carl used to attend service at the Catholic Church and participated as one of the ushers passing around the collection plate—that is, until he lost respect for them as well when someone insulted him. He decided to boycott church after that, as well as any form of personal hygiene.

Since the very first time that I met Carl, I couldn't help but run back to school each day and tell everyone the tales of the miser from Transylvania who lived in an old garage. The stories fascinated Roland more than anyone else. He was adamant about meeting Carl as soon as possible.

Roland's golden chance came one afternoon when I took him with me on my paper route. Even though it wasn't time to collect, we purposely knocked on Carl's door to get him to come out as an exhibit. As soon as Carl opened his door and showed his face, Roland burst out laughing. He didn't care if Carl got upset or not. Luckily, Carl's brain was deteriorating so rapidly that he didn't understand that we were making a mockery out of him. Each time Carl called us "bawd," Roland called him "bawd" right back.

After delivering the papers that afternoon and returning my paper bag to the house, Roland and I ventured back to Carl's place. Before we could reach his front door, we had to pass by the north garage bay. Through those windows, we immediately noticed a figure moving about inside. It was Carl. He was working on something and making a lot of noise in the process. When we got closer, we noticed that Carl had the table saw going and was sawing up large bones that looked like human femurs. Roland gasped in horror. He quickly jumped back and slammed himself up against the brick wall of the garage as if to keep from being spotted by the enemy.

"What is it?" I asked.

Terror filled Roland's eyes as he began to breathe in short, quick breaths. He braced himself with his palms against the bricks and started to hyperventilate. I asked him time and time again what the matter was. Roland whimpered and moved his lips, trying to speak. His behavior started to scare me. Finally, he gathered his thoughts enough to say, "He's … he's … sawing somebody up! He did somebody in, and those are the bones!"

I couldn't believe it. I just couldn't imagine that Roland could be so serious about it, but he put on such a good act that it began to frighten me. Meanwhile, the screeching and whining of the table saw echoed inside the garage bay just a few feet away from us.

"We've got to stop him!" Roland declared. He leaned over to the glass window and violently rapped on it with his knuckles. We both took off running for cover. I ran and hid with Roland around the far corner of the building. The noise subsided for a moment, but when the hideous sawing resumed, we knew that Carl wasn't coming out. Roland snuck back up to the bay door and beat even harder on the glass, and then he immediately dashed back to hide next to me.

Finally, the table saw stopped momentarily, and Carl peeked through the filthy glass. After seeing nothing outside, Carl returned to his bones and resumed his sawing. Roland insisted on beating on the glass again. He had to stop Carl from sawing those bones and murdering more people.

This time, when Roland rapped on the glass, the saw immediately stopped running. Roland took his spot next to me once again and then yelled out a word of warning for Carl. He cupped his hands to his mouth and yelled out, *"We know what you did, Carl! You won't get away with it!"*

Carl raised the garage door and took a few steps outside. After a quiet moment of looking up and down the street and not seeing anything, a baffled look came across Carl's face, and he lowered the door only to return to his saw. We let it go at that for the evening. Roland figured that Carl was onto us now and wouldn't kill anyone for a while, at least. Since I didn't want Roland to cause any more trouble with Carl, I made him go home. I never did know if Roland was seriously that frightened or if it was just an act he put on. It's one of the secrets that he'll probably take to his grave.

The next day at school, the stories were spun—and they went on for weeks. According to Roland, Carl ate dog food, did nasty things with his cats, and murdered people for a hobby. Most of our classmates were so fascinated with the tales that they wanted us to start a fan club. To keep the moment going, Roland desperately needed new material from Carl to work with. We somehow had to coax Carl into going public.

On one the nicest weekends during this particular autumn, Roland came over to our house and immediately attracted a following of intrigued neighborhood kids. They wanted to witness the great Roland Martell in action. So up and down the alley we strolled, looking for a heavenly sign. At one point, we started to pass a lush, green garden protected by a white picket fence. Roland suddenly spotted a long, thick, ripe squash still attached to its vine. He clumsily climbed over the fence (a rare feat for him) and ripped it up from its resting spot. Roland handed the forbidden squash to the rest of the kids as he climbed back over the fence. I asked Roland what he planned to do with it. With the usual Roland-type smile, he said, "I'm going to give it to my buddy Carl!"

The entire pack of kids followed Roland over to Carl's house. All we had to do is carry torches—we would have fit the bill perfectly for an audition for the *Frankenstein* lynching scene. Near the perimeter of Carl's house, most of the kids hid behind trees and even a garage a hundred yards away as Roland approached the carport. None of us wanted any part of this. Roland didn't want to get out of our sight just in case he fell victim to Carl's kidnapping and murder routine.

In a prime position, Roland stood next to Carl's Volkswagen and raised the huge squash over his head with both hands. He then used all his might and heaved it through the air at Carl's door. What ensued next was an earth-shattering bang that reverberated throughout the entire neighborhood. It was the squash heard around the world. The green vegetable slammed into the door and by all means should have smashed it in. We all ran like a bunch of cowards and regrouped in the safety of our backyard.

After patting Roland on the back and congratulating him for a job well done, we dismissed the rest of the neighborhood kids and told them to go home and get some hot cookies. Roland actually felt disdain for most of the other kids because they were too gutless to do anything themselves. He didn't mind performing for a sample stunt now and then, but enough was enough for the nonpaying audience.

About thirty minutes after the squash-throwing incident, Roland and I inconspicuously walked past Carl's place. The door looked perfectly intact, and to our surprise, there was no squash to be found anywhere. Roland's first conclusion: Carl had taken it inside to eat it. The following Monday at school, Roland broke the latest story about the miser from Transylvania. He told everyone that Carl took a break from eating dog food and switched to squash for a week.

Since Roland's condescending attitude toward the other kids became a little more evident, one of the kids from an economically challenged family decided to prove that he was worthy to hang out with us. This particular boy and his two less-than-hygienic siblings were known as the "Dirt, Grit, and Grime Brothers". "Grit", the middle brother, teamed up with me one day in an attempt to earn Roland's respect by committing his own audacious acts against the unsuspecting Carl. A week after the squash incident, Grit came with me on my paper route and got a real thrill of approaching Carl's mysterious carport so closely.

Grit wasn't the worst smelling of his brothers. He got better with time and kept his bed wetting down to only three days a week. Grit's pet peeve was washing his face. He just didn't do it very often. Regardless of hygiene, I liked a man with the spirit of adventure. Grit had it this day, and to pique his curiosity even more, I mentioned to him that I had discovered an interesting habit of Carl's. Carl always left his car parked on the cement pad without the parking brake on and with the transmission in neutral. I made reference to the slope of the carport that led right down into the road. We both got an idea. I was tempted to draw an illustration supporting the physics of my plan just like on the Coyote and Road Runner cartoons, but we went straight into action.

Grit came with me on the paper route and anxiously helped me do the deliveries. We then returned to the scene of our next crime. After quickly probing the surroundings, we felt that we were safe from any witnesses. While Carl sat inside watching *Frankenstein Meets. the Wolfman* on Channel 4 and sympathizing with Lon Chaney, Grit and I pulled on the bumper of the little Volkswagen and let it roll down the slope toward the street. Once it started to roll on its own, Grit and I ran down the street and toward the safety of my own backyard (which was a really stupid idea).

Dumb as we were by thinking no one was watching, we turned from the street and sprinted directly down our alley for the homestretch to safety. Meanwhile, a tall, neighborly man with rape-prevention glasses ('50s-style and black rimmed) had witnessed the entire event and instinctively dropped his garden hose and ran after us. Had we not been heading right for my house, I would have outrun this guy. But we were stupid enough to let him chase us right through our back gate. He caught up to us and grabbed both Grit and me by the shirt collars and led us straight back to Carl's house. This was bullshit. I had never been caught before.

The size of the crowd that had already assembled outside of Carl's place was unbelievable. There must have been twenty people gathered around Carl and consoling him over the terrible tragedy of his car rolling into the street. I could almost hear cheers from the people as we were dragged through the crowd to face our victim. "Here they are, Carl," the heroic bastard who apprehended us said with great pride and honor in front of the mob.

With us now standing before Carl, several of the men from the group jeered him into taking action. "I'd take them to the police if I were you, Carl," they kept saying over and over. Hell, I didn't want any police action, and neither did Carl. He probably had fresh squash garnished in Alpo waiting for him back at the house.

Instead, Carl gave us a warning that would send chills down my spine for decades to come. He stepped closer to us and made this ghastly statement: "No, bawd, not this time. But, if you boys ever do something like this again, I will grab you by the back of the neck, put you in my car, and take you to the police." I choked and coughed at the thought of being trapped in Carl's car, peering out with my hands against the window and gasping for air.

The crowd, after hearing this rather dull threat and feeling disappointed, began to reluctantly disperse. They mumbled among themselves about Carl's leniency with us. However, I did remember the faces and identities of the ones in the crowd who were for Carl taking us to the police. The ones who openly begged Carl had sealed their doom on the upcoming night called Halloween. My eggs and dog poop would be ready for them.

On the following day at school, I told the story to Roland, and he almost fell on the floor from laughing so hard. For years to come, he imitated Carl by saying, "Hey, bawd, if you ever do that again, I will grab

you by the back of the neck, put you in my car, and take you to the police."
He then pretended to have his hands pressed up against the car window
as he choked and gasped for fresh air.

Roland finally got his fill of Carl and left him alone the next few years
while he engaged in other activities with us. One of our favorites was what
we called "cherry knocking." The whole idea is to knock on someone's
door and then hide. When the victim answers the door, there is no one
there. But with Roland, we didn't do it just once to someone—we did it
repeatedly.

There happened to be one sad incident where the occupant of the
house down the street from us happened to be a crippled man who spent
the last years of his life on his stomach pushing himself around on wheeled
stretcher with a cane. I told Roland about the poor guy, but I think that
only encouraged him all the more to do it. One night that we went out,
Roland knocked on this guy's door and quickly hid behind the lone tree just
across the sidewalk, only yards from the house. The man kept answering
the door each time Roland knocked on it, but then he finally had enough
and rolled himself—stretcher and all—out onto the porch. He waived his
cane wildly and angrily swore out at the darkness. He couldn't see Roland
hiding behind the tree and giggling, but he knew he was there.

After that, we decided to give Mission Avenue a break and ended up
venturing over to another street. By this time, Tim had finished up his
latest Lego creation and came outside to team up with Roland and me.
In such a risky venture as this, we let Roland be the brave one and put
his neck on the line. Each time we chose a house for Roland to terrorize,
both Tim and I hid across the street behind a fence or a row of hedges.
Roland's eyes lit up when he picked out a humble rancher next to a small,
unlit side street. This poor guy didn't know what was coming, and neither
did Roland. Just like usual, Roland cautiously walked up to the door and
pounded on it. In a flash, he ran around to the side of the house and hid
in the shadows.

Someone we couldn't quite see answered the door and immediately
shut it after realizing that a prank had just been pulled. In his regular style,
Roland came out from his hiding place after a few minutes and beat on the
door again. Once more, the door opened and shut quickly. The third time
Roland pulled the trick and ran back to his hiding place, a man stepped
outside and very calmly shut the door behind him. I strained to look more
closely at the guy only to discover that he wielded a small pistol in one
hand. The prank had turned serious. This sucker wanted blood.

The man scanned his yard for a minute, looking from side to side. He then slowly pranced out onto the grass and around to the dark side of the house where Roland was hiding. A few minutes went by, and we didn't see the man emerge from the shadows. We didn't see Roland, either, or hear any gunshots. Tim and I waited longer and finally gave up on Roland. We went home and said our prayers for him.

The next day at school, Roland was alive and well and telling everyone his tale. He told us that the man walked right by his hiding spot. This guy, somewhat perplexed, supposedly stopped and stood directly in front of Roland without seeing him in the darkness. According to Roland, this pistol-wielding citizen even lit up a cigarette. As the man enjoyed his rush of tar and nicotine, all Roland could do is stay still, or he'd be detected. Naturally, the facts began to change the more Roland told the story. The small pistol the man had soon morphed into a submachine gun, and the guy was some wacko from a prisoner-of-war camp. Roland had to wrestle the guy and knock him out to make his escape. Half the kids actually believed Roland's story.

Soon enough after that incident, it was business as usual in our neighborhood. However, cherry knocking just didn't have the same excitement as running from the police or a raging motorist. We unanimously decided to taper off on our door-to-door efforts and concentrate on other trouble.

Tim and I invited Roland over one night for chili. Roland claimed that he loved chili because of all the fun stuff you can do once you get the gas. Right at the kitchen table, we decided to announce an unofficial chili-eating contest. Tim and I sat across the dining table from each other and slurped up the chili as fast as we could. With each refill, we counted out loud how many bowls it was for us. "*Two!*" "Well, this is *three* for me!" Roland was a great sport and played along just fine. Luckily, the beans didn't go right to work. We simply enjoyed the flavor that early in the evening.

After Roland left that night, Tim and I retired to our bedroom. As we tossed and turned throughout the night, the gas began seeping out from underneath our covers. Even the cats wouldn't sleep on our beds that particular night. I could explain it in scientific terms, but it's much simpler to just explain in layman's terms—our room was very small, and the fresh air supply was limited.

Throughout the night, we got comfortable enough with the odor that we slept right through the holocaust ourselves. But the first thing in the morning, Mom opened our door and walked across the room with an armful of freshly folded clothes. By the time she reached our dresser, the aroma had reached her nostrils. She screamed in horror and threw the clothes on the floor. Fearing loss of life or limb, she plugged her nose and ran out of the room, yelling, "Oh, you kids! It's the gas house blues!" Tim and I rolled over and looked at each other and gave the thumbs-up signal. At school, I let Roland know how well the chili worked, and he shook my hand.

One of the only classes we had together during the first year of junior high was social studies, and Roland, for some reason, didn't like our teacher. I personally thought our teacher was all right. He tried hard to inspire us to embrace the class instruction with such things as "Current Events Time." During every class, Mr. Murray came out from behind his desk with a newspaper. He paced the floor as if he were performing at a college symposium and enthusiastically announced, "Current Events Time! Current Events Time!"

He quizzed us on our knowledge of current events. Just that quirk alone set Mr. Murray apart from all the other teachers. In addition to his large, fuzzy beard, Mr. Murray spoke with a squeaky, raspy voice that Roland found very annoying. Many times when Mr. Murray left the room to go to the office, Roland would jump up from his seat and imitate him. Roland not only imitated Mr. Murray's voice, but he also imitated his fuzzy beard by balling his fists up and placing them up against his cheeks. Roland would then cock his head from side to side and announce, "Current Events Time! Current Events Time!" After enough practice, he got brave enough to do it right in front of Mr. Murray. He got sent to the office several times for that.

Not only did Mr. Murray and his odd demeanor disturb Roland, but so did a strange, curly-haired girl who looked like she just walked off a Charlie Brown cartoon. The girl had a very long face and a pointed chin with a Kirk Douglas-style dimple. She wore a set of old-fashioned, cat-eye glasses. Sadly, the girl didn't have many friends, and no one really knew her name. Roland rudely called her "Chinzle" because of her pointed chin. All she wanted was to be left alone, but she was forced to defend herself against Roland by jabbing at him with an overly sharpened pencil. Roland loved it when he got her fired up. He dodged the pencil lead on a daily basis and kept harassing her until the principal eventually threatened him with expulsion from school.

When he yelled, "Chinzle! Chinzle! Chinzle!" at her, I believe that all it meant was that he had a crush on her and didn't know any other way of showing it. Roland caused such a ruckus in junior high that he had to spend a lot of time in the office—even more time than I did.

Roland and I slowly drifted apart after the seventh grade because adolescence was getting the best of him. He delved into the drinking, smoking, and association with seedy types of people. Tim and I, as we began to grow up, hung on to the firecrackers, candy bars, and model rockets until the bitter end.

By the time Roland and I were in the eighth grade, I had never yet invited him to participate in any Halloween festivities with us. For some reason, I decided to include him this year—probably as an attempt to keep our friendship alive. This Halloween was to be even more special than any other one. We were very stocked up. We had eggs, eggs, and more eggs, and we were even armed with firecrackers. When Roland took us up on our offer and joined us, the night was still young, and we had not even begun our trouble-making. Traffic was slow in our neighborhood, and we were dying to find fresh targets.

Since we weren't finding many cars to bomb in our sector, I wanted to up the ante and get into a riskier area. Under my advisement, Roland, Tim, and a couple of stragglers followed me over to the main intersection where the local First National Bank branch, IGA, and the only stoplight in town were. The Hill Street highway overpass was less than a block away.

While we waited in the dark alley behind an unsuspecting neighbor's garage, I decided to kick off the festivities with a bang. I pulled a pack of one hundred firecrackers out of my coat pocket, unwrapped the waxed paper coating, and then I had Roland light the fuse.

Tiny orange sparks immediately spit off of the burning fuse as I heaved the whole pack into the middle of the street. I felt completely relaxed thinking that there wasn't anyone around at the time. But, just as the bundle landed and sent a burst of sparks all over the pavement, a slow-moving police car drove directly over the top of the pack. They instantly exploded in rapid succession like a machine gun. Oops! The cops in that car weren't going to like that.

Tim and I knew it was time for flight and took off running. We ran in a large loop, circling the block. In typical fashion, Roland attempted to hide instead of run. He braced himself on the other side of the motel near our original position and really didn't fool anyone. The police found him—again. However, this time, it wasn't just the local police that we assaulted and insulted—it was the Shoshone County sheriff himself, and he had plenty of experience with Roland. Even though Tim and I were long gone making our evasive maneuvers, the bystanders filled us in on the story the next day.

The sheriff's car made a quick move around the motel building and caught Roland hiding behind a stairway. Sheriff Crummly greeted Roland as if they were old friends. With a preponderance of eggs in teenagers' pockets that night, Crummly asked Roland what he had bulging in his pocket.

Roland hesitated.

"Give it to me, Roland!" Crummly demanded.

"Okay. Here it is," said Roland. His next move sealed his fate. Roland reached into his pocket, pulled out an egg, and purposely squished it just before he plopped it into Sheriff Crummly's outstretched hand.

The insulted sheriff shook the egg mess from his hand and pushed Roland into the back of his car. He slammed the door shut on my mischievous friend. I didn't see Roland again for four years. It was only when he made an unexpected but yet triumphant return during the beginning of my senior year in high school that I would see him again.

Chapter 3
Josh Mueller

Josh Mueller sent waves of terror through our neighborhood that were unparalleled by anyone—even Roland Martell. Roland happened to be a visitor on our turf, but Josh owned it. Born and raised in our neighborhood, Josh ran wild with impunity. Each time the police showed up on his doorstep, his overly protective mother warded them off with her proclamations of little Josh's innocence. "Not my little Joshy. Maybe it was another boy—like one of those Majors—but not my little Joshy."

Josh lived just a block behind us on the next street with his German father, Scottish mother, and his little brother Mitch. It took me several years to realize that Josh and Mitchy were both adopted. Until I knew the truth behind their heritage, I wondered why they didn't talk the same way as their father. Josh and Mitchy spoke as plainly and as arrogantly as any American kid could. Regardless of their roots, they were loved and coddled just the same by their overly caring mother.

Mr. Mueller was a great guy—always happy, always intrigued by what my brothers and I were up to, and always getting after Josh. Josh's father came from the old country and excelled at brewing beer. I had the privilege of seeing the basement brewery in action once. Josh popped off the ceramic cork on one of the hundreds of bottles of beer and let me sip it. Luckily, I didn't have a flare for fermented malt beverages until I got into high school—or else Josh and I would have drank up his dad's reserves.

For quite a number of years, Josh shared his equally active imagination with me as we drew pictures of spaceships and ray guns with our crayons and colored pencils each Saturday morning after we got back from swimming at the YMCA's indoor pool. It was somewhat uncanny how Josh and I became so close because he was actually a year younger than I and in my brother Steve's class all throughout grade school. There came a time when things between them no longer jelled, but our similarities became apparent.

Josh and I shared the same adventurous spirit and held the same motto in high esteem: "Be carefully careless." Although Josh rode the edge much closer than I, it seemed that—at least for a few years—we could share some common ground that most adolescents experienced. Sometimes for hours, after escaping the pressures of the school curriculum, we would find solace in the woods not far from our neighborhood and simply share our views of the expanding life before us—mainly in the arena of women. I could tell him everything about a crush I had on a certain girl in school. He'd listen intently, but then when he couldn't understand my hesitation, Josh would simply blurt out, "Shit, man, why don't you just f——— her?"

I appreciated his patience with me, but I grew somewhat frustrated with him. I actually had romantic intentions with the women I spoke of. He merely wanted to take advantage of his. How could he be so cavalier? He got his way much more than I did. I spent years frustrating the girls that I liked and even myself.

Another area in which Josh and I held a very strong bond was the sheer attraction to adventure. The origin of all of our efforts began at that stupid little pool that we met at every Saturday morning. The YMCA was fun for a while, but it was too normal. We showered. We swam. We ate candy in the TV room, and we behaved for a bit until one of our mothers came to pick us up. That routine naturally ended quickly when boredom set in. As usual, new ideas developed quickly after hanging around that bacteria-infested warehouse for a few weekends.

Kellogg, being quite behind the times, taught us to appreciate some of the simpler things in life. The YMCA was one of them. Although the local youth center had been built just after the turn of the century and was somewhat antiquated, it did have some of the modern amenities that are found at most contemporary health facilities. The small sauna was one of them. As much faith as the staff put into the thing, it turned out to be not so healthy for the old guys who dressed down in the locker room for a stint in the Swedish wonder.

Just before Kellogg's distinguished elderly men could hobble into the tiny, wood-lined chamber, Josh and I would often dash in just in front of them and relieve our bladders over the scalding-hot rocks. As we sprayed the hot coals with our kidney overflow, huge clouds of acrid ammonia vapors filled the room. We giggled and quickly ran out the other door and jumped directly into the pool.

Sometimes the old men went into the sauna immediately after our urinating spree and came out seconds later coughing and gagging into the pool area trying to find us. Luckily, with a pool full of kids, we remained safely anonymous.

Sometimes we swam next to some of those strange old men who had wrinkly skin grossly hanging off their bones. That gave me the willies. I never thought that someday I might look like that. Although those old guys seemed to be a constant in an ever-changing YMCA world, I did notice that all kinds of other strange people did visit the Y. Those were the days in which leukemia and the bubonic plague had special meanings to us, and I watched the other people closely.

Sometimes, during our lovely moments in the hellhole called an indoor pool, we got splashed by mentally handicapped people, thinking we wanted to have fun on a six-year-old level. My God, why couldn't we see some real girly action? Those assholes on the beach party shows saw it in every episode. Every once in a while, we'd get lucky and see a couple of really pretty girls come in for a dip, but that was rare. Most of the time, we got stuck with the fat, pizza-faced girls who were too unpopular to be sleeping in at weekend slumber parties with their Barbie-toting friends.

One Saturday morning, Josh and I were swimming in the chlorine-rich waters, testing our lung capacity by seeing how far we could go under water. Josh went first and popped up at the far end of the pool and gasped for air. Unexpectedly, he came face-to-face with a teenaged girl who suddenly burst out laughing uncontrollably at him.

What was the deal? He didn't do anything funny (at least not yet). After bumping into her and trying to avoid her from there on out, it seemed that everywhere Josh swam, this girl seemed to follow him. He splashed her a couple of times to get rid of her, but she continued to laugh throughout his ferocious spray of water. It soon became obvious that this girl was a little messed up in the head. Wow, that wasn't anything unusual for our neck of the woods. Any group fortunate to hook up in Kellogg was a like a box of chocolates—you didn't know what you were going to get. (I learned so much from Forrest Gump.).

After encountering the mentally challenged girl, we climbed out of the pool and went into the locker room for a quick recess. Josh warned me that he wanted this girl off his back or else he'd get dressed and leave. I didn't want that; if he left, all I could do is blow spitwads at the attendant behind the counter upstairs near the front door. So, to keep a good comrade, I came up with a great idea. "Let's bomb her from the diving board!"

Josh grinned and beamed with the thought of revenge. Just as expected, as we climbed up on the diving board, the girl treaded water closer to us. What in the hell did the girl see in us—bananas in our pockets?

Josh ran, bounced off the end of the board, and tucked himself into a cannonball shape. He hit the water hard, just a foot or two away from Silly Sally. She held her arms up to shield her eyes from the blast of water. Surprisingly, she wiped the water away from her face and burst out laughing again.

Josh seemed to enjoy himself now, knowing that he was going to splash this chick to death. He jumped off the board many times, making all kind of wild shapes and gestures with his body. Soon he was grabbing his crotch with both hands as he leaped through the air and into the water. Silly Sally got quite a kick out it. Josh surfaced right next to her after one tremendous splash. She giggled as hard as ever. As he wiped the water away from his eyes, he glanced over at her and screamed in horror. He pointed at her face. A large, greenish yellow slime stretched out of one of her nostrils and across her upper lip. "Oooooo!" he yelled.

I wasn't far from the slime scene—close enough to join Josh as he paddled hastily to the other end of the pool. We spent a few minutes catching our breath and trying not to laugh too hard at this idiotic girl. Josh thought for a moment and turned toward me with the most serious look on his face. "Hey, I've got one for her," he said.

"Yes, what's that?" I asked.

"She wants something funny? I'll show her something funny. Just watch," he replied. Josh climbed out of the pool and walked past the lifeguard, who was sitting on a bench and reading a magazine. He looked down at her to make sure she devoted her attention to something other than the diving board.

When Josh climbed up on the diving board, he posed like Charles Atlas for a second and then looked at me and pointed at his crotch. Then he stopped and paused, making the others in line wait. Josh wanted to make sure Silly Sally was watching.

Once he knew he had her attention, he took a running leap into the air. Just as he cleared the end of the diving board and bounced high above the water, Josh pulled his swimming trucks off to the side and let his genitals hang out for Silly Sally to see. It was a ghastly sight. The lifeguard looked up at the last second but was too late to notice what he did.

He splashed down next to the girl as planned, covering her with a wave of water. When he surfaced, he laughed so hard he almost couldn't climb up the ladder to get out of the pool. Finally, he topped the final rung and staggered to the locker room, holding his belly. I joined him by the showers. He kept giggling and giggling. All I wanted from him was some type of acknowledgment that I was there. It took him a minute to recuperate. Finally, he laughed for a few seconds and then asked my opinion.

"Just fine. You did just fine!" I assured him. That was all the swimming we did that day. Things were just getting a little too weird at the Y.

On days that we didn't go swimming, we had other favorite pastimes. Prank phone calls were just becoming popular in our social circle, and Josh and I decided to get creative. What would we say when we got someone on the phone? How could we freak people out? Since we were limited on jokes, we decided to challenge people like a game show host. Josh and I waited one day for his mother to leave to go grocery shopping. Once she had pulled out their driveway, Josh and I went into the house and headed straight for the black rotary dial phone sitting on a china hutch in the living room. Josh dialed a random number using our local exchange. He waited as the phone rang and rang on the other end.

Just as Josh was about to hang up the phone, an elderly man answered. "Hello?"

"Hey, who is this?" Josh immediately asked.

"This is Frank. Who are you?"

"It's me—Joe."

"I don't know any Joe."

"Of course you do. It's me, your old neighbor Joe. Don't you remember me?"

The old man paused for a moment and then continued, "No, I don't. I never had any neighbor named Joe."

Josh insisted that the old man knew him and continued to throw out fictitious clues regarding how and why the old man should remember him. There came a point where the old man's memory had been jarred enough to where he finally admitted, "Oh, yes, you are right. I do remember you now."

Josh was elated. As I held my ear up to the receiver, I held back my laughter. Josh was ready for the punch line. "Yeah, Frank, of course you remember me. I used to screw your wife all the time!"

The phone suddenly went dead.

Another one of our favorite pastimes was riding our bicycles all over the neighborhood pretending we were police interceptors. We chased down other kids on their bicycles and arrested them for no reason at all. We just liked to scare the hell out of them and watch them run home crying. At other times, we performed our little stunt jumps in the alley.

My brother Steve ended up outdoing both Josh and me with his seven-garbage-can jump he had performed during my 1974 backyard science fair. I had made several dollars charging admission for people to see my methane gas generator and model rocket display, but Steve stole their attention by claiming that if he didn't make the garbage-can jump, the bystanders could keep his knocked-out teeth free of charge. He made over twelve dollars on that one and didn't even wipe out. When he was done with the jump, the neighbors simply wanted their garbage cans returned.

During the summer months after giving up the YMCA swimming, Josh joined me in my tree house, which was nothing more than a little platform in the maple tree in front of our house. That was one great thing about Josh; for a few years there, he did everything with me. After we both watched the movie *The Great Escape,* he even helped me dig my three underground tunnels named Tom, Dick, and Harry.

Josh surprised me at times and could be quite industrious, even more creative than I originally imagined. One boring summer day, we were in dire need of cash, and he thought of a quick way to get some. Josh told me to go home and dig up any little trinkets that we could sell for a quick profit. That was fine, but to sell them to whom?Regardless, I wanted in on this adventure so desperately that I did what he said without question.

After rummaging through my bedroom for a while, we met outside and took inventory. I had a couple of little tools, and Josh had some souvenirs from his recent trip to Germany. My favorite trinket of his was the soapstone carving of the Wurzburg Castle. But it wasn't for me to have; it was for us to sell. If his mom only knew that he intended to sell precious remnants of his father's old country, she would have beat him severely, but Josh didn't ever worry about the consequences of anything.

We rode our bikes across town to the local retirement center. I saw the large, two-story complex and felt quite intimidated. Josh reassured me that he knew his way around the place well. After calming my nerves, Josh had me knocking on the doors one by one. We gave the sales pitch of a lifetime to the retirees who resided there. Although some of them were smart enough to know we were up to something, others fell for our ploy.

We invented a believable story about raising money for a Boy Scout campout. All of the residents turned us down except one old man with a giant wart on the end of his nose. He bought the soapstone carving of the Wurzburg Castle from Josh for two dollars and some change. Josh and I didn't make any more sales pitches that day; we were too ecstatic knowing that we actually suckered someone. Our next stop was the candy section at the local Circle K. (Naturally, we didn't bother going camping that day.)

Later that year, after I got tired of doing my paper route and collecting from all the weirdos, I turned the job over to Josh. He instantly became intrigued by Carl, just the same as Roland Martell did. The first and foremost feature Josh loved about Carl Zarkosky was that Carl was truly a Transylvanian miser. I believed that it actually had more to do with the rotten snuff around Carl's lips. Josh started calling it "snoz" and quite often asked Carl how the snoz tasted that day. Carl always responded nicely.

One Saturday, Josh and I got an idea. We came across two small library card envelopes while digging through my mom's paper stockpile. Something inspired us to draw our own unique labels on the front of them. Our artwork included portraits of Carl with his fuzzy hair, tuxedo, and rotten teeth. The labels read:

Snoz: Five Cents—Refreshing Taste!

Real snoz wasn't tobacco at all. It was Lipton tea taken out of the bags and poured into our little yellow envelopes. Just for effect before our sales presentation to Carl, we parted our hair in the middle like Carl did, and we filled our mouths with Lipton tea.

When we beat on Carl's door, Josh and I giggled at each other while we squished the tea leaves all over our lips and teeth. Carl slowly opened his door and asked us, "Yes, bawd?"

"Carl, we are here to sell you some snoz. It tastes great!" we replied in unison.

Immediately Carl said he wasn't interested and began to shut his door.

"No, wait! You don't want any?" I pleaded.

Carl opened his door a little wider to give us the common courtesy of a proper sales objection. "No, I don't think so, bawd."

"But you chew snoz, don't you? We do, and it's good," Josh said as he pointed at the caked tea leaves around his mouth.

Carl looked at Josh's mouth and then at mine as I pointed the same way at the snoz on my lips. Carl shook his head and began to back into his house. "Wait!" I yelled. "Don't you want to try some?"

Carl turned one more time to us and took the little yellow envelope that I held out for him. He quickly glanced at his portrait on the front of it and tore the package open with his grimy fingers. He poured the contents into his hand and fingered the material. "It looks like tea, bawd," he exclaimed.

"Oh, no, it's snoz, and it's good!" Josh responded.

Carl handed the package back and began to close his door. Josh and I were close to losing a sale. I shrieked, "But it's *free!*" Carl began to open his door. "For five cents!" Then Carl began to shut his door again. Once he slammed it shut, we knew we had just lost a customer. I had to hand it to Carl. He never wavered in his love for Copenhagen and never tried snoz at all.

Josh's true glory days arrived when he got involved with motorcycles. After I turned my paper route over to him, he started working hard to save for a bike of his own. Until that day came, Josh got some riding time in on his dad's prized Honda Trail 90. We thought it was a pretty girly looking machine, but that didn't stop Josh from seeing what she could do.

A few blocks away, up the little gulch, Josh ran the bike up to the end of the road and back. Each time he did it, he tried to do it faster and faster. Sometimes he wound up the engine so badly that I thought it was going to blow. Each time, he would come back down and stop. Sometimes he was so excited that he'd say something like "I got it up to forty in second gear!" His dad was hot tempered enough and would have really gone nuts and frothed at the mouth if he knew how Josh treated the bike.

Finally, in the spring after all the practice rides and months of paper route work, Josh amassed enough money to invest in his own bike. His dad escorted him to the local motorcycle shop, and they returned a few hours later with a new red Honda 100. I was so jealous, but I knew Josh worked hard for it where I had just spent my paper route money on useless—but interesting—science projects.

It wasn't long until Josh had to show off to a group of kids outside the junior high school. The enthusiastic crowd dared him to make a jump. More than willing, he hastily constructed a wooden ramp about three feet high. It was the tallest ramp I had seen yet. Josh didn't falter under the growing pressure of the crowd; come death or dismemberment, he was going to give them a show.

Josh made a quick practice run across the dirt field and then turned around for the final stretch. He held his right hand up to his helmet and made a mock salute to the spectators. Allowing the engine to rev up to a painful whine, he then let the clutch go. The bike engine screamed as he built up speed. Josh shifted through a couple of gears before he reached the bottom of the ramp. Up, off, and into the air he and the bike went. During his descent, I could see he wasn't going to land quite right. His trajectory was off. He bumped the ground, front wheel first, just like Evel Knievel did at Caesar's Palace in Las Vegas in 1967.

The handlebars shook and twisted until he lost control and crashed into the thick, dark soil. Josh flew over the handlebars and rolled a couple of times, lying there for only a second. He immediately climbed to his feet and brushed the dirt off of his sleeves. Josh increasingly revived himself as the applause grew louder. The only damage realized was a set of slightly bent handlebars and a broken brake lever. Even without broken bones, Josh became instantly famous with the prepubescent youths.

After only a few months of riding, this motorcycle became too slow for Josh. He worked harder yet and a year later bought a giant of a bike, a screaming racer—a bright red Honda CR125. It was twice the size of his first one. Josh raced up and down the hills for hours at a time, spraying dirt off the back tire as the engine screamed like a nest of hornets. Not knowing when enough was enough, he soon realized that the hills may be fun to ride on, but they weren't interactive. A foolish idea entered his mind: the streets of Kellogg could be a blast—especially since the police were able to respond. Shortly thereafter, he boldly ventured into town and dared the local police to join him in risky games of cat and mouse.

One autumn day, I borrowed my brother's Kawasaki 400 road bike and rode with Josh to school. He naturally rode his dirt bike, and that was strictly illegal.

The high school in Kellogg is nestled beautifully a quarter mile up a lovely little gulch named Jacob's Gulch. The school can be seen from the edge of town and particularly from the highway overpass that crosses over the interstate and leads down to the junior high. Most of the foot traffic to the high school is directed up a very small, overgrown, dirt road that traverses the bottom of the eastern hill. The road was so overgrown that it wasn't known anymore as an old road but instead as "the trail."

Our most direct way to school took our two-bike procession down Mission Avenue for half a mile and then up the trail. Our route led us straight from the pavement to the mountainside and made an easy getaway from the police. We considered that possibility since we were both driving illegally. Josh's bike wasn't street legal, and Phil's Kawasaki had no registration.

At lunch time, following all the oohs and aahs, we drove across the high school parking lot, down the trail, and onto the stretches of Mission

Avenue. Part of Mission Avenue runs along the south side of the hill, similar to the school trail. Although Mission Avenue is a maintained city street, erosion each year causes part of the hill to spill into the roadway. The naturally formed bank entices people to swerve partway up it just for fun. It doesn't matter whether they are in cars, on bicycles, or motorcycles.

On our way home during lunch, Josh drove up and down the bank. He looked over at me and smiled at his little stunt. Just as a natural precaution, I looked over my shoulder. To my surprise, a city patrol car had been following us with its blue lights flashing. I motioned to Josh to look behind us. He did and then looked back at me with a smile. Immediately, he turned back at the officer and flashed his middle finger at him. Josh then twisted the throttle of the bike and leaped ahead of me. He sped away at an incredible speed and shifted wildly through the gears. The blue exhaust streamed out of the exhaust pipe on Josh's bike and looked like a vapor trail from a jet. The squad car passed me in hot pursuit.

As I rounded the bend, I looked as far as I could in front of me and could barely see both car and bike screaming through the intersection down by our house. At the end of our block, Josh turned left and shot up the side of another hill. When he reached the top of the small ridge, he shut off the bike. In his typical style, he waved arrogantly to the police car waiting at the base of the hill.

Even though the pursuing officer fumed over losing the chase, they would get another chance very soon. This particular episode made Josh a wanted man by the local police. Doughnut sales at the local bakery rose sharply for the next few weeks from all the effort the department put forth. They wanted him badly and were going to throw the book and the pastry box at him once they apprehended him.

Our favorite time of the year finally came—Halloween. Tim and I had our eggings all planned out, as usual. New friends joined our party this year because of all the tales they had heard about us and our years of mischievous activity. These adventure-starved students wanted in on the action—all of them except Josh. He excused himself from the egg throwing this night because he had devised a new way to torment the local cops.

In attempts to disguise his motorcycle, Josh cut up brown grocery bags and taped them over every red part of his bike. Instead of a red dirt bike, it was now a tan-colored dirt bike. At night, under the streetlights, who could tell, anyway?

Josh stood with us in the shadows of our driveway, proudly mounted upon his bike like the Lone Ranger. The rest of us, huddled around him in our driveway, acted like the pit crew and aided him in any way we could. Since the air was a bit chilly, he borrowed a face shield from Tim to attach to his helmet. The only problem with the shield that Tim gave him was the dark blue tint. With its vision-impairing quality, it would prove to be a very bad idea.

Just as the local kids began their door-to-door trick-or-treating, Josh started up his bike and idled out into the road. He wanted so badly to drag a jelly doughnut behind his bike to bait the cops, but the rope just wouldn't hold the crumbling thing. Josh finally disappeared around the corner and began combing the back streets for the police. Even though he was out of sight, we tracked him by the sound of his noisy engine. After mildly driving a few blocks to the west, he turned down the next street and slowly made his way a few blocks back to the east.

After a few minutes, we heard him downshift. Then the engine wailed. The bike screamed like a hellish demon as he punched it through the gears. "He's got one now!" I said as we all laughed.

We traced the sound eastward down the back of our neighborhood and around to the base of the hill. The engine screamed, cried, and gnawed angrily at the mountainside. Only a few seconds passed before he began to slow down and fight his way up the dark, overgrown trail. Moments later, the sound muffled slightly and then died. Josh had made it to the safety of the obscure hillside. According to his plan, he would sneak down the adjoining trail to an alley and quietly push the bike back to his house.

The rest of us waited and waited. After the longest while, Josh still didn't show up. I looked up at the side of the hill in wonder and suddenly noticed two sets of flashlights bobbing through the darkness on top of the ridge. The police were going all-out to catch their man. There were two different sets of officers scouring the mountainside. The flashlight beams soon split up as the team of police set out to cover both ridges. The officers huffed and puffed all the way up to the top and then dropped down through the draw where Josh hid with his bike.

By then, too much valuable egg-throwing time had slipped away, and if we wanted to bomb the cops, we had better get to it. For the next two hours, the rest of us jumped fences, dived over hedges, and splattered as many moving vehicles with lights on top as we could. At the end of the evening, we still had not heard from Josh. The next day, I saw him at school. He was as proud as ever. The police had found him and arrested him. The story unfolded in the hallway among a group of his fans.

The blue face shield that he borrowed from Tim had virtually blinded him in the darkness under the trees. Josh didn't go far up the trail before he was forced to simply shut the bike off and wait. The police nearly missed him until one of the officers dropped his thermos of coffee and stumbled over the bike in the middle of the trail while he sobbed. At first, Josh didn't want to give himself up, but when the proud officers of the Kellogg PD began to push his bike down the hill, Josh surrendered himself and volunteered to do the pushing.

After the judge gloated in his chambers over the capture of the so called "Evil" Josh, all the charges were reduced to one—reckless driving. Josh's license would be suspended after that. (The suspension was supposedly enough to teach him a lesson—but not enough to doom him for life.)

A year later, Josh was at it again when he and some of his friends snuck into the drive-in theater. The owner knew the trick well and kept a good vigil over the exit. He had seen them come in and hastily ran out to kick them out. When he came up and tapped on the driver's window, merely asking them to leave, Josh pulled out and brandished a large hunting knife. The owner took it as a threat of violence and backed up a few steps. He wasted no time in placing a call to the sheriff's office. Although Josh quickly left the drive-in, the police were onto him again and arrested him across town. Josh didn't mean anything by it. He just wanted the guy to envision death by buck knife.

This arrest didn't stop Josh from getting into trouble time and time again. The ironic part about Josh Mueller's life is that he went on to become a respectable deputy in a little-known county far away from Kellogg, Idaho. He once returned to town to attend one of the class reunions. There he told of the joy and pleasure he experienced using pepper spray on defiant citizens! God help us!

Josh, good luck with protecting and serving.

Chapter 4

RodThompson

On the other side of Mission Avenue lived the greatest nemesis to the Major family—Rod Thompson, the hardware store owner. Rod's presence was more prominent than the rest of the neighbors because he voiced his opinion quite openly. One thing to be said about Rod was that he wasn't two-faced. He had one—and it was ugly. Most of the other neighbors acted nice up front, but we knew that behind our backs, their feelings were different. They anonymously called the police and reported us for infringing on their rights to peace and quietness on our little street. At least Rod made it very clear publicly that he thought we were a bunch of wild hellions with no parental guidance or discipline, and for that attitude he paid dearly and suffered many eggings.

Rod was an aging, self-employed hardware man and a very chunky, bald man at that. Across the street and a few houses down, he owned and operated a little, old-fashioned hardware/general store. The locals loved his tiny store and flocked to it during the evenings because he had a TV mounted upon the wall for his favorite patrons to watch. The broadcasted football games attracted every old coot that had nothing better to do with his time. Seven cement steps lead up the entrance to Rod's store. Upon the landing in front of the door, Rod placed his command post. From there, he could gaze all the way up the street in each direction and spot anything juvenile in progress. Rod glowed with pride over his thriving establishment right along with the bright red, white, and yellow Olympia neon beer sign that glowed in the window of his store during all business hours.

Because of all the patronizing customers who paid homage to Rod's bar stools and almighty TV set, the city strategically installed a streetlight directly across the road from Rod's store, squarely in front of the white church building. Although the extremely powerful lamp lit up the street quite well, it cast beautiful shadows all around the perimeter. The shadows were so dark that we could hide virtually in plain sight and never be seen because of the dark contrast. The shadows made it ideal for us to infiltrate the area and cause mischief. We didn't even need to paint our faces.

Rod got on my bad side when I was about five. While rummaging around in the shop attic, I found a can of gold spray paint. I instantly caught gold fever! I took the can out to the alley and sprayed a couple of coats of gold paint over a flat, round rock that I had found during the excavations behind our shop. My first entrepreneurial venture failed when Rod flatly rejected my offer. All I asked of him was a straight trade—pure gold for a mere handful of candy. This SOB could have simply traded a few pieces of penny candy, and everything between us would have been all right—but oh, no, he had to be a jerk. Boy, was I mad! All the pudds sitting on the bar stools started laughing, and it angered me so much that I wanted to throw the gold rock right through the window at them.

Some time after that incident, Rod openly made derogatory comments about our family. For this offense, Mom instituted a familywide boycott of his store. This proclamation by my mother made Rod open game for us kids—we looked for anything to antagonize this old grump.

It's a fact of life that everyone has a weakness, and Rod's soft spot was his CB radio. Rod, being the astute businessman he was, invested his hard-earned hardware profits (instead of easily acquired gold) in a newly famed Citizens' Band radio. My brothers and I couldn't afford such useless luxuries. All we had were cheap walkie-talkies that Santa gave us for Christmas. Strangely, with them, we could hear all the CBers yapping away no matter what channel they were on, but for some reason, they couldn't hear us trying to talk back.

During this era in American history, the whole country raved over CBs and doing the ole stupid "breaker one nine" bullshit, and we were missing out! Even our school buddy down the street, Mark Torkelson, had a big CB with a huge antenna. I refused to be shown up by Rod or even Mark. I decided to study up on electronics, and by doing so, I soon discovered that my brother Steve's *Star Trek* walkie-talkies actually transmitted on the CB Channel 14. The engineers were such lazy bastards that they designed the receiver circuits as a broadband receiver that picked up all of the CB channels without any way to select them individually. All the truckers we happened to tune in to were calling back and forth on Channel 19—the "call" channel. I then knew how to fix ourselves up. It would cost a couple of bucks, but that didn't stop me. If I didn't have the money to upgrade, I would get the money.

Rod's candy department came in handy for the financing of my latest project. I ordered a friend of mine to go across the street and invest our spare change into a big bag of one-cent candy. After counting out my newly acquired candy inventory, I invited all the neighborhood kids to come over with their piggy banks and play a little bingo at our kitchen table. My strategy was simple. Each game cost the participants one cent to participate. Each round we played grossed me nearly a dime, but I only had to pay out one cent in prizes. After many "fourteen-under-Is," I earned enough money for the project with a few Tootsie Rolls to spare.

Corporate America served me well by planting a Radio Shack store only two blocks from my house. I walked over, accompanied with an armed guard (Josh Mueller with his BB gun), and strutted through the door with my profits. I plopped the cash down on the counter and bought that precious Channel 19 transmit crystal for only $4.99 plus 5 percent Idaho sales tax. I held the tiny little package securely in my hands and almost kissed it a couple of times. Our new access to the radio waves would validate our position among the neighborhood CBers.

Back at the house, I dumped my box of gizmos out on the kitchen table, heated up my soldering iron, and performed surgery on Spock's communicator. With the skill of a brain surgeon, I installed the new crystal in our *Star Trek* walkie-talkie. Presto! We were able to call out and talk to any trucker or CBer.

Not only did I change the transmit frequency, I also thought of a way to get a little extra range out of our walkie-talkie. I climbed up one of our plum trees and got onto our roof. On the peak of the roof, I mounted an old aluminum ski pole as an antenna. From there, I routed a wire down and in through our bedroom window. The antenna setup looked like hell, but it worked wonders. The ski pole had at least tripled the range of our little device.

It didn't take Rod long to walk out onto his command post and spot the strange apparatus up on our roof. The first time he noticed it, he took his glasses off, wiped the lenses clean, and took a second look. He knew instantly that we were up to something. Within minutes of our first radio test, we discovered some really neat stuff. We found out that we could really freak the other CBers out by utilizing a special button built into the side of our walkie-talkie. Pushing the button transmitted an irritating, pulsating "phaser" sound. If a person wasn't a Star Trek fan and couldn't recognize the sound as that of a phaser, they could have mistaken it for a civil emergency warning.

With a simple push of a button, we pretended that Scotty was trying to beam up Captain Kirk. In doing so, we sent out a tone that bled over into every CB radio within five blocks. We loved it almost as bad as cussing and swearing on the radio. Some of the CBers got so angry at the noise that they almost had seizures and swallowed their tongues. They wanted to kill us badly. But they were never smart enough to catch on to where we were. Only Rod knew.

We played the game and talked the stupid "breaker one-nine" bullshit and amazingly managed to buffalo a few people into thinking that we actual CBers. The Tobias brothers came over to visit our brother Phil one day, but our little contraption immediately caught their attention.

"What in the hell is that?" Greg asked, knowing it was something out of the ordinary.

"Hey, man," I explained. "We're CBers."

Rather than do any more explaining, I demonstrated. I held the newly modified walkie-talkie and depressed the transmit button.

"Breaker, breaker one nine."

Within seconds, a voice crackled over the speaker. "Go ahead, breaker." Greg's eyes widened, and he smiled.

"No shit!" he said. "Let me try that."

Greg talked back and forth for a minute with the trucker, asking about the weather over the pass and where he was going. But Greg learned quickly that everyone conversing on the radio has to have a call sign.

Some trucker responded to Greg's next call and asked him what channel to go to. Greg told him to go to Channel 14. So, instead of flipping a knob on a real CB, we gave Greg the other walkie-talkie that still transmitted on Channel 14, and we switched the antenna wire to the unit Greg now held. Greg resumed the conversation with the trucker but was soon asked for his call sign. Greg stuttered for a second, and I whispered the first thing that I could think of. "Popcorn Man."

"Ah, ah ... it's Popcorn Man," Greg told the guy. Instantly, Popcorn Man became a known entity in the CB world.

Right from the beginning, most people on the radio accepted Popcorn Man as a real CBer. Rod was doubtful. That became evident by various comments he interjected over the air when someone asked about the identity of Popcorn Man. When someone on the airwaves asked Rod if he knew Popcorn Man, Rod mumbled back something about "them damned kids."

Weeks later, we heard some trucker calling over the airwaves looking for Popcorn Man. Greg just happened to be over at our house at the time, and I ran into the other room to get him.

"Greg, hurry! Get your ass in here. Someone is calling for Popcorn Man!" I hollered.

"No shit!" Greg replied with his typical response. Once in my room, he grabbed the walkie-talkie and spoke into it. "Yeah, this is Popcorn Man. What's the matter? You want some popcorn, you faggot?"

The trucker paused for a moment and asked, "What?"

"You heard me, you faggy-ass mother," Greg answered back.

Suddenly, the once calm trucker became frantic. He yelled. We laughed. He yelled some more. We laughed some more. Wow! We discovered a new game—pissing off CBers. This special breed of idiots actually took this CB stuff seriously, almost as if it were some kind of religion. We just had fun with the radio; to them, it was their life. After that initial exchange between teenager and trucker, we were verbally warned and threatened with many ass beatings time and time again. An article even came out in the newspaper describing an incident where an irate CBer whipped a fellow CBer with his own CB antenna for being discourteous on the radio. If they caught us, it would be a whipping with a ski pole!

If it wasn't for Rod with his big antenna, big radio, and big mouth, we probably would have never gotten involved. But now it was a CB war. Even Tim got involved. Being only about eleven at the time, he got the hang of provoking CBers, too. Not only did he make them irate, he made them actually believe they were talking to a doped-up juvenile delinquent. Tim anxiously grabbed the little blue walkie-talkie and yelled into it, "Hey, you jive-ass mother-f——r! Whatcha mean, Dude?"

He once did that in the middle of a conversation between two truckers and disrupted their little intercourse. One of the truckers heard it and said to his friend, "We ought to pull over and whip that punk's ass!" Afterward, I worried that they might pull over at one of the Kellogg exits and actually run into some random teenager and really whale on him. We didn't want to cause any serious trouble for anyone except Rod.

Rod kept the airwaves alive with his deep, gruff voice and snide remarks about the pack of troublemakers across the street from him. That was fine with us because we kept him alive by making him wash his truck all the time. He left it in a very vulnerable spot, and we took the liberty of messing it up at every chance we could.

I'm not sure at what time Mrs. Welman and Rod became friends or what incident prompted the friendship, but Rod chummed up with her during this harrowing time frame. Somehow he got the bright idea that if he parked his red Ford truck on her property in front of the popper-berry bushes, no one would mess with it. That was really stupid because he may just as well have parked his truck down range at a missile test site. Tim saw the bright red truck on the other side of Mrs. Welman's yard as a definite target of opportunity. As a morning, noon, and nightly ritual, Tim used Rod's truck as a test bed for projectiles.

Weather permitting, Tim threw snowballs, eggs, apples, plums, grapefruit rinds, dried cupcakes, shriveled-up baked potatoes, dog poop, Almond Rocha chunks from the litter box, and on occasion, small rocks. Rod's truck really took a beating in the line of duty. Just for a little extra spice, Tim snuck up to it in the dark and put gravel in the hubcaps. Tim became obsessed with destroying the truck. He sometimes became so obsessed that he lost his grip on reality, and Rod then became a true victim.

My feelings soon changed toward Rod. That's the way I was. If the underdog was getting his butt kicked too badly, I was always first at breaking up the fight. Just ask Steve about the time he and Ben Carter, one of the "Dirt, Grit, and Grime Brothers" (I think Ben was "Grit") got into a fight. Grit fought dirty by trying to scratch Steve's eyes out and by kicking for the balls. That really upset Steve. Although Steve was a year and half younger than I was, he always seemed to be the same height and weight. For example, I had to wrestle the same weight class as Steve all during junior high only to have him jumped a couple of weight classes above me in high school. This growth spurt eventually filled Steve with an inflated sense of toughness.

During this fight, Steve went toe-to-toe with Ben and simply waited for the next slipup that this poor kid would make. Ben swung wildly and lost his balance. Steve tackled him and pinned him to the ground. As the skirmish continued, Steve shimmied around on his knees and began to sit on Ben's head. Steve teetered back and forth, rubbing the side of Ben's face into the pavement. The wild screams of sheer pain and terror were too much for me. Although the rest of the bystanders cheered at the gruesome sight, I simply had had enough.

When I dragged Steve off of Ben, I figured that Ben would run off or at least relent, but instead, he stood there quivering as he wiped the blood and gravel chunks off the side of his face and head. After a brief moment of catching his breath, he unexpectedly lunged back at Steve, and the fight ensued once more. The fight could have been over the first time if I hadn't prolonged it by pulling them apart, and Steve reminded me of that for years.

I now contemplated pulling Tim off of Rod. If I did, would Rod learn not to mess with us, or would he do like did Ben did and keep up his shit? Some people never learn, but for Rod's sake, I had hoped he was learning not to mess with the kids on Mission Avenue.

Eventually, at one point during Tim's bombings, I felt that Rod's paint job had taken enough abuse. I made it my duty to be like a United Nations peacekeeper. There came a night where I was sitting on the couch watching *The Waltons* (the episode where John Boy gets mugged in town and loses his first paycheck) and Tim wandered aimlessly around the house. I knew I had to keep an eye on him. He learned to be really sneaky (taking too many tips from Roland Martell).

On this particular night, Tim acted exceptionally strange. He meandered around the house, almost as if he were an ant searching for his lost anthill. During a lapse in my vigil, I heard the refrigerator door open and quickly shut. Tim immediately turned from the fridge and marched directly for the front door at combat speed. I barely had time to jump up and stop him. As I stood blocking the front door, Tim pushed, squirmed, and even whimpered. "Where are you going?" I asked.

Tim refused to answer.

"Where are you going?" I asked again.

He squirmed, whimpering some more as he clawed at the doorknob with his one free hand.

"What in the hell is going on!" I yelled. We wrestled over the door handle for a minute, and I finally gave up and let him go. Like a prison escapee, he flew out the door and off the front steps. He stopped in the middle of the yard, reached his arm back in a perfect hand grenade stance, and then let a white object fly. It arced through the air and came down splattering yellow goo and white fragments all over the side of Rod's truck. It was indeed another egg. Tim chuckled. He had gotten his fix.

Later that winter, Rod had grown a little wiser and moved his truck back across the street so that it could lick its wounds. When he did, we could see half-decayed chicken bones on the top of the canopy. Tim had thrown them, too, when he got done ordering out at Kentucky Fried Chicken.

With the snow gone and the spring rains vanishing, firecracker season soon came. Tim found a new trick. He just loved to throw smoke bombs and firecrackers on Rod's porch. One afternoon, the hostilities became so hot that Rod closed his store early and declared a cease-fire. Tim had dropped a live smoke bomb down the mail slot in his front door. There wasn't any immediate response. It was kind of like the calm before the storm. An hour later, Rod timed his retaliation perfectly.

That fine June day just happened to be Tim's birthday. After all his friends gathered around our kitchen table with their presents, the birthday party started. As my mother finished lighting the candles on the cake, there was one more knock on the door. She blew out the match and walked over to the front door and opened it. Standing there, huffing and puffing in his grocer's apron, was Rod.

"Your kids have done it this time. I won't put up with it!" Rod yelled. He flung the expended smoke bomb across the room at Tim sitting behind his huge birthday cake. My mother slammed the door on Rod as he stuck his foot in the way. She slammed it again, and he finally removed his foot and stormed off back to the store, slamming our gate behind him.

When we told Dad about the story, he said, "Oh, yes, I would have invited him in, all right! For a real good beating!" We loved hearing that from Dad. We had never seen two men fight before and would have loved to have seen that.

Rod never gained any ground during our wars with him. I think the real problem was that he didn't have any fun. If he had laughed and chuckled every time he called the police on us or foiled our plans, he would have been a happier man.

There was one and only one time that Rod tried to have a little fun with us, and it backfired severely. It was one of the best Halloweens I had ever experienced. We had more eggs and more participants than ever before, and it was the most target-rich environment that I could ever remember. The police assigned most of their patrol cars to duty in our neighborhood. On this particular Halloween, we had a foreign exchange student from Sweden. He wanted to celebrate Halloween the American way, so we definitely wanted to accommodate him and show him how to do it right.

Our first barrage against the moving vehicles would be launched at the end of our alley. Our anxious group of egg-throwers met on our back porch. With eggs in everyone's hands, we strutted out of our back gate and into the darkness of the unlit alley. Once at the end of the alley, we stood nervously in the darkness while I handed the confused, blond Swede an egg. In choppy English, I told him to throw them at a car when it drove by. He appeared to get the idea by the way he nodded and smiled stupidly.

Approaching headlights signaled us to take our positions in the shadows. Just as the car came by, we threw our eggs. Splat! Splat! A couple of them hit, and a couple of them missed. Our Swedish friend still had his egg in his hands. I scolded him for his cowardice. I told him that if he didn't throw them at a moving automobile, I'd kick him out of NATO. He grinned wildly through his big Nordic teeth. Luckily for our foreign friend, this particular car knew better than to stop.

A minute later, another car came by. I peeked around the corner and identified the rack of lights on top of the car. It was a patrol car. Perfect! As it cruised by, we cut loose with all the eggs. Yellow and white debris exploded and ricocheted off of the side of the car. The officer choked on his doughnut and screeched the patrol car to an angry halt. "Run!" I yelled. "Run!" Everyone ran except our Swedish friend. His didn't know what was going on. It was one of those moments when proverbs and antecedents come clearly to mind. Anyone who is not panicking doesn't fully understand the situation!

The police officer slammed the transmission in reverse and gunned the engine. With the danger of capture becoming imminent, I yelled again, "Run! Police! Police!" The word "police" triggered the correct response and proper levels of adrenaline in our Swedish friend. His eyes shot wide open, and he gasped. Finally, he turned and ran after the pack of kids already sprinting ahead of us. But when most of us diverted away from the alley and into our escape paths through the various neighbors' yard, he kept running down the empty alley. He didn't stop running for a long time. We didn't see him again until school the following Monday. He allegedly hooked up with some other kids from our school who were a little more normal and were simply cruising town.

After the bombing of that patrol car and getting away scot-free, the night was still young, and Rod hadn't provoked us yet. When I took the time to look over at his store, I couldn't believe that he had the nerve to pull something over on us on the worst night ever to be out on our street. We were too engrossed in bombing cop cars to even think about Rod. He was perfectly safe until he purposely made his presence known. It would have been better for him if he had just stayed in bed.

We didn't know exactly what Rod was up to until our little gang split up for a while and searched for new killing zones for the local police. We agreed that it just might be fun to go our own ways for a while. We could all share our stories later.

Soon after Tim and some of the others left, Mitchy Mueller came running back with an intelligence report about Rod. Apparently, both Tim and his friend Mitch reported that they were tiptoeing up the sidewalk past Rod's store when a set of headlights flashed on them from the dark abyss of Bronson's long, dark driveway. It was Rod. He posted himself in the cab of his red Ford pickup and backed it all the way down to the back of Bronson's property and up against the garage. Rod had properly used the darkness as perfect concealment—that is, until he was stupid enough to alert us to his whereabouts by turning on his headlights.

If Rod was going to be a wiling participant in the Halloween games, we were going to count him in. First off, we tried launching long, mortar-style shots from the alley behind the church. But he was a little out of range, and our eggs fell short—some couldn't make it through the thick maple tree branches. I wanted to see Rod's spotlighting firsthand, so I sent Tim across the road as bait. I told Tim to be as conspicuous as possible and fool Rod into thinking he had a live mischief-maker in his clutches.

Tim crossed the street and walked up to the edge of Rod's store. He then slinked slowly down the dark sidewalk, peering from side to side and acting like an escaped convict. Just as he made it in front of Bronson's driveway, Rod quickly flashed on his truck headlights. Tim performed well and ran like he was frightened to death. Rod, that sneaky bastard! What in the hell was he thinking? It took me about two seconds to devise a ruthless counteroffensive.

We armed ourselves with as many eggs as we all could carry, and then we looped around to the far end of the block. I ordered my team to take flanking positions at the corner of Rod's store. I gave everyone a few seconds to grip their eggs for combat. Once everyone was in place, I yelled, "Go!"

We all bolted out of the darkness and stopped directly in front of his truck. We lobbed egg after egg until all were expended. Splat! Splat! Splat! Splat! Splat! Rod fumbled for his light switch as the eggs rained down on the windshield and hood of his truck. He finally opened the door and stepped out. All we heard him say as we ran away was, "Goddamned kids!"

Rod threw in the towel and reluctantly parked his truck back in front of his store. Once back inside his house, he sadly donned his pajamas, drank his warm milk, and went to bed hugging his teddy bear. Rod didn't give us any more trouble again, ever!

Chapter 5
The Witch Next Door

Since the beginning of our childhood, a witch lived within crawling distance of our house (twelve feet to the east.) She was a bona fide witch, or so we thought as kids. Jeri-anne was supposed to have solved that mystery when she interviewed old Mrs. Welman for a high school project. Being highly intelligent and immensely creative, Jeri-anne could also slip up. She never came right out and asked Mrs. Welman if she was a witch just like Barbara Walters would have. Jeri-anne did have experience, though. She wrote articles for the school newspaper and even the *Kellogg Evening Press* when she tried her hand at promoting the Kellogg High School wrestling team. During this historic interview, Jeri-anne nervously fumbled with her notepad during the entire visit and forgot to pop the big question on our aging friend. The rest of us kids found the results of Jeri-anne's interview to be inconclusive. (Not knowing the truth merely kept us in fear for a few more years—like we should have been).

Mrs. Welman was sharp for ninety-nine and a half. She minded her own business and ours, too. She was so weak and frail that she rarely made an appearance outside of her castle. For her to ever come out into the open, something really big had to happen. It had to be something life-threatening because her life was threatened every time she ventured outside.

In addition to her age, her house appeared to be the same vintage. Based on the data I recovered from some old planning and zoning maps in the library archives, her old house had been built just after the turn of the century and probably hadn't been painted since its initial construction. Actually, the house didn't really have a color. The closest hue must have been black because if you brushed up against the side of it, a blackish charcoal residue rubbed off on your clothes or skin. Knowing she was a witch led us to believe that Mrs. Welman had changed the color of her house from white to black during a violent thunderstorm that she had caused herself.

(What? It could have happened!)

Mrs. Welman turned out to be the perfect scapegoat for all that went wrong around our place. If a window got smashed and no one 'fessed up to it, Dad bellowed out, "Who did it, then? Mrs. Welman?" Yep, that's right, Dad! Mrs. Welman did it. Mrs. Welman played with matches, got into old paint cans, ate the rest of our ice cream, and even broke some of your power tools!

Just like all the other neighbors, Mrs. Welman deserved to get harassed by us. We couldn't play a simple game of kickball in the churchyard without trouble from her. Although her house stood only twelve feet from ours on the east side, there was all kinds of room on the other side of her property since it bordered the churchyard.

Mrs. Welman didn't believe in fences—just shrubs, bushes, and mystical force fields that didn't always work. If someone missed the ball during a game in the churchyard, it rolled unabated into her yard. Oops! Now someone had to go in and get it! As soon as someone tiptoed into her yard and picked it up, the blinds in her window wiggled as she peeked out at us. Not only did she spy on us, she incessantly called the police when we played too close to her perimeter or infringed on her property rights. She alerted them no matter how small the infraction.

Mrs. Welman knew about everything that went on in the neighborhood. It was that damned crystal ball! Sometimes she made mistakes, though, especially in identity, since she needed to have nine different mug shots to identify each one of us kids.

One afternoon, my friend Dan and I walked down the alley and noticed her infamous iron weights. These irksome weights dangled from the end of a frayed rope that was strung through a pulley. The simple mechanical wonder hung over her back porch like an exotic gallows. The sight of it definitely kept us in awe. Actually, after years of scientific analysis, we discovered that the weights were there only to help open the trap door that led down to her dungeon. Seeing them blow in the wind, hanging from those ancient hemp ropes, became too much for Dan. They made him glassy-eyed and neurotic. He would begin to twitch. Finally, he had to do something about it, and I knew if he did, he would involve me.

Despite the jilting, Dan still looked for action, but he never expected it again from young sweethearts. In the current crisis of the mysterious swinging weights, Mrs. Welman happened to be a much older woman, and that suited Dan just fine. We were going to take care of those creepy iron weights on her porch once and for all.

Late one evening, Dan pulled a black stocking cap down over his curly hair and armed himself with a sharp piece of kitchen cutlery. He insisted that I accompany him out to the alley, but first we had to turn off our porch light. Once out back, we went over behind Mrs. Welman's yard and took our positions. I posted myself in a thick clump of bushes at the edge of her yard while Dan stealthily crawled up to her porch in the total darkness. As he leaned over the porch railing, tugging and cutting at the ropes, I waited impatiently. I continued to wait until I almost panicked. What was taking so long? Finally, a loud thud shook the back of her house. Dan bolted for the alley, steak knife in hand.

I scurried out of the bushes and ran with him to the safety of our own backyard. We laughed and laughed, slapping each other high-fives and wondered what we had really accomplished. If nothing else, at least those weights wouldn't bother Dan again!

Within minutes and after catching our breath, we were back in the house, seated at the kitchen table and setting up the Monopoly game. The phone rang. My older brother Phil, lounging on the couch and sucking on a Popsicle, reached over and answered it. He stopped paying attention to the TV for a moment and tried to make out the eerie voice crackling in the receiver. It said, "Tell Philip ... thank-you ... for ... cutting my ropes."

Phil immediately recognized the voice but had no clue what she was talking about. He slammed down the phone, dazed. In his bewilderment, he got off the couch and came into the kitchen. He walked past Dan and I and went directly to the fridge to fetch another Popsicle. I asked him what the call was about, and he disgustedly said, "That old bag next door just called and said, 'Tell Philip thank-you for cutting my ropes.' I don't know what the hell that means, but I ought to burn that bitch's house down!"

A large smile grew across Dan's face (which was rare because Dan never smiled). We played our game and laughed sporadically throughout the evening. I wondered how she could have possibly seen us in the darkness— or better yet, how she could have guessed that it was Phil. Nevertheless, Mrs. Welman was determined to take care of the damage.

The next day, the weights hung once again, dangling from a rope with a large, square knot tied in it.

Mrs. Welman not only saw things at night or in her crystal ball, but sometimes she simply peeked out her windows. Every time we got near her house, the window blinds shook. Often, when they did, we saw her eyeballs peering at us through her thick glasses.

Each year, just before winter, Mrs. Welman had an elderly gentleman come by and meticulously install plastic sheets over all of her windows. He did a good job, making it as tight as a drum, just like modern shrink-wrap. Immediately after the old man finished her plastic job, Mrs. Welman went right back at it, peeking around her blinds and trying to track every move we made.

One quiet Saturday morning, Dan and I found ourselves in my bedroom, directly across from Mrs. Welman's kitchen window. Boredom set in. Luckily, it didn't last long, because those were the times we found the neatest things to do. Dan remembered an old hobby of his and decided to revamp it. With his precise instructions, we started an assembly line on top of my dresser.

From memory alone, Dan showed me a new breed of homemade blow darts. He demonstrated the construction process by cutting the heads off of straight pins and installing them into the end of wooden matchsticks. He finished the job with thread and hot candle wax. Utilizing plain, drinking straws as blow tubes, we had just developed a deadly weapon.

Together that morning, we made about fifty of these blow darts and noticed Mrs. Welman peering across the neutral zone at us the entire time. Her crystal ball told her that something was brewing in our sector. During our labors, she just happened to peek at us one too many times, and Dan just couldn't take it anymore. He opened my bedroom window just a crack and nosed the end of a straw out. With one deep breath and one deadly arrow chambered, he blew. *Whoosh!* The trajectory was perfect. The needle sailed through the air and stuck in the plastic directly in front of her window like a porcupine quill in a dog's snout.

Dan and I began an onslaught of flying arrows that lasted several minutes. Soon her window plastic was peppered. It looked like Mrs. Welman's last stand. Dan and I were having the time of our lives until our phone rang. I knew who was calling. My father picked up the living room phone and muttered something to the caller. Dan and I frantically tried to get rid of our evidence. I knew we had been had.

Immediately, my dad's footsteps came tromping through the house. They grew louder and louder. They headed right toward my room. The door flung open, and Dad yelled, "What in the hell are you doing?"

He marched up to my window and looked across the firing line at the dozens of expended blow darts. Behind the plastic sheet, two beady eyes peered back through the crack of the blinds. Now my dad was under her evil eye. He had to perform his fatherly duty now, or she'd put a hex on him.

"Get out there right now and get those off of there!" he screamed. "Are you guys goofy? Do you want a strap?"

We frantically ran outside and got all the darts down out of her plastic. (The window covering didn't quite have the R-value that it was supposed to after that.) Unfortunately, when we were done, Dad forced us to surrender all the ammo to him. I thought for sure that he'd turn my ass into hamburger with his belt, but this particular time, I made it through the episode without a whipping. Dad must have found it somewhat humorous because he spent the rest of the afternoon sketching the scene of Mrs. Welman's house with her two beady eyes peeking out of the window. At the bottom of his drawing, the caption read: "You naughty boys, I see you!" He chuckled for a day, proud of his fine art, and left it out for display for everyone to see. It eventually got framed, and to this day, that sketch hangs proudly on my wall.

I started to get tired of being caught red-handed, so I soon found the perfect ambassador of ill will. In our neighborhood lived a tall, chubby, bulbous-headed, fourth grader named Robbie. Robbie bordered on retardation and really wasn't supposed to be accepted to the normal school system, but he cheated on his school IQ exams and luckily qualified to stay in regular school.

Robbie would do almost anything to gain our acceptance since he didn't have any friends of his own. We had him lapping water out of a mud puddle like a dog because we told him it would make him tough. We also tried to get him to lift a car engine block and offered him sugar cubes if he could do it. Robbie even volunteered to help me practice my skateboarding stunts. I told him to grab my legs when I stood on my hands. Unfortunately, his coordination was off, and he was a little slow at reaching for my feet. I accidentally rabbit-kicked him under the chin. It almost knocked him out, but his head was quite hard.

Since we always got into trouble for messing around near Mrs. Welman's property, we started to train our moronic friend. Actually, Phil had the best program. You see, we tried to get Robbie to go up onto Mrs. Welman's porch one day, but he knew better. Robbie had heard all the scary tales of the witch and what she might do to you if she caught you. She would put you down in her dungeon.

Several of us were leaning on the fence at the edge of Mrs. Welman's yard, trying to coax Robbie into going up onto the porch. After being asked several times and with fear in his eyes, Robbie shook his head and adamantly replied, "Noooooo!"

Phil was a little more experienced at manipulating the mentally challenged than we were and just happened to be out in the yard with us that day. He realized that our skills in persuasion were weak. He reached into his pocket and pulled out a nice, shiny penny for Robbie. Instead of giving it to him, he threw it out onto the narrow cement walkway leading up to her porch. Robbie gulped and paused. He eyeballed that penny. "Go get it!" Phil ordered him. Robbie ran over, picked it up, and ran back. He glowed with pride over his newfound wealth.

Phil threw another penny, but this time it landed on one of the steps leading up the porch. Robbie swallowed. Again Phil ordered him, "Go get it! Get it and it's yours, Robbie!" Robbie spent a few moments mustering up enough courage to run over and grab the second penny. He dashed over and came back somewhat winded (and one penny richer).

I'm not sure how badly Robbie or his family needed the money because we didn't have much social contact with them, but for some reason, Robbie thought a few pennies were quite the fortune. We knew little about his family except that he had a little brother named Harold who rarely left the confines of their yard.

While Robbie's mom stayed in the house and kept a really low profile, Robbie's dad caused a scene almost daily. He drove a large, beat-up station wagon and always exceeded the speed limit on our street. Time and time again, Robbie stayed too long at our house, and his father came looking for him in the car. In style with the Pontiac test laboratories, Robbie's dad sped down Mission Avenue. Just as he reached the front of our home, he must have seen imaginary checkered flags, because he slammed on the brakes and skidded the two tons of metal and glass to a screeching halt. He then yelled out the window with a roar that would wake the dead, "Robbie! Get you butt home now!"

Robbie's facial expressions displayed sheer terror. They were the same every time. He dropped everything and bolted home in utter desperation. Robbie feared his dad.

Although I felt concern for Robbie's well-being that day, Phil didn't because he was all ready with another coin. He kept flipping the coins, and Robbie kept retrieving them. Soon, the pennies landed up on the porch. Robbie didn't want to go onto the porch—she might see him. He got down on his hands and knees and carefully crawled as close to the coins as he could get. Finally, he reached out and grabbed the last penny.

Phil threw two more on the porch, directly in front of the screen door. Now that was going too far! Robbie refused to go that close.

If pennies weren't enough, maybe the stakes needed to be higher. With an ingenious insight to human psychology, Phil pulled out a quarter and showed it to Robbie. Robbie salivated. With spittle forming in the corners of his mouth and his tongue slithering through his crooked teeth with anticipation, Robbie pleaded, "I can't. Oh, no, I can't. She'll see me!" He almost cried. But the temptation was too great. He sure wanted that quarter.

Phil didn't blink an eye. He threw the twenty-five cent piece. It plopped onto the porch and began to roll around in large circles. As it lost its momentum, it rolled in smaller and smaller circles until it finally flopped over and fluttered for a second. The quarter lay still just inches away from the door. "Go get it, Robbie. You'll be rich!" Phil commanded him.

Robbie paused for a minute. His lower lip quivered. He rolled his eyes back into his head as if he were having a seizure. Finally, he turned as if headed to the gallows and marched across the grass. At the bottom of Mrs. Welman's steps, he got back down on his hands and knees and crawled. He stopped at the edge of the porch and reached out as far as he could. Still a couple of feet away from the prized coin, he turned and looked at Phil with desperation. He whispered as loudly as he could, "I can't reach it. She'll see me!"

Phil pointed and ordered Robbie to get it. Robbie obeyed and crawled a few more feet. Soon, he was completely on the porch. Despite his orders, he continued to reach out at the distant quarter. He looked back at us with the same plea. Phil just pointed. Finally, Robbie dropped his head and whimpered to himself. He resumed the pursuit and stretched out the twelve inches. A wide grin spread across his face and as he reached down and secured the quarter between his fingers.

At that precise moment, Mrs. Welman's door creaked open. Robbie shrieked. A slow, torturous death down in the depths of her dungeon was imminent. As fast as he could possibly move his large frame, he jumped to his feet and raced off of the porch. He leaped, and with his legs peddling in midair, he landed on the grass and ran for his life toward the safety of his home.

Damn! Mrs. Welman shut the door too quickly for us to get a glimpse of her. However, a moment later, we saw the corner of her blinds moving. We were under her evil eye once again. I could feel it.

Robbie eventually came back again like always. On the day he did, Phil happened to be gone, but my oldest brother, Pete, was home and very busy cleaning out the shop. Pete grumbled to himself about the slobs that he and Mom had to deal with. The biggest offender was our other brother Kit and all his automotive junk. After a few minutes of making rare, civil conversation with Robbie, Pete got a brilliant idea and offered Robbie the deal of a lifetime. Pete told Robbie to go home and tell his dad that he'd sell the "squad car" for only one dollar. We called it the "squad car" for many years, ever since Dad mounted a CB antenna on top of it. Resembling an unmarked police car, it became a family joke.

The old Chevy had broken down months earlier, and instead of repairing it, Kit began to part it out, selling a piece of it here and a piece of it there. The radiator and engine were pulled out, and miscellaneous components were strewn all over the porch. Pete had had enough of the mess and wanted to do Mom a favor by getting rid of it. Every time Dad was away, Pete played the father figure. We often referred to him as "Papa Peter."

"Yep, that's right, Robbie—one dollar," Pete reassured him. Robbie's eyes grew big. He looked likc he had just seen a ghost. He turned and sprinted home, excited instead of frightened this time. In a matter of minutes, Robbie's dad showed up. After talking with Pete for a moment to validate the offer, he handed Pete the one dollar that he just withheld from Robbie's allowance. Pete accepted it and then commenced helping Robbie's dad load the engine parts up. He also helped push the hulk out into the road so it could be towed the rest of the way down the street.

The dollar sale of the old '65 Chevy Impala became a sore spot with Kit for many years to come. He had great plans to market the car parts and reap hundreds of dollars in sales. Pete, being the acting papa, made the decision to get rid of the eyesore, and he stuck with it. While the two of them angrily hashed it out, the rest of us were too young and too busy to nurse any grudges. We knew each day held more wild adventures.

After the dollar squad car sale, my younger brothers and I went right back to mischief. We used our uncanny ability to find new uses for old items. One item was the ole wrist rocket slingshot. That thing, we discovered, with the wrist brace and surgical tubing, could hurtle almost anything you could get into its pouch. I could launch the miniature pool balls from our half-sized pool table (that we got as joint Christmas present) halfway down the block. If one went through someone's window, the occupants could never tell where it came from without triangulating our coordinates.

My friends and I launched crab apples, plums, three-foot wooden dowels, chunks of gravel, etc. Best of all was the ole firecracker in the green apple! The old lady across the alley was once hoeing her garden with her pacemaker cranked up to ten when one of our apples landed next to her. She looked down at it for a second and noticed the little puff of blue smoke rising from the stem. Then it blew. *Blam!* Everything came apart—her bean sprouts, her fertilizer, her eardrums, and even her bowels. After that, my brother Steve recommended that they make a new adult diaper called "Just In Case."

That poor elderly lady got some real shocks from us without ever provoking us first. Phil's friend Juan Delgado just loved some of the neat gadgets we had around our place—especially the machetes. He had seen *Animal House* with John Belushi and adored the end scene when Belushi dressed up like a pirate.

After having a mock duel with us, clanging machete blades, Juan climbed up high on our eight-foot backyard fence and looked out at the neighborhood. Immediately, he spotted the old lady across the alley, once again hoeing in her garden.

Juan conspicuously grunted. When the old lady looked up at him, he swung the machete over his head and yelled, "We take no prisoners, veggie!" The old lady reached for her chest, expecting the big one to come. After almost having to call the ambulance for her, we laid off the poor senior citizen. She didn't deserve our guff, but Mrs. Welman did.

In addition to discovering all the things we could launch with my wrist rocket, we also found plenty of new targets. With the high fence and structures surrounding our backyard, there wasn't much else visible but the mountain ridges, telephone lines, and ... the lone brick sitting on the top of Mrs. Welman's crumbling chimney.

We launched salvos of rocks, marbles, ball bearings, nuts, bolts, and dried dog poop at that brick trying to topple it down. News got around fast about our quest, and soon the neighbor kids came over with a cache of BB guns and bows and arrows. Each time we launched a rock and missed the chimney, the rock vanished over the top of her house. A second later, we heard a *tink* of it hitting someone's car out on the street. Oh, well.

Chips flew off the brick every time we made a direct hit with a BB or rock. It quickly became evident that the mortar was still too well intact to let the brick break free and fall down into her chimney. Robbie eventually showed up. When he saw the firing range, he and all his grey matter couldn't contain the excitement. He mumbled something about going home and getting his dad's 30.06 hunting rifle. Shortly after Robbie darted home to get the gun, we heard the sound of my dad's truck pulling into the driveway. Everyone scattered. Target practice was over.

Dad surprisingly didn't find out about our day at the range. Apparently, Mrs. Welman's crystal ball had been in the repair shop, because she didn't know what we were up to, either. That's what we concluded, because the police never arrived on the scene like they should have.

One of the rare times Mrs. Welman did show her face was when Tim and his friend Mitch crawled up our back fence and leaped onto the roof of one of her sheds. The rotted roof had already exposed the ancient sawdust insulation. Tim and Mitch ripped open the roof just a tad bit more and began to play with their toy dump trucks. After a couple of hours, most of her roof was torn off, and a large pile of sawdust developed at the base of the shed.

A little later that afternoon, we heard a faint knock on the door, almost like the light tapping of a dog's tail. My mother answered it and found Mrs. Welman standing there with a crooked, wooden cane. The old fossil wrapped herself in an ancient, knitted, white shawl and trembled as if she were experiencing the dying quivers. In her tiny, wavering voice, she explained to Mom the atrocities that were currently taking place on the roof of her shed. Mrs. Welman must have been freezing by the way she shivered all over. I wanted to get her a blanket, but it was the middle of July and quite hot outside. Well, if she survived the trip over to our house, I was sure she could survive it back. (She did.)

When my dad got home that afternoon, Mom cracked the news to him about the roof damage. He went bananas, cussing and swearing and inventing new words again. With no chance of getting out of it, he gathered up all his tools and spent the next several hours rebuilding the obliterated roof. As we got ready for bed that night, we knew Dad was still working because of his incessant cursing in Pig Latin.

Tim and Phil weren't the only ones Mrs. Welman had fingered in a Major family lineup. Kit had once changed the oil in his car, and instead of taking it to the service station to get it recycled, he took it out into the alley and poured it along the side of her back shed. The black, carbon-rich oil splattered all along the lower part of the siding (which was rotten, anyway), and the rest of it soaked into the mossy soil.

This scene was identical to the roof incident. Mrs. Welman showed up at the door once again, quivering all over, and told Mom of the severity of the oil spill. No one had yet heard of the *Exxon Valdez*, so Mom couldn't have put the blame on its Captain, Joe Hazelwood. When Dad came home and the news was broken to him, he went berserk just like always. (No wonder he stayed away so much when we were kids!) Since he could only call us "goofy" so many times, on this occasion, he chose to simply call Kit "the boob."

Over the years, each of us had our own share of run-ins with Mrs. Welman, and each of us described her in slightly different ways. Steve had a strange experience involving her—or should I say her spirit?

We had a birthday party for Tim in the later part of June. The sun shone brightly, and the weather was nice enough for a little kickball in the backyard. Some of our neighborhood friends had come to join the fun. Accidentally, one of them kicked the ball over the top of Mrs. Welman's garage. It sailed right into her yard. Steve volunteered to run over and get it, but just before he made it out of our yard, the ball came flying back over. We all looked at each other dumbfounded.

We didn't think much of it and continued our game—that is, until someone kicked the ball over the garage again. Moments later, before someone could even run around and retrieve it, the ball returned over the garage to us. That had to have been quite a throw for the old mummy next door. The mystery disturbed Steve severely. Mrs. Welman must have been working out at the gym.

Steve decided to test her again. He threw a plastic baseball over. It came flying back. Frantically, he picked up a little yellow bucket and heaved it over into her yard with the "you'll take it and like it" gesture. Amazingly, the bucket came flying back. In a rage, Steve dashed out of our yard and ran around through the alley to catch Mrs. Welman on the pitcher's mound. We held up the game waiting for him.

Minutes later, Steve slowly ambled back a broken man. We forced a testimony out of him. He said that there was no one—no one at all—in Mrs. Welman's yard. We never did find out who kept throwing the ball and other objects back into our yard. We labeled it as an unexplained phenomenon.

Mrs. Welman haunted us for many years until she finally passed away one summer while we were in Canada. By the time we returned in late

August that year, the city had already bulldozed her house down. We were spared any supernatural incidents emanating from her property after her death. No poltergeists or anything. She went into the other world and left nothing behind. Thank God.

Robbie and his family moved away before he made it out of the sixth grade and was never heard from again, either. Who knows what government research lab he's in now? I hope that he and the Roswell debris are getting along well.

Chapter 6

The Icy Streets and Tim's Incarceration

As we all know, every Christmas season, the children's shows *Frosty the Snowman* and *How the Grinch Stole Christmas* air several times on a variety of channels in the weeks before the great holiday. If you have the means, I recommend watching them. One of the reasons why Frosty and the Grinch are my two favorite Christmas characters is that they those two guys were troublemakers. Frosty jaywalked, mouthed off to an officer of the law, broke into a greenhouse, stole a ride on the train without paying, and even used blackmail to keep the magic hat. My kind of guy! The Grinch was even worse—grand theft, false testimony, and breaking and entering to name a few.

The memories of cuddling on the couch in my pajamas and watching them are indelibly etched in the deep recesses of my mind. The winter scenes of the snow-covered Kellogg mentally come to life each time I watch those two programs. In the midst of each winter, the snowfall transformed our neighborhood into a new kind of world. Our sleigh-riding spot was within walking distance to our house (we lived only a half a block from the hillside).

Because Kellogg's city traffic director instituted a permanent, full-time, four-way stop at the end of our block, both the drivers of passing vehicles and we children benefited. The mandatory stop became the perfect trap for cars to stop on the icy street and for us to grab onto their bumpers and hang on for the ride. To us, it was known as "hooky-bobbing." In certain parts of the country, it's called other things, and in other parts of the world, the sport is unheard of.

Josh Mueller was the best hooky-bobbing comrade of all. He had no fear. He didn't care what type of vehicle it was or who was driving. In fact, Josh even managed to latch onto the bumper of a police patrol car and was taken a few blocks down the road to the doughnut shop. Josh and the officer even went inside together and ordered a couple of jellies. (Just kidding about that one.)

Both Josh and I began adding up how many blocks we covered one winter. Sometimes we only went a half block per jaunt—at other times, we went as many as seven or eight. That was quite a feat. Some of the reasons we had to terminate our body-to-bumper interface were such things as encountering rough terrain. A slight change in the weather could turn the snow into deep slush one afternoon and then freeze it back into ice, forming deep grooves and high ridges running down the middle of the road. Other hazards caused us to bail off—like another car coming up behind us.

Rare, but not unheard of, was a driver that just went too fast. A couple of maniacs had detected our presence on the bumper before and panicked behind the wheel. They drove faster and faster, trying to throw us off. (Hell, we were the closest things to Hollywood stuntmen.) Trailing behind oil-burning cars was unpleasant, as well.

I hooky-bobbed with Tim a lot. Just like always, he went a little further with the pranks. He once went all the way across town behind a car. Besides experiencing some frustration in teaching Tim the ropes, I had a real problem with gloves that stuck to the bumpers. While other kids wore thick, warm gloves, I wanted to look cool and always bought myself a pair of longneck, welding-style gloves. I froze the shit out of my fingers most of the time with them.

I once lost a glove when Tim and I latched onto the bumper of an innocent car that happened to unfortunately stumble into our neighborhood. We made it through the four-way stop and were just starting to get up to speed when we encountered a frozen slush barrier. I was ripped right out of my squatting position and was dragged on my belly for a few seconds before gravity and plain old friction finally detached me from the bumper.

Tim continued to hang on but looked back at me lying on the road behind him. Right next to him, only twelve inches away, my longneck glove hung off the bumper with no hand inside it. I yelled and yelled at Tim and even pointed. "My glove! My glove! Get my glove!" Tim had no idea what I was yelling about, so he let go. I pounded on the ground with my fist. Damn! Another glove down the tube! That wasn't the only time I lost a glove. The other I time I did, I actually had a chance to get it back.

There I was, casually delivering my papers and had stopped to collect from a nice elderly couple. As the old lady was counting out the money, her husband slipped on his coat and went out the back door to his car, which had been idling and warming up for him. Just as I thanked the lady and began to leave, the old guy climbed into his car and backed out of his driveway and into the street. I couldn't believe my eyes. A beautiful opportunity lay right in the palm of my hand—an old fart in a car!

I rushed out, dove down to the edge of the tall snowbank, and did a perfectly executed combat roll. I lay near the edge of the street. From there, I quickly crawled up to the back of the car as the old coot fiddled around trying to shift from reverse into drive.

General Motors must have put Braille on the dash of the car, because the old man had to feel around with his fingers to turn on his lights, find the ignition switch, and engage the automatic transmission.

He started down the road at a moderate speed until he had to slowly brake for the stop sign. Somehow, the proper directions to the grocery store started to become clear in his feeble mind. It took him a few seconds to figure out which way was right and which was left. I stood up and looked into back window. When I saw his right hand slap his left hand—and each hand point in opposite directions—I realized this guy's brain was rotted out, and he shouldn't even have been on the road. I figured he was good for another few blocks before he went up the off-ramp to the highway and killed a few innocent motorists in a head-on collision.

Finally, after plugging his nose and farting to blow the cobwebs out of his mind, he turned down another road that headed right for a busy part of town. After two more blocks, he slowed again for another stop sign. There he stopped. I stayed in the hooky-bob squat position waiting for him to go, but I heard him unexpectedly put the car into park at the stop sign.

Oh, shit! He knew I was on his bumper, and he was coming to get me! No way did I want to get beat with an aluminum cane or oxygen hose. It was time to flee for my life. When I started to turn and run, one of my gloves refused to let go. One of the screws that held his license plate on had snagged it. I tugged and tugged. Although the glove stretched, it wouldn't break free. I heard his car door open. Oh, shit, now he was coming for me! I tugged harder and harder on the glove, stretching it even further. I heard the old man's footsteps. Oh, crap! Here he comes!

Finally, I left the glove for dead and ran off slipping and sliding down a dark alley. I didn't even look back at the guy for fear of him seeing my face. However, the newspaper bag still draping around my neck had to have been a dead giveaway to who I was.

The next day, I delivered my papers and came to his house. I expected to see a wanted poster on his front door. As I walked up his front steps and opened the door to his veranda to lay his paper inside, his front door burst open. Now, this old fart could have just called me on it and told me that he didn't appreciate me hooky-bobbing behind his car, but instead, he gave me the old Mr. Roger's act. "Hello, young man. How are you today? Isn't it a wonderful day in the neighborhood? I found this glove. Does this happen to be your glove?"

I played dumb.

"Well, boys and girls, I'm going to leave this little glovie right here. Whoever it belongs to can just come up here and get it." The old pervert finally went back inside and left the glove sitting on the rocking chair next to his front door. I was getting the glove back, but not at that moment. I was going to get it back when I wanted to get it back, and that would be when Josh was with me.

Josh and I went back later that night. Josh eagerly snatched it off the rocking chair for me for only a quarter.

Just like during our car-bombing days, word must have gotten around to the police that they had a hot LZ on Mission Avenue. This called for the attention of the department's toughest cop—a reckless Clint Eastwood wannabe—the illustrious Officer Meyers.

Like any other city in America, Kellogg had certain individuals who, when they got a badge put on their chest, thought they were God's gift to law enforcement. One overweight punk with a badge even pulled over his own mom and gave her a ticket. She was as brain fried as he was because she took it in stride and continued to be very proud of her little boy.

Meyers read the local police blotter, *True Detective* magazine, and he also listened intently to his own private police scanner. It was only discovered after his downfall that he was quite demented. Despite his hidden quirks, Officer Meyers took his job very seriously—actually, *too* serious. He became so obsessed with his job that he even patrolled the neighborhoods while off duty in his beat-up Chevy pickup, equipped with a loaded pistol and a box of day-old doughnuts.

After weeks of successful hooky-bobbing, Tim recruited a small group of grade-school friends and began teaching them how to be a pro at the growing sport. They violated one major rule of engagement, though. One night, the five of them latched onto the bumper of a car at the stop sign while another vehicle approached from the rear. Behind the beaming headlights of the tattered pickup was none other than the magnificent Officer Meyers.

He had been patrolling for weeks, and now he spotted his quarry. Damn, wouldn't the chief be proud! Meyers immediately pulled the truck over to the side of the road, and its front bumper smashed into a high snowbank. He jumped out and yelled, "Stop, you kids! Stop in the name of the law!"

The car at the stop sign pulled away, while the five kids released their grips and all ran in different directions. Meyers yelled again. He grew extremely upset over the fact that the youth of Kellogg had no respect for authority, especially his divinely ordained authority. Heads would roll this time!

Somehow, Meyers chased down and captured one of the kids and forced the ten-year-old (under sheer duress) to disclose the identity of his coconspirators. Damn, wouldn't Perry Mason be proud!

I was home that night, working at the kitchen table on a new radio transmitter, while Steve sat by himself on the couch watching TV. After having fled the scene, Tim bolted through the front door and dove into one of the bedrooms. I didn't pay much attention to his entrance because, with eight brothers and sisters, kids were coming and going all the time, so I simply continued on with my work.

Steve, at this time, was in a phase of his life when he wanted to be a cop. He watched all the cop shows and had even gotten a book from a novelty company that illustrated fifty-two different police apprehension techniques. Since Steve didn't run around much with Tim and me, a slight rift between us had formed a few years earlier. Tim and Steve's differences came to a head this particular night when, shortly after Tim's hasty return, we heard a knock on the door.

It was either up to Steve or me to answer the door. My mother had left for the evening to attend one of Allyson's dance recitals. Everyone else was gone, as well; that left only Steve, Tim, and me at home. Steve happened to be the closest to the door, so he got up and opened it. Standing there with his chest puffed out, snowflakes in his hair, and his head arrogantly cocked to one side was Officer Meyers. "Good evening. I'm looking for Timothy Major."

I then realized how peculiar Tim's behavior actually was. He was in some sort of trouble, but I knew when to keep my mouth shut. Meyers inquired again for the whereabouts of the one and only Timothy

Major. Steve seized the golden chance to further his involvement in law enforcement. He had seen enough cop movies to qualify him to work for Scotland Yard, and now he was going to finally get his feet wet. Steve yelled down through our long, narrow kitchen, "Okay, Tim, you can come out now. They're here for you!"

He repeated himself one more time. Finally, the bedroom door slowly creaked open, and Tim sheepishly stepped out. Giving himself over to the authorities, he submissively walked up to Officer Meyers, who stood there out of uniform—off duty but yet still on the job protecting the citizens of Kellogg from dangerous hooky-bobbers.

"You are coming with me, young man!" Meyers ordered Tim. Tim glared over at Steve and gave him a look of true hate. How dare he betray his own brother? There wasn't much I could do except yell at Steve about turning him in. Steve claimed that he wanted to be a cop someday and would turn in even his own brother if he broke the law.

Tim left with his captor and was ushered out to Officer Meyers's beat-up truck. From there, he was driven uptown to our local police station.

Mom came home an hour later with Allyson and learned what had happened to Tim. Her jaw dropped in total disbelief. She immediately rushed out the door and headed to the police station where they held her youngest son. It was crazy. Hell, Officer Meyers could have been home drinking eggnog or doing something productive like making Christmas cookies. Instead, he spent his spare time taking the law into his own hands, patrolling the streets at night and looking for bandits.

At the police station, my mother grew absolutely appalled. Meyers had taken her son out of the safety of her house, across town, and up to police headquarters—a place for true criminals. To detain him until Mom could arrive, Meyers had the audacity to haul Tim downstairs and lock him behind the bars of a prison cell.

Sitting on the worn-out, blue-striped mattress, the undersized ten-year-old Timothy Winthorp Major pondered the thought of punishment for hooky-bobbing in a communist country. Would he be put in front of a firing squad or sent up Vergobbi Gulch for ten years of hard labor breaking up boulders with a sledge hammer thus making little ones out of big ones?

After pacing the cell for an hour, Tim spotted a folded-up wad of paper under the bunk. He reached down and picked up what seemed to be a familiar shade of green. It was a two-dollar bill. Life wasn't so bad, after all. Tim scored!

Shortly after the great find, Mom arrived to rescue Tim, and the ordeal ended with her engaging in a fierce argument with Officer Meyers over the unjust incarceration. Meyers's biggest defense was, "Do you know that I could have shot him for running?" It was a good thing for Meyers that my dad wasn't still in town. My father would have chewed this guy up and spit him out.

Fate had it that a couple of short years later, Meyers did shoot—and kill—someone for a minor infraction. His trial was painful for a lot of people, especially him. The facts about his sick personal obsessions came out. The wannabe cop went too far and killed someone. He was the one who was sent to prison. I wonder if he found any dollar bills on the floor?

Chapter 7
Summer Camp

Uncle Bill's lake place wasn't the only location on Lake Coeur d'Alene in which we frolicked in the summer sun. At a nearby Boy Scout camp called Camp Easton, the YMCA sponsored a weeklong summer camp. Initially, I had no intention of going to this silly, structured event which I felt had been designed specifically for wimps. It took me years to understand that the average child in America didn't engage in camping, crafts, swimming, and outdoor activities like we did on a daily basis. And for some reason, I never could handle any type of prearranged activity—whether it be laborious (a job) or recreational (sports teams). Organization meant no spontaneity—and mischief was purely spontaneous. Besides, my type of pals just didn't go to summer camp. They went to juvenile detention centers.

After I terrorized the pool and staff members at the YMCA for so long with Josh Mueller, the management tried to redirect our energy into more meaningful activities. One Saturday morning, they asked us if we wanted to earn our way to summer camp. These well-meaning community leaders informed us that thousands of other happy campers had earned their own way to camp by selling the famous YMCA peanuts.

Unfortunately, I had to turn the offer down without having to think twice about it. I had my taste of door-to-door sales selling the flower and vegetable seeds that I was stupid enough to order out of the comic book. On that endeavor, even though I knew I hated doing anything with the public, I gave the seeds a whirl, anyway.

My first prospective buyer for a pack of petunia seeds was a very nice elderly lady who lived just around the corner from our egg-throwing spot. We had raided her garden during many of the previous autumns. I was totally astonished when she sincerely told me that she wasn't interested in seeds since her newly acquired wheelchair wasn't four-wheel drive, and she couldn't get out to the garden anymore.

In fact, I was outraged! How dare she reject my sales offer? I thought about throwing her into a full nelson wrestling hold and slapping her upside the refrigerator to try to convince her to buy, but her walker was in my way. (I'm just joking.) Within five seconds of her refusal, I knew that I was through with sales as a career. Shit, one rejection was enough for me. So, when the YMCA staff extended their offer, I knew right away that there wasn't a chance at trying again with peanuts. So, for the next few weeks, we gave our mom such a hard time that she ended up paying for us to go only to get rid of us for a week.

The other kids who didn't sell seeds or have parents who forked over the money somehow qualified for assistance. Although kids from all the social classes attended camp, there were a group of underprivileged ones, and my heart actually went out to them. Our family wasn't poor by any means, but money was tight with my parents having to support nine of us. But these kids were poor, and their hygiene wasn't the best. In fact, some of them resembled the youngster who came over for breakfast in the movie *To Kill a Mockingbird*.

All these kids had to do was prove that they wet the bed three times a week, were unable to recognize two items called a toothbrush and a comb, and that they successfully survived a year eating only peanut butter and jelly sandwiches. They had the worst moth-eaten sleeping bags and suitcases and had the chitty-chitty-bang-bang dirt on their faces. Regardless, they were okay in my book. As tough as I could act on the surface, I always felt compassion for others. It was the other arrogant assholes that thought they were better than the rest that I usually got into the fistfights with.

Summer camp was where I met Dan. He didn't seem to fit in any more than I did. Neither of us liked the structured activities where we had some simpleton talking at us like we were three-year-olds, walking us through a simple task like driving a tent stake into the ground. Even though I had befriended a lot of other kids there, each time the weeklong camp sessions ended, we said our good-byes with shallow feelings. I couldn't accurately classify many of them as friends. They were more like victims of our pranks.

Not only were many of the other campers not overly brilliant, the head of the entire program had reached a ripe old age and was mentally slowing down. We poked a lot of fun at this elderly man when we should have been more supportive. It was evident that he put his whole heart and soul into providing the younger generation with a positive experience. His name was Mr. Williams. We simply called him Willie just like the Americans called the Japanese "Japs." If one remembers the old World War II propaganda newsreels, the commentator always talked about the enemy in a particular way. "The Japs did this, and the Japs did that, but the high-spirited American GIs kicked the Japs' asses, ladies and gentlemen." In those days, they didn't say "Japanese." They simply said "Japs."

Our reference to Mr. Williams was in the same style. When we were busy digging tiger pits for the other campers or sneaking out of our tents at night, we were warned, "The Japs … oops! I mean *Willie*. Willie's coming! Willie's coming! Willie's going to kick your ass!" Everyone used the threat of Ole Willie too loosely. Willie couldn't fight himself out of wet paper bag nor win a game of chess with an amoeba. The poor guy was just too old and decrepit and should have retired years earlier. Each time someone caught Tim or I in the middle of carrying out one of our secret plans, they cried out, "I'm telling Willie." (Whoopie shit!)

"Oh, crap! Not Willie!" we'd reply as we reached up with our fingers to stop our bottom lips from quivering. By the time they could go and get Willie, we had already run through the woods and arrived on the other side of camp. Willie was so senile that once he'd arrived on the scene, he usually wasn't able to identify the culprits. So, to humor himself and the other tattling campers, he yelled mightily at some other kids who had nothing to do with our crimes. We ended up getting a lot of other people in trouble for our mischief. As a last resort If Willy couldn't find any kids to yell at, he scolded the nearest pine tree. He and Mr. Magoo, I found out, were related.

Mrs. Williams, by chance, was a little sharper stick than Willie. She watched over the female campers and knew that they were vulnerable to mischief themselves as well as to an invasion by sneaky boys. During one of the best summers we spent there, Tim assisted me in building a couple of booby traps. At first, our favorite one was a simple trip wire across the trail that would topple any kids who stumbled to the outhouse at night. A few days later, I tried to rig an elaborate water-spilling bucket that would dump on anyone who flushed the toilet.

While I snuck around the bathroom working out the mechanics, Tim spent his time at the crossroads in the trail digging a couple of man-eating pits. To add to the victim's confusion, he spun a complex web of fishing line in between the surrounding group of trees.

One day, a little girl no more than eight years old accidentally discovered what we were up to. She ran down to the main camp to get Mrs. Williams. Tim and I scurried off and hid in the nearby bushes. We risked getting into trouble, but the opportunity to watch someone get snared in the traps would be worth it.

We kept busy for a short while inventing our own burp, belch, and barf terminology. For example: a burp and belch executed at the same time is a "bellurp." If you're really sick and try to burp only but end up barfing, then you "barpped." But if you let go with a really long belch and ended up barfing, that was a "bellarf."

A few minutes later, the girl returned tugging on Mrs. Williams's hand. Mrs. Williams displayed great interest in what this little girl may have seen. "Now show me what you saw, Missy," Mrs. Williams instructed her.

"Right over here. I saw the two boys," she said as she pulled Mrs. Williams along and pointed.

Nearer and nearer they came. Tim and I held our breath. Close and closer they went toward the fresh patch of pine bows on the ground. Finally, Mrs. Williams walked right over the first tiger pit. The skimpy branches and leaves gave way under her weight. She fell forward, pulling the little girl down to the ground with her. Oommph! Luckily, that first pit was only a foot and half deep, and Tim had only filled it with mud. This one didn't have any punji sticks or fermenting human excrement in it.

Mrs. Williams gasped as she fell, but she managed to catch herself with her other hand. She lay for a second, hanging her head in silent rage. After Mrs. Williams caught her breath and regained her bearings, the little girl pulled on her arms, trying to help her up. Mrs. Williams pulled her foot out of the pit and stood up. Her leg was covered with mud halfway to the knee. She was no weenie. A simple tiger pit wasn't going to stop her. She asked the little girl to show her more. Tim and I started to giggle. They headed right for the fishing line web that Tim had so craftily spun. Tim had imagined himself to be a spider on LSD. Mrs. Williams swore that the boys who created this mess were on LSD.

In this case, just like always, Tim had taken the things that I had showed him and pushed them to the nth degree. All I did was instruct him about how to run a couple low-profile trip wires six inches off the ground.

After that first lesson, Tim took a huge roll of fine fishing line and strung hundreds of feet of it throughout a group of trees where two of the trails met. He placed the lines not only at ground level but also at ankle level, waist level, eye level, and some of it so high that I thought he was trying to trip up a few birds. Inadvertently, he left plenty of slack in all his lines. Most of his trap was one continuous line that he spun around the forest. Fortunately, that proved to have unique consequences when Mrs. Williams and this little girl walked a short distance into Tim's labyrinth. They were getting strands tangled around their ankles without even knowing it. As they pulled the lines tighter with their feet, it raised new adjoining lines into their faces and around their necks.

The little girl continued with her account and said, "I saw the one boy over here," as she pointed and dragged Mrs. Williams (and a couple of fish lines with them) along a little further. A few yards deeper into the trap, one line rose up to Mrs. Williams's neck. She shrieked and clawed at it. When she pulled it down and out of her way, another one rose up between her legs. When she stepped forward, trying to scale it, it only wrapped around her ankle, causing her to trip and stumble forward into even more wires. Mrs. Williams finally decided to head out of the trap by turning down a different path. That only led her into countless other tangling fish lines. She grew frustrated, entwined in Tim's little mess. Finally, she yelled down at the little girl, "Go, Missy! Go get Mr. Williams. Please, please hurry. I'm stuck."

As the girl ran down the trail to get Willie, Mrs. Williams mumbled under her breath, "I'm going to catch those bad boys if it's the last thing I do!" Willie arrived a few minutes later with the First Cavalry and a Barlow pocketknife and released his loving wife from Tim's snare.

After that near-fatal incident, word spread fast about a campwide sabotage, and the teenaged counselors began interrogating the other campers. To my surprise, the other kids were so impressed with our traps that they formed their own unofficial code of honor and did not rat on us. With this incident—like most of them—we didn't get caught. We rarely got caught at anything we did.

If people would only look at life more openly, they would be able to see that inside every experience, there lies many undiscovered benefits. I found that out after two summers of listening to Willie blow that damned bugle ten times a day. One summer, I decided to play dueling bugles with him. I was shocked that it took several days for everyone to catch on that there were two bugles in camp.

Willie used bugle calls to muster all the campers together on the parade field. He had an old, tarnished, dented bugle that he used several times a day for the purpose of assembling the campers before launching each scheduled activity. When Willie bugled, everyone came running. When I bugled, everyone came running, too, but they ended up swearing.

I had been a trumpet player for several years and quickly learned that, by holding down the first and third valves on a trumpet, it essentially became a bugle. So I brought mine to camp, and on the first day, shortly after setting up our tents, I pulled it out of its case and gave it a try. "Dah-di-dah, di-dah-*dah*!" The kids began to run at high speed down the parade ground. It worked!

A day later, Willie blew his bugle shortly after lunch, and we all came running. In accordance with his established routine, he sent everyone to their appropriate activities and then went to his cabin to retire for his afternoon of exertion (and for a swig of Geritol).

About five minutes later, I snuck up to my tent to get my swimsuit; the plaster mold painting started to bore me. I pulled my trumpet out of its case and blew a nice "Willie" call. Everyone from all corners of the camp dropped what they were doing and came running. I had already fooled them a few times over the previous few days, and by this time, most of them were getting fed up with it. This time when they arrived to find no Willie, some of the kids wanted his hide. That damned Willie!

I never felt sorry for Willie because he didn't have enough brainpower left to distinguish between insult and compliment. The kid I felt sorriest for was a dumb, underprivileged boy by the name of Alfie Brumfield. Alfie was tall, skinny, and just plain dumb looking with his over-inflated lower lip.

We attended summer camp in the midseventies, just about the time when streakers were famous all over the country. On this particular summer campsite, we had just gotten all of our tents set up in the woods a few hundred yards away from the cookhouse. I got a wild idea when I was changing into my shorts. I would streak across camp with everything I had hanging out in the wind. At eleven years old, I didn't have much to catch on the thistles, so I didn't worry about it.

I stepped out of my tent and yelled, "*Streaker! Streaker!*" Then I made such a quick dash across camp that few of the other campers had time to come out of their tents to see me. With the lack of witnesses, I did it again. For their amusement, I ran back and forth between tents a couple of times. After laughing about it for a few minutes, I got dressed.

In the meantime, Alfie had been watching, and he noticed all the attention that I was getting. He became envious. Somehow in his warped mind, he thought he could win friends and influence women by streaking across camp like I did. The only thing that he could accomplish would be to be mistaken as a Vienna sausage salesman. He undressed and stepped one foot outside his tent. In his deep, monotone voice, he weakly yelled out, "Streaker! Streaker!" Then he stepped back inside his tent. I figured that Alfie was either too afraid to really streak or that he didn't understand the procedure.

By this time, the rest of the campers had their cots set up and their bags unpacked, and they were now ready to see this supposed real streaker. Alfie tried again. This time, he stepped two feet outside his tent and yelled out, "Streaker! Streaker!" But just like before, he stepped back into his tent. Now the other campers were getting antsy and wanted to see this phantom streaker. But after each announcement, Alfie was nowhere to be seen. He was hiding in his tent.

Each time Alfie attempted to do a real streak, he grew braver and stepped a few more feet away from his tent, yelling, "Streaker! Streaker!" Like the previous attempts, he quickly dashed back inside the canvas flaps to safety. After the fifth time, he had a few pretty fed-up campers wanting to lynch him. Ignorant of this, and braver than ever, Alfie carefully stepped out one last time, about ten feet away from his tent.

Unbeknownst to him, about eight other campers had sneaked up behind him and were waiting to pounce on him. Alfie yelled his last "Streaker! Streaker!" and as he turned to run back into his tent and awaiting harem (or the one he wished he had after all the fame he achieved by streaking), eight angry campers tackled his naked body to the ground.

Poor Alfie got a pinecone up the butt, sticks and rocks jammed into his bony back, and eight perturbed campers jumping on top of him. One guy sat on Alfie's chest and began banging his head on the ground. A couple of other kids pinned his arms and legs down. A few more were kicking him in the ribs while one sadistic soul reached out with one hand and grabbed Alfie's penis, testicles, and scrotum. In one tight handful, he tugged on the package with all his might. From that second on, Alfie sang soprano. He painfully moaned from the beating he was undergoing.

Finally, Jerry Fulmer unfolded a large pocketknife and said, "Why don't we just castrate him?" Now, back in those days, everything was fun and play. No one was going to do any castrating, but for a moment there, I started to get worried and was ready to jump in and break it all up. Alfie had had enough.

Somewhere in the back of the mob stood a frail, little, wimpy kid who had a striking resemblance to Alfalfa from *The Little Rascals*. He was the first to buckle under the pressure, and so he yelled out, "Willie's coming! Willie's coming!" On perfect cue, the mob hastily dispersed.

With his genitals now snapped back into place and turning blue, Alfie slowly crawled back to his tent and collapsed onto his cot. I couldn't say he licked his wounds because Alfie wasn't a dog. He was a boy, and he was in pain. Later on, I befriended Alfie during a few camp activities and attempted to let him know that at least someone cared to be his friend. It was the least I could do.

The reason I said that many of the other campers were kind of stupid is that so many of them thought that all the little, goofy, "happy camper" bullshit we did was cool. I couldn't stand holding hands at night around a campfire with some strange kid who picked his boogers and had warts on his fingers, just so we could all sing, "He's Got the Whole World in His Hands." With that kid, it was like "he's got his whole mucus membranes in his hands." And "Kumbaya" really gave me the willies. I didn't want to be caught singing. That wasn't manlike. Years later, when karaoke become so popular, my stomach turned every time I heard someone attempting to sing a popular song because of all the horrible renditions from the past.

Each day when arts and crafts time came, I didn't like Willie showing us a plaster mold of a bouquet of tulips and talking to us in his Uncle Pervie voice. "Isn't this nice, boys and girls?" If he put his hand on my knee one more time, I was going to stick an ice pick in it. I wanted to lose the crowd and find fun stuff to do. If it wasn't mischief, it was conflict.

Camp Easton wasn't big enough for two bullies. During one of our summers there, a scroungy-looking camper went around bullying the little kids. The only mistake he made was that one of those kids happened to be my little brother Tim. Tim gave me a couple of reports on this retard, so I hunted him down. I caught up with him outside the outhouse one afternoon and confronted him. I often talked tough, but when it came down to the reality of fighting, I always felt fear. Still, it never seemed to stop me. This bully and I instantly started duking it out. The punches were flying, and most of mine were connecting. Tim was cheering.

After only a minute into our bout, this guy grew upset from being punched in the chops time and time again. Finally, in one heated frenzy, he took a couple wild swings. He squealed like a retarded kid having an embolism, so I backed up to avoid him. Strangely enough, I tripped over a large root protruding out from a huge pine tree. I immediately fell down onto my back, keeping my eyes on him the entire time. My opponent had swung so hard and uncontrollably that he tripped and fell right on top of me.

When he snapped out of his little seizure and realized our positions, he immediately pinned me to the ground. I wisely called a truce. Without another thought, he said, "Okay," and he let me up. I knew there was always another chance for a rematch, but I doubted that he'd ever bother Tim again, and I hoped he wouldn't bother the rest of the younger campers, either.

After I brushed the dust off of me, I thought to myself, "What a sap!" This dumb bastard could have pulverized me. I had punched his face in for five minutes and almost made him cry, and then he ends up falling right on top me. What luck for him. Although I got off of the ground unscathed and scored a ten-to-one hit ratio, several kids went running wildly through camp telling of how I got my butt kicked. So much for the facts—that was yellow journalism at its finest.

In addition to having to take out a camp bully that year, I was also forced into dealing with a surprise rivalry between a close friend and I that started the very first day of camp. One of our old neighborhood friends, a toe-headed, chubby kid named Joe Yergler, came again that year but was beginning to act differently right from the beginning. Maybe we had all matured more than we realized since the year before, because something was definitely up with his attitude.

We had just finished getting our tents set up and our sleeping bags unrolled and then began to greet our old comrades that attended camp the year before. The incident that freaked out Joe was when my other friend Dizzy Dan pulled the first prank of the season. Dan cracked open a smelling salt from a first-aid kit and bombed another kid's tent with it. This became Joe's moment in the sun. A huge halo glowed over his head while the angel wings sprouted out from his shoulder blades. Joe jumped in and admonished Dan severely. Since I was a much closer friend with Dan than Joe, I rushed to Dan's defense. Words were said.

After our little skirmish with Joe acting like a dickhead, I didn't call him by his formal name of Joe Yergler anymore; I shortened it and just called him Jergler. Naturally, he didn't like that, but I didn't dare fight him. Joe was pretty tough. We had seen him fight a couple of the local bullies, and he even challenged both of the Tobias brothers. During one incident, he punched out Greg's little brother Tom, and instead of defending his little brother, Greg ran away scared. We had reason to fear Joe. He could easily knock my block off. So I had to outwit him.

So that night, after we were ordered to go to bed, I snuck outside my tent and began to bomb Jergler's tent with pinecones. He knew I was doing it. Threats were yelled out through the fabric, and I finally subsided. I had succeeded in agitating him enough for one night in perfect accordance with *The Art of War*; if your enemy is stronger, then anger him.

The next day, Jergler took the offensive by sneaking into my tent and eating my entire box of Ritz crackers. He purposely laid the box out in front of my door so that I would discover it right away. Worse than that, he laughed about it right in front of me. That did it.

"They tasted pretty good, didn't they?" I asked him.

"Oh, yeah, very good. Thank-you very much!" he said sarcastically.

"Well, good. Maybe I'll have another snack for you later," I promised him. While he was away from his tent the next day, I did pull a stunt on him that blew his mind so severely that he never bothered me again. In fact, he grew so disturbed over the incident that he spent the next four days shaking his head.

Jergler and I drifted apart from then on. I only saw him once after that, and that was during a quick visit he made to our house several years later. He was a changed man. He had found religion. Who knows where he is now? Mixing up a batch of Kool-Aid for all his friends?

Chapter 8

Uncle Bill and the Safari Wagon

Uncle Bill stood nearly six foot three and weighed over three hundred pounds. With his wit, he charmed—and usually terrorized—all those he came in contact with. Sober, he could be as docile as a teddy bear. Inebriated, he unleashed his verbal wrath on anyone within slurring distance. At his United Airlines job on the ramp at Sea-Tac Airport, he touted many nicknames. Some of his coworkers called him "Belly 310" because of his weight. I once got into trouble as a child for referring to him as "Uncle Bilge." My mother demanded that I show him more respect. Regardless of what impact he made on people or what anyone would think of him, he simply didn't care. After witnessing Bill offending hundreds of people over the years, I've watched them verbally strike back at him. Being impervious to insult himself, Bill would only cock his head back and chuckle.

I once flew from Fort Bragg, North Carolina, into Tacoma on a military transport plane and then made my way to Seattle unannounced. After bursting though the doors of Bill's favorite drinking establishment—the Derby—I was surprised to find that he wasn't there. The Derby was his favorite hangout, just walking distance from his trailer court.

From there, I ran across the crowded highway 99 to The White Shutter and asked for him by name. At first, they didn't know who I was talking about. Finally, the trashy, wrinkle-faced waitress and the rotten-toothed bartender glanced at each other and in unison blurted out, "You mean 'Loudmouth Bill?'"

"Yeah, that's him!" I replied with a large grin spreading across my face. Jackpot!

In his early military photos, with his slightly upturned lip, casual smile, and greased-back hair, Bill strongly resembled Elvis Presley. However, unlike Elvis, Bill never married nor made much mention of any female companions, except the German girl he met in a haystack. Bill claimed that she couldn't speak English, but she did know sign language. The story always ended with Bill displaying his linguistic genius by making obscene gestures with his fingers.

In confidence, he made it clear to me that he was once bitten and twice shy. Because of something that went awry in his past, Bill treated women with great contempt and disrespect. With any level of alcohol in his blood at all, he severely insulted women in general. But worse that engaging in a casual conversation with him was to be out in public with him and get him going. He'd make rude, gross comments loud enough for any nearby women to hear. He had seen too many good men "bite the dust" by getting married. To Bill, women were all conniving witches.

When any of Bill's coworkers or nephews got married, he would describe the horror of marriage by gritting his teeth and shaking his head from side to side as if he were experiencing sharp chest pains. Just before you could reach over to give him a pre-cardio thump, he would squeak off with, "She shot the poor son of a bitch down before he ever got off the ground. Keeeeeeee Reist!"

Everything about Uncle Bill was unique—the way he lived, the way he drank, and the way he spoke. He seemed to growl as he talked, and when he did, he talked somewhat out of the side of the mouth as if everything he said was a wisecrack. With each beer or slug of whiskey, he talked proportionally louder. Sometimes he used the excuse that he lost his hearing in one ear from working around the jets. It may have been true; there were times you could be carrying on with your own little monologue when you had actually intended it to be a dialogue. Meanwhile, Bill would just nod and "uh-hum" periodically at your story. Even after a perfectly structured tale with a carefully planned climax and subplot, at the end of your little discourse, he'd pop off with the strangest reply because the whole time he had no idea what you were saying. At least when Bill got caught feigning intense interest, he was man enough to admit he tried to wing it because he couldn't clearly hear you.

Bill spent twenty-seven years in Seattle living near the airport, close to his job. Because of his solitary lifestyle and bizarre behavior, Bill at one time was on the list of suspects during the hunt for the Green River Killer. Years later, Bill gave a wonderful, drunken confession (performance) for me while I activated my handheld tape recorder. While we sat one summer afternoon sunning on his front porch, he held a whisky drink in one hand,

and he yelled into the small Sony device, "*I am the Green River Killer!* I've been doin' it for years and getting off scot-f——g-free! But you don't blab it around!"

My nephew and I almost wet our pants because we were laughing so hard. Luckily, none of the neighbors called the police because they knew Uncle Bill quite well and knew how full of crap he was. And besides—the murderer had already been caught.

Despite his shortcomings in the social graces, Bill was the most parsimonious bastard I have ever known. He paid cash for everything, never bought anything new, and never used credit—ever. The decrepit (but totally owned), eight-by-thirty-foot, 1957 trailer in a Seattle mobile home park became an exciting place for us kids to spend the night while en route to our summer home in Canada.

After a grueling, seven-hour car ride all the way from Kellogg to his abode in a Seattle suburb, we rested our weary selves at his place. Bill called the old heap "the dumpster," and we totally appreciated the nickname. He had pinned so much junk on the walls over the years that some of it was actually historic. At times, we got glimpses of *Hustler* magazine centerfolds before my mom could tear them down. While we slept at night, the jet airliners from Sea-Tac Airport incessantly screamed overhead until dawn broke.

During the seventies, Bill encouraged an old German friend by the name of Helmut to fly into Seattle and tour the Emerald City with him. Although Bill and Helmut had kept in touch via handwritten letters over all the years, Bill didn't really know that much about his old German friend. For all he knew, Helmut may have been a wealthy German executive with Lufthansa Airlines or a washed-up brewery worker. Regardless of anyone's social status, flying eight thousand miles and being introduced to "the dumpster" could ultimately be a culture shock, but during this historic visit, Helmut took it all in stride.

The night that Helmut arrived in Seattle, Bill took his old comrade out on a drinking spree to celebrate their golden reunion. They visited a few of the lower-class pubs within walking distance of Bill's trailer and saturated their brain cells with grain alcohol. (Yes, they got all boozed up.) Despite the fact that Helmut had never been to the United States before and also the fact that he could barely speak English, the beer had finally begun to make him feel a little more at home and relaxed as the night wore on—that is, until they arrived back at Bill's trailer.

Standing outside the door of his humble little hooch, Bill stuck his hands into his pockets and fumbled around for a moment. A sober expression appeared on his face. The neurons in his brain began to fire, and there became of flurry of activity in his nerve synapses. Just like an answer being spit out of a slot on an ancient computer, Bill quickly arrived at the awful conclusion that he had locked his keys inside the trailer before they had left. Helmut, in between burps, began to suspect by Bill's demeanor that something was wrong. With a few reassuring waves of his hands, Bill calmly communicated to his foreign visitor that all was well. Then, having no recourse, Bill began beating and prying on his door with a tire iron that he had just retrieved from the back of his '61 Rambler station wagon that lay in the driveway with one flattened tire.

Within moments, Bill skillfully popped the door open and climbed up the tiny, metal steps into his home-sweet-home. Cocktail hour ensued once again under the illumination of a cigarette smoke-stained, 40-watt bulb. Bill proudly held up his glass of gin and backwash and proposed a toast. Just as they began to drink up, enjoying the peak of their triumph, several King County police cars raced through the trailer court and skidded to an abrupt halt in front of Bill's trailer. The squad cars' blue and red lights flashed, and the bullhorn began to blare out commands. "Come out with your hands up!"

The noise scared Helmut so much that he dropped down on the floor and crawled under the opened hide-a-bed, frightened to death.

Since Bill believed himself to be a law-abiding citizen and considered the police to be dutiful public servants, he staggered out of the trailer to aid the officers. They only ended up happily throwing him against a squad car and handcuffing him.

After the police ordered Helmut to come out from under the hide-a-bed and slapped the handcuffs on him, as well, one of the officers opened up the inviting door of the squad car. Bill froze in place for a moment and respectfully asked the head officer, "Officer, do you mind if I lock up my trailer before we go?"

"What? This is *your* trailer?" the patrolman responded.

A neighbor had called the police and reported that two intruders were breaking into Bill's trailer. He and Helmut were they!

Few people understood Bill's drinking, but take away the alcohol and you have taken away half the man. Wrong or right—it doesn't matter; it's just the truth. Of course, without the drinking, Bill was a big, gentle panda. But Bill's role in life wasn't to be a public benefactor. He didn't believe in dishing out warm-and-fuzzies. His role was that of the obnoxious, belligerent drunk, and he was proud of it. He became a true icon to the Major family and only grew more famous as the years flew by.

In his own defense, Bill spent years perfecting his short list of reasons for his habitual inebriation. First off, "Having a few drinks takes the edge off of life as we know it today." Secondly, "You've got to get drunk and be somebody." And thirdly, if you were a married man, "That bitch must drive you to drink. Don't go home and beat the piss out of her. It's not worth it. Let me pour you another drink."

Downing a few refreshing cocktails for the sheer enjoyment of the flavor wasn't Bill's objective. He had to get as loaded as he could before 2:00 am. He'd always tell me, "You know, having that first drink is just like priming a carburetor. Once I get started, I can't stop."

Sometimes I'd ask, "Bill, you're supposedly a devout Catholic. How can justify drinking like you do?"

He always looked shocked at my ignorance and would reply with something that bordered on blasphemy. "What do you mean? Jesus and the twelve apostles got ripped out of their gourds at the Last Supper! They were all fishermen, and you know how they drink!"

My oldest brother Peter studying engineering at Animal House in Butte, Montana. Having unlimited energy and focus, he earned the nickname "the Bionic Man" among his South African colleagues.

My older brother Chris "Kit" winning a bodybuilding contest in Washington State University in Pullman, WA. He possessed a terrific blend of brains and brawn. With his fast car, rock band, and physique he was the envy of the local male youth.

Philip sitting on his Kawasaki 400; the same motorcycle that I road during the police chase with Josh Mueller. Phil, being fiercely independent and self-reliant, had little need for showing off like the rest of us. This bike was one of his few toys.

I just arrived in Kellogg for Christmas after a grueling 3000 mile flight home from Fort Bragg. Once home, I discovered that the mischief had only continued in my absence. Tim and Steve kept up their antics in full force.

My younger brother Stephen on the bow of the Merlamac II off the coast of British Columbia heading toward our summer home. While I snuck around pulling my pranks, he committed all of his acts of audacity in plain sight.

My youngest brother Timothy "Blue Eyes" standing in front of Steve's 1970 Ford Mach I Mustang. His meticulous ways spilled over from his Lego building days to engine rebuilding and then eventually on to finances. He went on to be an ultra successful stock broker, never missing a beat on anything.

My three sisters shown here in a rare photo torn from an old family photo album. Jeri-anne, the oldest, named after my father. Kimmerly, slightly older than me was the last sibling born in Canada. Allyson being the last, longed so badly to keep up with her six older brothers.

Timmy grinning just after mouthing off to a trucker on a walkie-talkie that I had modified. Visible behind him are various walkie-talkies and electronic gadgets, including the wires coming in through the window that led to the ski pole antenna on top of our roof.

*Steve behind the wheel off The Death Machine. The graffiti,
the buckled metal of the hatch that they cut through the roof,
and even an ax chop mark are visible in this photo.*

*My chemistry set days. No matter how big of a chemistry set I got, Josh
Mueller always got a bigger one. Motorcycles always intrigued me as well.
The brochures of the latest Kawasaki mini-bikes are taped to the wall.*

Pete and Phil at the kitchen table with an assortment of firecrackers and rockets. The details of their raids are strictly confidential to this day.

Me, Steve, and Tim during the winter of 1970 throwing snowballs at passing cars in our alley—not really a smart move. The motorists knew where we were.

Uncle Bill and Kit being towed back to the dock in Jaws after a test run with the new V-8 engine at Rose Lake, Idaho. Electrical problems caused the motor to die.

I am goofing off doing a wheelie on my Yamaha XT550. This photo was taken just days after a five-mile, high-speed police chase at over 100 mph. Like always, they never caught me.

One of the go carts that I had built from total scratch.

Uncle Bill working on the ramp at SeaTac Airport for United Airlines. Rumors had it that there was more than just Pepsi in the cups that he drank from.

Uncle Bill shown here piloting Jaws up the Coeur d'alene River not far from Harrison, Idaho just as they passed another speedboat. My brother Kit is water skiing in the far left of the photo. He rode the skis from Uncle Bill's lake property on Coeur d'Alene Lake all the way up the river to the Cataldo Mission, a total of 31 miles—a local record. In the lower part of the photo the rusty, inverted car headers jet up and out from the beefed-up Chevy 327 with the velocity stack air intake in the middle.

Uncle Bill with the Safari Wagon after the lug nuts had sheered off near Avery, Idaho, a town that resembled Aintree off of the movie Deliverance. Bill left his friend to guard the car but didn't make it back for three days because it was a holiday weekend—his friend felt traumatized.

*During his army days Uncle Bill had an uncanny resemblance
to Elvis Presley. In fact, Bill was stationed in Germany at
the same time as Elvis and had actually met him.*

Pete's 1969 AMC Javelin.

Kit's 1970 Ford Torino GT Fastback.

Tim's 1968 Ford Torino GT Fastback.

*The Hill Street highway over pass that Dizzy Dan
and I hung the Halloween dummy from.*

The Kellogg Civic Building. The Police station is at the far left. A mid-1960's model police car with a single light on the roof is parked in front. This photo is courtesy of the Kellogg Public Library.

The Major House on Mission Avenue, home to nine children. Visible in the lower right corner is the family station wagon and the bow of Jaws with the painted shark's teeth and eyes on it.

Once, when I was a kid, I went shopping with Uncle Bill. Booze was first on the agenda. Inside the liquor store, I knew exactly what he wanted and anxiously grabbed a fifth of Black Velvet off the shelf. I handed it to Bill and got chastised for my grave error.

"No, no, no!" He pointed down to the row of half-gallon bottles on the bottom shelf. "I only buy family size!" I never made the mistake again of grabbing a small bottle.

There came a time after I had reached adulthood that my mother and Aunt Jackie really baffled me with their lack of understanding of Bill. On this particular beautiful, hot, and balmy August afternoon, Uncle Bill had joined us for picnic at his Lake Coeur d'Alene beach property. Halfway through the sultry day, I wander up the hill to the refuge of Bill's tiny camper. Apparently, he had purposely abstained from drinking until the opportune time.

He had just finished a nice swim awhile earlier (which more resembled a rhino wading through a swamp) and was waiting patiently for me to arrive. By the time I wandered up the hill to his old camper trailer, the droplets of condensation were already rolling down the outside of the chilled Black Velvet whiskey bottle. I thoroughly understood his pain. So I gave in and allowed him to pour us a drink of whiskey.

Naturally, since his property had always been the family recreational spot, there were young children present on this occasion, just as usual. But they were down the hill on the beach and somewhat sheltered from Bill and his obscenities by sheer virtue of distance. And besides, it was common knowledge that once Bill started drinking, he would become loud, foul mouthed, and with certitude offend (if not scare) most of the women and children. That is one reason the supervising adults always kept the children carefully contained to the safety of the beach.

On this meaningless afternoon, the instant my mother and aunt realized that Bill and I were beginning to immerse ourselves into our cocktail hour, they simply went to pieces. I thought they were going to have a nervous breakdown by the way they shook their heads, wailed, and quivered all over. They acted like they had never seen Bill drunk at his lake place. I scratched my head in total bewilderment. Bill had been getting soused at the lake with everyone there for over thirty years. That was an irrefutable fact of life. My mom and aunt acted like they were having POW flashbacks. What did they think he was going to do—come down to the lake, read the comics, and eat cookies?

Bill was at least somewhat predictable. He usually drank in precise patterns of one day on, one day off. He complained about the jesters at work who hounded him the morning after a good drunk. "Hey, Bill, was it an *on* night? Did you have an *on* night last night, Bill?" Catching Bill just after an *on* night was not a good idea.

Surprising enough, there were times when Bill could be very crude without even trying. Sometimes the situation was a matter of being at the wrong place at the wrong time. He proved it one day at the bus stop in Seattle.

One morning, Bill arrived on the job too drunk to work, and his boss found him laying on one of the tables in the cafeteria, moaning in pain. Fortunately, his boss ordered him off the job. There was no way Bill was going to be allowed to drive the small tractors around on the tarmac within collision distance of the passenger planes. Following orders, Bill punched out on the time clock like any loyal union employee and staggered out to the bus stop.

Out at the long bench, he joined a group of elderly ladies who were waiting for the same bus. While he sat there wilting the flowers in the large, decorative cement pot with his breath, his head began to spin, and his stomach started to bubble uncontrollably.

When he couldn't hold it down any longer, he scrambled to the garbage can at the end of the cement bench and began vomiting with screaming, violent convulsions. His large frame quivered, gripped with spasms. With one last bow and deadly roar, he dry-heaved so hard that he messed his pants—the ole famous Hershey Squirts.

The old women on the bench hid their faces in horror at the spectacle before them. The vivid sounds of chunky fluid splattering on the sides of the garbage can and the ferocious hacking and coughing from Bill turned their stomachs.

Eventually, the bus came, and he climbed aboard with the load in his pants and with the invisible stench of death following him. Bill had no choice but to sit in it all the way home. The passengers on the bus twitched their noses like curious rabbits. When asked about what happened at the bus stop in later years, he claimed he "got hit at both ends!"

My earliest encounters with Uncle Bill's drinking came when I was a very young child sleeping in my bed. His screaming at my dad in our living room during their many drinking sessions awakened me countless times.

When Bill drank, everything he said became a scream instead of normal speech. And sometimes, if he knew he couldn't properly pronounce certain words, he'd just make up something witty. For instance, when Princess Di was killed in the tragic car wreck, Bill said the "Pepperonis" had been her. And in regard to international politics, he called South Africa's Mandela "Mandoli" after an old neighbor of ours.

For many years, Uncle Bill's favorite line was, "Have you ever made a jump at Bragg?" He asked that year after year until he finally talked me into going into the army as a paratrooper and getting stationed at Fort Bragg with the famed Eighty-Second Airborne Division. (I then made lots of jumps at Bragg—only to find out that Uncle Bill had never made a jump in his life. However, Bill would eventually get his chance.)

Bill and my dad were great drinking buddies, yelling and screaming in our living room until the wee hours of the morning. They did that until my dad finally moved back to Canada. After that, Uncle Bill only got to drink with my dad two or three times when he flew the four hundred miles north on a small pontoon plane to see him.

I once made the comment to my dad, "Boy, Uncle Bill sure has a big gut!"

My dad disgustedly glanced over at me and said, "What do you mean? That's not his gut. That's his liver all swelled up from the drinking!"

Somehow the story surfaced about Dad and Uncle Bill getting into a fight at our summer home at Jennis Bay. When I asked Dad about it and how he could beat up a man over twice his size, Dad disclosed to me a little-known secret. He claimed that he used opposing force on Bill somewhat like a piston in an engine coming up at the wrong time during the explosion. It's supposed to tear everything all to hell—that's what he did to Bill. My brother Pete laughed at that one. Pete said that Dad was probably bombed out of his mind as badly as Bill, and both their brains were probably torn all to hell like the supposed piston.

Although Uncle Bill's moments in the sun with us nephews were plentiful, he actually didn't make it over that often to Kellogg because the job at Sea-Tac International Airport kept him quite busy. But being employed by the airlines did give him the opportunity to do a little traveling. In his younger years, Bill ventured away a few times to places like Hawaii, and then he went on to attempt to reach Lima, Peru.

During that fateful trip, he experienced a very unfortunate, extended layover in Panama. Not surprisingly, Bill didn't last long there because he annoyed the officials so severely that they kicked him out of the country. Rumor has it that he got drunk and made fun of a Panamanian general in full dress uniform sitting across the lounge from him. It happened to be one of Noriega's lieutenants. When the Panamanian police apprehended Bill, instead of executing him, they politely sent him back to the United States on the first available plane.

As each of my brothers came of age to drive, they became the designated drivers to make the trips to Spokane to pick up Bill for his visits to Kellogg. Each trip was no less than an epic adventure because Bill usually had a fast, hard, cocktail hour on the forty-five minute flight to Spokane and wanted more when he touched down. Although he got drunk and obnoxious, he was very generous. He always treated his chauffeurs to a quick meal somewhere along the way—usually burgers. However, even a seemingly innocent stop could become incredibly precarious at times (especially when Bill did things like urinate in the middle of the McDonald's parking lot).

After many years of flying into Geiger Field in Spokane, Bill uncharacteristically decided to make a special trip over by car. The news of his impending arrival seemed quite peculiar because Bill hadn't owned an automobile for years—since his third drunk-driving offense. This time around, he was going to make a fresh start as a responsible driver.

I don't know if he won the car in a lucky hand at poker or if his claim was true that he picked up a real bargain machine for only $125.00. It was a car, all right, but there was a catch. It was missing its gas tank. Problem immediately solved! Bill quickly hired a local garage to install a used tank pulled from an identical model at a nearby junkyard.

After prepping the vehicle for his historic journey to Idaho, Bill acted on one more of his brilliant ideas. He figured that if could only add one more bargain to his list of prized acquisitions, his mission would be complete.

In addition to a beast of a car for $125.00, he made a deal (with undisclosed details) for an old, aluminum-hulled speedboat. Bill was now a budding yachtsman as well as an exquisite limo owner. On the day of his departure, he latched the nonfunctioning boat on its rusty trailer to the bumper of his car and climbed aboard, completely equipped with a good drinking buddy and a fresh (family-sized) jug of whiskey.

The route from Seattle to Kellogg began with nearly thirty miles of dense, inner-city and suburban traffic on crowded arterials, followed by fifty additional miles over the steep Snoqualmie Mountain Pass, with three more hours of desolate desert driving ahead, and then a final stretch of seventy-five miles through Spokane and into the Idaho Panhandle. Kellogg lay just past Lake Coeur d'Alene over one last mountain pass that separated the rest of the world from the secluded valley. Depending on a traveler's speed and condition, the trip could take anywhere from six to ten hours.

By the time Uncle Bill rolled up in front of our house on Mission Avenue, it was already late in the afternoon, and he caught me right in the middle of assembling the latest of my inventions in the front yard. I immediately dropped everything and jumped the fence. I ended up reaching the car before he and his copilot could even get out. The moment he pulled the key out the ignition, Uncle Bill, just like a senator's wife christening a new battleship, marked the beginning of a wildly adventurous era remembered as the life and times of the Safari Wagon and Jaws—the boat from hell.

After climbing out of the car, Bill secured his jug of whiskey and staggered up the steps and through our door with his friend in tow. On the living room welcome mat, Bill attempted to introduce his friend Louie to my mother. Louie reached out to shake Mom's hand, but instead of making hand contact, he fell flat on his face and rolled onto the rug, consequently bumping his head on our coffee table.

Meanwhile, as the introductions were coming to a close in our living room, my younger brothers and I checked out the car. It was nothing more than a 1968 Oldsmobile Vista Cruiser station wagon, a real pile of junk. Luckily, we spotted an opened but uneaten pack of raspberry jelly-filled Hostess doughnuts sitting on the seat. That was the best part of the whole car/boat deal. And boy, did they taste good! The doughnuts left white powder rings around our mouths, and I was hoping I wasn't going to be accused of eating cocaine.

Looking back at the boat, I wondered what in the hell Bill was thinking. The boat motor lay in pieces that were strewn all over the floorboard. In addition to its age, this wasn't a regular speedboat. The steering wheel was placed off to the starboard side, protected by its own tiny Plexiglas windshield. This jalopy looked like shit and couldn't even run. What good was it? Nothing Uncle Bill ever owned was normal. For some reason, he always gravitated toward all the freakish products that the world had to offer. His cars, motorcycles, or anything mechanical always had to be some type of reject.

During that weekend, several of us kids jumped in the car with Bill and joined him for a ride up the river. From that trip on, the car became known as the Safari Wagon. But a short while later, we watched a film called the *Gnome-Mobile* at the theater, and we decided to alter the name of the car and call it the "Moldmobile" because of all the rotten carpeting, dumpster debris, burger wrappers, and dried french fries on the floor. The odor inside was enough to gag anyone.

An innocent housefly accidentally got trapped inside the car a short time later. I watched it land on the dashboard and crawl up to the windshield gagging, coughing, and begging me to open the window so it could fly out to fresher air. Hot, steamy dog poop … anything—just get him out of the moldy automobile. The color of the car could not have been more perfect. It was dark green with wood-grain paneling. It even had a tiny, green-tinted sunroof just in front of the luggage rack. My God, a Motown masterpiece!

Near the end of that first summer on the weekend before school started, Bill took Steve, Tim, and me with him in the Safari Wagon on a trip high in the mountains on the border of Idaho and Montana. Steve rode up front with Bill and tried to act mature and grown up. Tim and I sat in the back seat with the warm, summer air blowing in our faces. The back roads and Bill's slow driving began to bore us.

Although the stench of the car wasn't bothering me at the time with all the windows rolled down, all the garbage piled up on the floorboard and seat was. I nudged Tim with my elbow. When he looked over at me, I inconspicuously lifted an old Burger King bag up to the window and let the wind suck it out. Behind us, it tumbled down the road like a leaf. Tim and I giggled. It was his turn to find something to eject from the car. Mile after mile, we kept launching garbage out into the breeze. With each dump, we giggled uncontrollably. Steve kept looking back and giving us the evil eye. Neither he nor Bill knew what we were doing. We were actually doing Bill a great service by cleaning out his car.

Eventually, we turned off the pavement and drove for almost an hour up a windy, dirt road to the top of a high mountain ridge. Supposedly, we were looking for huckleberries. That was surprising because I could never pick more than a handful at a time without eating them. All I wanted to do on this particular trip was crack into the fresh watermelon that we'd just bought at the store.

We finally arrived at the top of the mountain. The view thrilled me intensely because I could see all the way to Canada and more than one hundred miles in any direction. Bill let Tim and me goof off in one spot while he and Steve drove down the road a short distance to find their own patch of berries. I think we were actually getting on Bill's nerves, and he merely needed a break from us.

After a while, I began to wonder what happened to them. I had eaten enough handfuls of berries. I had utilized the chance to light up a cigar that I had saved for months in my underwear drawer. A half hour later, Steve came walking up the road by himself and said that the car had gotten a flat tire. That came as no shock to me since all the tires were bald and looked like big doughnuts on rims. Walking down to help Bill seemed better than staying in the bushes bored out of my mind. When we arrived at the scene, we found Bill swearing and wrestling with the bumper jack like a real pro mechanic.

Uncle Bill had managed to get the spare tire on the car, but there was one problem—the spare tire had virtually no air in it, either. It flattened out immediately as Bill lowered the jack. As enthusiastic children, we didn't fret, but Bill took it a little harder. He decided to drive the car the way it was up to the main dirt road so we could at least try to flag someone down.

At the top where the roads forked, Bill parked the car and waited for another sightseer to come along. A while later, a car came down the road. Bill waved his arms in the air. As the vehicle approached, I recognized the driver. She was the grouchy old bitch from our neighborhood, Mrs. Bowman. We had thrown eggs at her house on several occasions. It didn't take her a second glance to identify Bill. The old hag gunned the engine and sped past him with the tires spewing gravel. A huge cloud of dust engulfed him. Bill gagged and coughed and used a few choice words. We giggled and irritated Bill even more.

Steve, Tim, and I didn't mind waiting around for Bill to get us out of the jam, just as long as the watermelon held out. During our wait, we drew paper targets of our favorite schoolteachers and neighbors and hung them on stumps. We took turns shooting at them with our .22 rifles.

After two hours of our incessant shooting and eating watermelon, Bill finally caught a ride with an elderly gentleman. The sun had just set. Seconds before Bill slammed the car door, he gave us a quick pep talk and told us to hold out until he returned. A few hours went by until it actually got very dark, and the stars started to shine. Even then, we didn't worry. Instead, we continued to wait patiently in the safety of the Safari Wagon cracking jokes—crude ones, of course.

Finally, we saw a set of headlights flickering in the distance. The pair of high beams grew brighter and brighter until they reached our position. The vehicle came to a stop, and both doors immediately opened. Uncle Bill and one of our other uncles got out. It was none other than Uncle Bob, the world's greatest tinkerer. They opened up the back hatch on Bob's Jeepster Commando and pulled out a good spare tire. I held the flashlight as Bob hastily changed the tire and got us on our way.

The following spring, Bill was involved in an accident in Seattle where he broke his collarbone. The huge cast encased all of his arm, shoulder, and part of his chest. The doctors ingeniously propped up his arm, stretched it out at chest level, and encased it in plaster. It was to remain in that position until the cast was removed. Because of the extent of the injury, the airline gave Bill time off to recover. Naturally, Bill flew over to visit his favorite hell-raising spot.

After Pete picked him up and drove him back into Kellogg, they both started up the Safari Wagon after its long winter hibernation and prepared it for a road trip. Pete went to the cupboard and packed up some goodies for their excursion along the scenic back roads of the North Fork of the Coeur d' Alene River.

While they were out driving on one desolate road and enjoying the scenery, a large, four-wheel drive truck barreled around a corner and headed directly for them. Since the road wasn't wide enough for both vehicles, Pete quickly flung the steering wheel to one side to avert a head-on collision. For a split second, they were in safety's arms … until the car plowed into a two-ton boulder concealed in the grass on the side of the road. The car careened through the weeds and came to an abrupt stop. Unfortunately, Bill, unsecured in the passenger seat, flew forward like a crash-test dummy headfirst into the windshield.

The impact wasn't enough to send Bill through. It was just enough to jam his head into the safety glass, leaving a dome-shaped impression. With a cracked-up windshield, mangled bumper, and a severe headache, Bill still regarded Pete as a hero.

When they got back into town and pulled the Safari Wagon into the driveway, Pete strolled into the house laughing about the incident. Bill gently climbed out of the car and leaned over the windshield, inspecting the damage. I peered out of the kitchen window, and when Bill saw me, he pointed at the impression in the windshield and rubbed the top of his head. Later on, I took a closer look from inside the car. Chunks of Bill's hair were still stuck in the glass. Ouch!

The real fun in the Safari Wagon didn't come until yet another spring when boredom overtook me, and I became really good friends with the car. I had just gotten out of the eleventh grade, and as usual, Uncle Bill had mothballed the car in our driveway for the winter while he stayed in

Seattle and worked his job at the airlines. The snow had piled up on the top of it and kept it buried most of the time. The name "the Moldmobile" stuck in our minds as strongly as the "Safari Wagon" did, especially after I opened up the doors this particular spring to check out the possibility of getting the car running on my own. I found out instantly that the stench would knock you down.

That year's adventure began when Dan and I were leaning against the car one afternoon and discussing our plans for the weekend. As I tapped my fingers on the hood, it sent increasingly louder and louder signals to my brain. "Tony, Tony, Tony … help me! Help me!" the car subliminally called out. At first, I thought it said, "Help me, Forrest," but that wasn't it. It was definitely something like "Tony … drive me!"

To no surprise on my part, I discovered that the doors had been left unlocked, and one of the windows had remained halfway rolled down since the previous autumn. The winter rains formed a puddle of water in the passenger-side floorboard. Mosquito larvae and other gooey things were squirming around in the slime. The smell of mold and the vile smell of maggot-filled hamburger remnants turned my stomach. Just to make sure the conditions in the car were safe for human occupancy, I threw our dog Oscar in there and locked him inside for several hours. He didn't seem to mind the odor and showed no signs of the black plague, tuberculosis, or scurvy, so I let him out, and I climbed in. Now, if I only had the key.

I rummaged through the hanger in our kitchen window but couldn't find the brass key with the fob attached to it that at one time read "Oldsmobile." I knew that fob well because I scratched an *M* in front of the name so it read "Moldsmobile." It was nowhere in sight. Without the key, I would just have to be creative.

Many, many times, I watched people in the movies hot-wire cars, so I knew I could do it, too. Dan said he'd be happy to do his part and dump the gas into the carburetor, but he couldn't help with the electrical. When I pulled the ignition switch away from the dashboard and pried on it with a screwdriver, tiny springs and gizmos went flying all over the floor. One piece flew into the pool of slime and got swallowed by some mutated creature with three eyes. *Forget trying to recover that piece—give me a paper clip,* I thought to myself.

After making one jumper with a bent paper clip and inserting it into the proper slots, I shorted across it with a small screwdriver. Despite the few sparks, the engine turned over and came to life. Bingo! Dan and I cheered. As we pumped up the tires and let the engine warm up, we kept looking over at each other with macho-type gestures. We were going to be big shots now. There was a chance that we may be able to pass ourselves off as mighty, back-road adventurers with the guys at the local sporting goods shop. But, other than that, I just didn't think the girls were going to rave over two punks in the Moldsmobile.

By the time Dan and I had the car ready to go, the sun had set, and darkness overtook Kellogg. My mother had just gotten home from a school meeting and noticed the sound of a running car engine emanating from the driveway. She pulled open the back door and glanced out at Dan and me fiddling with a siphon hose and air pump. Immediately, she knew what we were up to. Panic overcame her. She shook her head from side to side. "Oh, my God! You guys can't. You just can't!" She paused for a few seconds and then continued, "If the police come here, I don't know anything!" She trembled for an instant and then slammed the door as she stormed back inside the house. Mom was seriously worried about us. I wasn't worried. I knew we would be careful, and she would have no explaining to do to the police.

Dan and I went for a little test ride—nothing big. We had only gone on a short jaunt down the old highway and on a rumble through the cemetery, daring goblins to jump in front of us. I somehow knew that fate wouldn't allow us to get pulled over that night, and Mom wouldn't have to deny that she had a son named Tony. I was right.

A couple of weeks later, the school season ended, and we were released for the summer. I then had all the time in the world to sneak off with the car. By this time, Tim had just gotten out of the eighth grade and was in his prime for mischief. He actually goaded me to pull a few tricks with the car. Out of all the crazy stunts that I had pulled with the Safari Wagon, his favorite was the drag racing by the garbage dump. We often would drive a few miles out of town to a stretch of road just below the county landfill and do some no-nos with Bill's car, inflicting great pain to the drivetrain.

The pavement by the landfill had grown very smooth after the many years of traffic. With the hot sun beating down on the black asphalt, bubbles of tar sprouted up from the cracks. I only had to show Tim my drag racing start once; after that, he was hooked. I would put the car in reverse, speed backward a short distance, and then slam the transmission into drive and mash on the accelerator. Each time, we heard a loud *clunk* come from beneath the car. While the engine roared and the tires squealed wildly, blue smoke poured out from the back of the Safari Wagon. Slowly, the car picked up speed in a forward direction as the smoking tires regained their traction. Tim almost wet his pants. "Do it again! Do it again!" he yelled as he pounded on the seat. So I did—again and again. (The engineers did a wonderful job designing that transmission. It held up to the abuse.)

The summer grew hotter and hotter, and the desire to go camping became unbearable. One day, I yelled across the street to my friend Josh, "Hey, let's get the heck out of here! Campout tonight!"

We had our own little tradition with our outings. We never planned anything; we just did it. When I announced that we were having a campout, word got out. After I made the announcement to Josh, Tim and I began throwing sleeping bags, fishing poles, tarps, and Mom's old pots and pans into the Safari Wagon. Josh came back across the street with an armload of his stuff—including his .22 rifle—and threw it in with ours.

We backed out of the driveway and almost made it into the street when someone slapped the side of the car. "Where ya guys going?" a familiar voice demanded.

It was Ted Mulligan. Oh, great—my good friend Ted. Actually, we were friends at the time, but our past relations had been a little rough. Ted was a wild man. He rebelled against all kinds of authority, even flipping both his middle fingers at our sixth-grade teacher after he was sent out to the hallway (my favorite hangout).

Ted was the first guy to smoke cigars with us. We didn't even know how to light them, but he was sure delighted to show us. Ted was slightly bigger than I was and had picked on a lot of kids in the neighborhood. Ironically, after I assumed we were friends, he had turned on me a few times. For some reason, he had gotten the urge to start a fistfight with me. My big mouth irritated him a little too much, I suppose.

On one of the occasions that he accosted me, I was scared out of my wits. After he dragged me around by the shirt collar and attracted a mob of kids, he decided to punch me in the face. Okay, you bastard! I then let him have it. Every time I socked it to him, he grew more upset. Finally, I bloodied his lip. Ted wiped his mouth with the back of his hand. When he saw the red streaks, he looked back up at me and paused for a second. Then, without warning, he screamed in a frenzy and dived at me. I easily took him down to the ground since I wrestled every year. The spectators loved the turn in the fight and cheered wildly until a young family man in the neighborhood broke up our senseless brawl.

There was another time Ted goofed around a tad too much with me. He cleared his throat and goobered in my ear. The glob was a real "sidewalk oyster." I touched the mucus ball that dripped off my earlobe, and I almost threw up. I let Ted have it again. When that fight stopped, he explained to me that I shouldn't have done anything to him for doing that because when he got in a fight at school, someone goobered in his ear, too. (I loved the reasoning power of this guy!)

Several years had passed since those incidents, and the two of us just wanted to collaborate on the fun. We did on occasion, too, since he lived only a block away. This time, Ted could smell some fun just beginning to happen. The fishing poles, sleeping bags, and backpacks stuffed with grub kind of gave us away.

"Camping. Do you want to go?" I asked him.

"Sure. Give me a few minutes to get my stuff." He ran home and came back with his arms loaded with gear.

We had the gear, we had the grub, but we didn't have any beer. To go camping and have a really wild time, we had to have booze. Mom wasn't aware of that, though. Although none of us were old enough to buy anything, I still took my chances by driving over to the grocery store. We hoped that we could convince someone to purchase some beer on our behalf.

Almost immediately, good fortune struck us. We spotted Tom Tobias. Just before he got to his car, we waved him over and explained our predicament. He agreed to buy us beer as long as we had enough money and we didn't rat on him. Josh, Ted Mulligan, and I pooled our change together and had enough to buy a case (barely). However, we were forgetting one thing—gas. The car didn't run off of water. Oh, well. When Tom brought us our change, we reasoned that the remaining $2.16 should buy enough to get us somewhere.

After fueling up at the station across from IGA, we drove out of town past the stretch of road where I tested the transmission's durability and headed up into the mountains toward Lake Elsie. We abstained from drinking until we got out of city limits, thinking we were being so smart. But some of the motorists coming down the mountain road spotted the irregularities. They looked a little shocked when they saw Josh and Ted Mulligan on top of the luggage rack guzzling beer and especially Josh holding a .22 rifle in his hands. Any one of them could have called the sheriff if they wanted to.

During the ride up the steep mountain road, Josh randomly shot at the bank and yelled at imaginary rabbits as if he were Elmer Fudd. He and Ted Mulligan were having too much fun up there. I was missing out on it. I thought about it for a minute and then decided to pull over, stop the car, and do something about it. "Hey, Tim," I said to my little brother. "I need you to drive."

He looked surprised and poked one of his own fingers into his chest and said, "Me?"

"Yes, you! It's real easy," I reassured him.

After a quick lesson on how to use the gas pedal and the brake, I laid a few sleeping bags down for him to sit on so he could see over the dashboard. Within minutes, we were back on the road. But this time, Josh, Ted, and I all sat on the roof, sipping our beers and holding our rifles. Tim drove the car carefully, slowing around the windy turns that took us higher and higher into the mountains. A half mile before the top of the mountain ridge, Tim yelled out to me something about a red light on the instrument panel that kept coming on.

"Shut up and keep driving," I told him. I just wanted to get there.

The engine didn't blow up or anything. We did make it safely to the top. However, shortly after rounding the corner, when we caught a glimpse of the tiny, beautiful Lake Elsie, the radiator began to boil over. I relieved Tim, patted him on the shoulder, and promoted him to official First Officer. From there, I took over the driving myself. Uncle Bill couldn't kill me yet. The engine cooled off just fine as we coasted down the hill to the lake—it still had plenty of life in it!

To simply find an unoccupied spot, we had to drive to the far side of the lake. More campers than usual were setting up their accommodations for the night. They were everywhere. Even though they had the fancy campers and motorcycles, the four of us still felt proud that we had the Safari Wagon, our beer, and fine Swisher Sweets cigars.

Once we had stopped, smelled the air, and began setting up camp, I realized that we were running short on two things: beer and firewood. Finding wood at Lake Elsie was always tough. Over the years, all the previous campers had thoroughly gleaned the surrounding area of any firewood. We pulled what we could from the shore of the lake but knew it just wasn't going to last long. The time came for a command decision. I looked up at the sky and squinted at the setting sun. I knew I had to go back to town regardless of the time.

Ted had been busy building a cozy little fire when I mentioned my plan. He thought it was a great idea and agreed to stay with my brother Tim while Josh and I made the trip. I was all ready to go, but the car wouldn't start. The battery had died. I couldn't understand why it went dead, but it did. There remained one alternative. I had to borrow a battery from the nearby group of drunken fishermen. That turned out to be really easy. They were so friendly. One told me to take his ugly wife, too, but to just be sure to bring back the battery. With their help, we finally got the car started and left for town.

Sixteen miles separated Lake Elsie from the main road to town, and from there it was still seven miles into Kellogg. The trip was no short jaunt. Forty-five minutes later when we pulled onto Mission Avenue, the stars were already out in full glory. I thought about the dismal situation at the lake and hoped Ted and Tim didn't freeze before we got back. I didn't have any real worries about heating material because Josh devised a brilliant plan. He mentioned the fact that his dad sawed firewood all summer long and stacked up several cords on their back porch. (The firewood had to be Tamarack, though.) Josh, being an heir to a firewood fortune, declared that wood was ours for the taking.

I was easy and didn't have any problem with that, so I parked the Safari Wagon in front of Josh's house and lowered the tailgate. Josh led the way up the dark driveway leading to the back of his house. Unfortunately, his dad had recently ordered a truckload of fresh gravel to be put in the driveway. Although we tried to be sneaky, the fresh rocks crunched loudly beneath each step we took. *Crunch, crunch, crunch.*

Loading the chunks of firewood into our arms was the quiet part. It was each trip that we took back down the driveway that made the conspicuous *crunch, crunch* sounds. Just like happy box boys at the grocery store, we dumped each load of wood into the back of the car and went back to get more. During our third trip for wood, something startled us enough to make Josh and me jump back and slither up against the wall. It was his dad. He knew something was going on and began poking his head through the curtains, peering out at the dark porch.

We held tight for a few minutes, hoping the coast was clear, before we headed out with another load. Finally, with one more armload, we crunched down the driveway, step by step, carrying our booty. Just as we dumped the wood into the car, we heard a loud shout blasting at us from behind. "What zee hell du you zink yur doin!" yelled a heavy German voice. It was Josh's dad.

Josh's dad loved his sons deeply, but to maintain discipline and respect, he knew he couldn't let them do whatever they wanted without putting up some type of resistance. He was aware that Josh drank beer and probably even smoked dope with his teenaged friends. His dad was probably even secretly proud of him when he got down a few girls' panties. But still, he had to put up some sort of fight. I had seen Josh and his dad on many occasions hash out their differences. Young Josh seemed to always win.

During this scuffle, I backed off to the sidelines and watched them yell back and forth. "Yur not goin' nowhere. Now git back in zee haus!" his father ordered.

"Shut the hell up, Dad, and give me five bucks!" Josh demanded.

"I told you to git back in zee haus right now!"

"Dad, shut up and give me five bucks. I've got to get going!" Josh screamed back.

The entire time they argued, his dad fought the temptation to give in, but he ended up reluctantly reaching for his wallet and slowly handing Josh the five dollars that he demanded.

Soon, we tracked down another dupe wandering around the grocery store parking lot and had him buy us a half case of beer before we heading back to the lake.

Once again, I found myself sipping on a cold can of beer and handling the wheel of the car like a brain surgeon (just like Uncle Bill always said). At times while I drove, Josh probably never noticed, but I lurched forward and stared out the window at the stars and full moon that loomed overhead. Josh was a great friend with whom I shared all my intimate secrets, but not even he could know what I felt when I smelled the fresh, night air and looked up at those stars. To me, it was life in the making, and I knew I would never be freer in my life.

Josh and I didn't talk much on the way back; we simply sipped on the cold beer all the way up the windy mountain road to Lake Elsie. Upon our arrival, we happily found out that Tim and Ted Mulligan were still alive and warm. Josh handed them a couple cans of beer. They cracked them open and celebrated the firewood and beer triumph by clanging their cans together and toasting our return.

A few beers later, we spread out in our sleeping bags, giggling about our many episodes of mischief. Our laughter echoed across the lake and probably annoyed the other campers, but we didn't give a shit. Finally, we fell asleep and let the fire burned itself out.

Morning came quickly—almost as quickly as the ache in my back and hips did from sleeping on the hard ground with no mattress. Oh, well. It was just another day for me—a bruised shin, a backache, a hangover. What the heck?

As we cooked our bacon and scrambled eggs over the roaring fire, I remembered telling my younger brother Steve that we planned to camp at

Lake Elsie, and if he found a way to do it, he should jump on a motorcycle and join us. So far, we had seen no sign of him, and I was just too hungry to wait around and serve him breakfast. Once we ate, we decided to head out. Our fun was over (or so we thought).

The four of us threw our sleeping bags and gear into the car and headed up the small slope that took us out of the shallow basin and to the top of the ridge. Just as we reached the crest of the hill and began to gently idle down the other side, the car engine sputtered and died. I looked through steering wheel at the fuel gauge and realized that it had never risen above the *E* mark. There wasn't any gas left. The Oldsmobile V-8 guzzled every last drop. That pig! I guess that $2.16 worth of unleaded plus the original fumes couldn't last forever. There wasn't any need for me to pull over and stop. I knew there was nothing I could do but let gravity do its part for the next eight miles.

At that stage in my life—without a job, a wife, children, or anyone to answer to—panic never entered my mind. I was literally along for the ride. But, besides taking care of myself, I did have three passengers who counted on me to pull them out of the jam. Luckily, my passengers were optimists. Before we considered our current situation a jam, we were going to have a little fun. No gas? No problem.

Less than a quarter of a mile down the hill, the road made a very sharp switchback. I reassured everyone in the car that everything was under complete control. I let the car build up its speed, and when we reached the turn, I cranked the limp steering wheel over very sharply to make the corner. With the excess momentum of the Safari Wagon in direct competition with the dirt and gravel, we slid in a death-defying broad slide around that first switchback and fishtailed a few times. I maintained control and continued on down the road. My passengers cheered. It had been a spectacular show of vehicular control.

Further along the road, we encountered several more sharp turns, and I performed the same maneuver. In addition to the sharp turns, we faced extremely smooth banks where prior motorists had veered off the road and partway up the side. I did the same thing, swerving so high that we thought the Safari Wagon was going to overturn. After I executed that move perfectly, everyone cheered again. They actually egged me on, encouraging me to go faster and faster or to swerve higher and higher up the bank. I couldn't resist the challenge, so I complied. However, driving the dead beast became increasingly difficult. I had to bear in mind that the power brakes and power steering barely worked without the assistance of the running motor.

For several miles, we had a blast. With each corner, the stakes got higher. I merely drove faster. After successfully negotiating all the steep banks and sharp turns, I decided to give them one last big thrill by letting the car loose. I got the car coasting as fast as it could through one last corner. Both my hands gripped the wheel in preparation. The corner came fast, and the transmission whined as if the engine were actually running. I swerved hard. The centrifugal force flung us sideways. Oops! I steered too hard, so I immediately corrected our heading, but the car fishtailed the other way this time. I had overcorrected.

The valley several thousand feet below us burst into view. We shot out of the turn and fishtailed back again in the other direction. We came very close to the edge. Left, right, left, right. Oh, shit! We were out of control. No more cheers erupted in the car. I could proudly say there was no screaming, either. We weren't women. There were white knuckles and pale faces only.

Luckily, the road leveled out, and we lost momentum with each swerve. I fought the wheel, and finally I regained control and straightened the car out. Once under control, I eased on the brake to slow us down to only a creep. I breathed deeply and then slowly turned my head toward Josh and Ted Mulligan. The color had left their faces, and they, too, gulped and breathed deeply. After a minute of silence and of staring at each other, we began to chuckle a little, and then we erupted into ferocious laughter. We were survivors.

Near the bottom of the mountain, we came across a few dips. The car lost its momentum, and we had to get out and push just to get us up and over so that we could begin coasting again. On the final stretch of road, the Safari Wagon rolled slower and slower until it stopped and declared defeat. That's when we got out and waited. The vultures circled overhead. Ted Mulligan began to sob. We were even out of toilet paper, and several of us had to go.

After each of us found our own private spot in the bushes to dump a load, we heard motorcycles approaching. We wiped quickly with thimbleberry bush leaves and ran out to the road. When the bikes came into view, we determined that the drivers were none other than Steve and Brad Curry. They flew past us, leaving a cloud of dust for us to eat. Luckily, they identified the car and turned around. Both Steve and Brad laughed at us when we told them of the eight-mile coast-a-car ride from hell that we just experienced. Steve and Brad willingly agreed to go back into town and get us the desperately needed gas to complete our journey.

Once back in Kellogg, I left the car to sit for a few weeks before I touched it again. I almost felt overwhelmed by the camping experience. I felt like holding off for a while.

The next time out in the Safari Wagon was after Uncle Bill came. Uncle Bill's arrival became a decisive moment in my life. He caught me completely off guard. I had only forgotten one thing for a perfect cover-up on the Safari Wagon scandal. The entire time I drove the car around, I neglected to install a proper ignition switch. I had gotten so used to using the old paper clip and screwdriver trick that all the fun had kept me from preparing the car for its rightful owner's arrival.

Eventually, Uncle Bill did show up, and when he did, he wanted to immediately get the car geared up for a road trip. That happened right in the middle of a peanut butter sandwich that I was eating at our kitchen table.

Uncle Bill showed up—but not alone. He did have allies in town, and the one he chose to help him out with certain mechanical issues happened to be my Uncle Bob. Sadly enough, Uncle Bob broke more crap than he ever fixed. Not only did he break things, but he also liked to overuse certain words ... words like "utilize." During his garbage dump runs, he collected all types of good stuff that he was going to "utilize." He not only "utilized" stuff in private, he'd always have to tell you about how he "utilized" it. Bob loved flicking his thumbs in complex hand gestures. He wiggled his hands nervously and sprayed spit into the air as he talked. When he talked about his "utilizing," he also spit into your face. Any spittle not sent flying into the air or into your face formed globs in the corners of his mouth. He tried so hard to illustrate to you how certain mechanical things worked. But one of the problems with the spit-spraying, hand and thumb-flicking, and his intense attempts to demonstrate a mechanism was that he always chose the wrong audience. At six years old, I didn't know or care how a planetary-geared automatic transmission worked.

On this particular family occasion, it happened to be the middle of July. While I munched on my peanut butter sandwich, my mother saw Bill and Bob pulling up outside the house in Bob's Jeepster Commando. She knew that there would be a showdown between us, so she instinctively pulled her hands out of the dishwater, wiped them off, and walked over to me. Out of thin air, she produced the authentic key to the Safari Wagon and laid it down next to me. It was almost like she wanted me to get into the trouble I deserved, and she didn't want to get caught in the crossfire.

I froze in my seat and waited for Uncle Bill to come into the house. He came through the living room into the kitchen and stood in front of me. Someone had tipped him off that I had the key to the car (which was a sheer fabrication). I had to at least hand it to Bill. He was up to speed on current events.

Uncle Bob must have been pretty far behind the times, because he was unloading a spare tire, a bumper jack, and a freshly charged battery. He was thinking that he'd be the first to give CPR to the Safari Wagon when I had already been rodding the piss out of her for over two months.

Bill's demeanor at first seemed so calm and casual. "Hey, Tony, I'd like the key to the Safari Wagon. I want to stoke it up for a road trip."

This was one of those times when I needed milk with my peanut butter sandwich. My mom looked across the room at me, her hands slowing down the washing motions in the soapy dishwater. She feared for me. I drew in a deep breath and realized the moment of truth had come. Since honesty is the best policy, I laid it on the line for him. "Bill, I ... I broke the ignition switch when I hot-wired the car," I said as he reached out and snatched the key from my hand.

His eyes grew really wide, and he paused for just a second while his brain computed what I'd just said. A moment later, he raised both arms in the air and exploded with, "All right, you just bought yourself a —— car!" He threw the key down on the table and stormed back out of the house. Uncle Bob sniffled a little as he loaded the supplies back into the Jeepster. I had ruined his summer project. Both Bill and Bob hastily climbed into the jeep and retreated back to Granny's place. Since the painful part was over so quickly, I felt very relieved and immediately began making more plans for the Safari—oops! I mean the Moldsmobile.

Chapter 9

Jaws

Despite the negative incident with the Safari Wagon, we had no need to worry—Bill had several other toys to keep him busy. The Safari Wagon just happened to be one of many. After his fateful trip across the expanse of Washington towing the old boat with the Safari Wagon, Bill put Kit up to the challenge of whipping the old vessel into seaworthiness. Kit may have been a hot rod mechanic, but he was not a marine engineer. However, he combined the two sciences, and the result of his efforts resembled a Frankenstein of a watercraft known better as "Jaws."

Luckily, the small, four-cylinder marine engine that lay in pieces on the floorboards of Bill's boat was made by General Motors—thus, parts were easy to find. Kit had the engine back together and running in one weekend. While we watched Saturday morning cartoons, he had the engine burping away in the driveway with the garden hose attached to it for cooling purposes.

Once the motor ran okay in the driveway, Kit took the boat to the small, lily pad-infested Rose Lake and gave it a few trial runs. Soon enough, a cracked block was discovered. The engine itself ran okay, but water leaked through a crack into the crankcase and mixed with the oil. Not a good sign.

Like most optimists, Kit didn't sweat it and calmed Bill's nerves with the vague details of his well-thought-out backup plan. Kit already had a spare engine in mind. The master plan determining the future of the boat began to unfold. One slight detail remained. Before Kit could install the new engine, we had to blow up the first one. To help facilitate the procedure, Kit made a few modifications—things I had never seen before—like a homemade wooden gas pedal. That way, we could take turns driving it and mash on the gas as hard as we could until the engine disintegrated.

Out on the lake during the first few outings, Kit encouraged my friends and me to run the boat and run it hard. We stomped down the accelerator and whipped the boat into all kinds of wild turns. Other boaters looked at us with disdain because they had real speedboats—fancy ones with fiberglass hulls. Our boat was an old aluminum tub with a faded green and white paint job.

Before Kit got around to installing the hot rod engine, he had one special touch to give the boat. One sunny Saturday morning, he prepped the bow of the boat with masking tape and newspaper and commenced spray painting two huge eyeballs and a large, red shark's mouth full of frightening teeth. The boat resembled one of the Flying Tigers' airplanes. From that day on, the craft was known as "Jaws."

After a couple more hot-rodding sessions on the lake, the engine finally blew. A nearby boat towed Kit back to the dock. Kit, being the philosopher he was, exclaimed, "With no death, there would be no life!" Once Jaws was pulled out of the lake, she would never go back in the same.

Kit worked like a fiend. Wrenches turned, nuts and bolts flew, hoses were rerouted, and wires were reconnected. The old engine was scrapped, and a freshly rebuilt Chevy Corvette engine was installed. The bolt pattern for the new engine block happened to be the same as the original engine because they were both made by our friend General Motors. The new engine bolted right up to the outdrive without a problem. One last problem to solve—how do you route the exhaust without the expensive marine manifolds?

Some people tour garage sales, and others go to gun shows. Kit snooped for car parts. After a small bidding session, he returned from a fellow car aficionado's junk pile with a set of rusty headers. Kit used the left side of his brain and turned both headers upside down and mounted them on opposite sides of the engine. They stuck up, out, and over the back of the boat. The eight twisted tubes looked like gruesome tentacles from an alien beast. When Kit started the engine up, every window in the house shook. When he revved up the engine higher, every house in the neighborhood shook. Forget finishing anything else. We were going to the lake!

On the first trial runs on the lake with the new Jaws, there were no dump pipes routing the exhaust down to the water. It didn't matter. Kit ran it as it was. A few spectators stood on the dock and watched the monster being launched down the boat ramp.

Once in the water, Kit turned the key, and the engine whined as it turned over and over. Finally, it fired to life with a grotesquely painful roar. The spectators backed off, plugging their ears. Some of them appeared to be very frightened. The headers were wide open, jetting backward and spewing orange flames like two rocket engines.

When Kit felt the engine had warmed up sufficiently, he let off the gas, and the engine quieted down to a slow, unsteady idle. It loped. Kit smiled with the same joy as a new father. He had installed a mild racing cam in the engine.

During a few high-speed runs across the lake, people stopped their barbecues and strained their eyes, gazing at Jaws with fingers pointing at the shark's teeth painted on the bow and the flames blowing out of the open headers. In addition to the flames being a sight, the prop was simply too small for the size of the engine. The prop created a forty-foot rooster tail of water spraying behind the boat as it sped around the lake. Kit gave all the spectators their money's worth.

Soon enough, Kit made a deal with Reco's, the local muffler shop, and got two pipes made to dump the exhaust down to the water. This quieted it down immensely and reduced the hazard of burning something up. Finally, Kit installed a new prop, and that alone doubled Jaws's speed. Now the boat was ugly, loud, scary, and fast. After all the minute mechanical problems were solved, Uncle Bill then took command of the ship. The coolers had to be loaded with beer, and he definitely didn't forget the ice. With a pack of Marlboros in the shirtsleeve, a set of oars (just in case), and plenty of potato chips, Captain Bill said, "Let's go, boys!"

Bill owned several secluded lots of beachfront property on the far side of the lake near Harrison. Unlike Lake Tahoe, this part of Lake Coeur d'Alene had limited neighbors. With his new pride and joy, Bill had to find someone to terrorize. A wild idea flashed through his mind. Uncle Rupert owned a small mobile home on a lot about ten miles down the lake nearer to Coeur d'Alene. In the past, the ten miles of water happened to be enough distance to keep Bill and the alcohol away from Rupert and his group of refined neighbors. Jaws closed the gap between the two properties and made Rupert's quiet haven readily accessible.

When Bill purchased his property outside of Harrison, he specifically chose it because it was at the very end of a dirt road. The seclusion and privacy appealed to him most of all. Bill refused to develop the land in any way. For over thirty years, the family and all visitors walked down the dry, dusty path below the pine trees and simply sat on logs on the beach and laid blankets down on the lava-type shoreline pebbles. That's the way Bill wanted it. At the beginning of each summer, we had to clear the beach of driftwood and rake the rocky shoreline. It became a labor of love.

Uncle Rupert, on the other hand, bought his little mobile home getaway in a small community of quiet, relaxed, and somewhat classy people who shared the same tastes and enjoyed the same pleasures that he did. The dock out in front of Rupert's retreat belonged to all the surrounding neighbors and was mutually respected. The grounds were well groomed with the soft, green grass engulfing the entire area, and lawn chairs were placed in the shady areas.

Once Uncle Bill got the idea of a visit to Rupert's place in his head, he simply couldn't resist the temptation of popping in. He knew that Rupert and his neighbors wouldn't always welcome him. The quiet people on that part of the lake would not tolerate a loud, belligerent drunk—and neither would Rupert. Bill, knowing that, grew more determined than ever. He knew a prized moment awaited him, and it was his for the taking.

On one beautiful, sunny day while we swam in the warm lake water and dived from the top of the dock pylons, Bill arrived in Jaws with his chief mechanic—my brother Kit. The day had come. Bill just had to do it. Being troublemakers ourselves, Tim and I just had to go, and so we anxiously piled into the boat along with Kit. My mother stayed on the beach and shook her head at us as she scooped herself another helping of potato salad.

Soon, we cruised down the lake with the engine roaring away and the water spraying up into the air behind us. The entire craft vibrated from the engine racing with no cover over it. From several feet away, I could feel the heat radiating from the rusty headers. Bill sat in the captain's seat with a cigarette in one hand and a can of beer in the other. He looked around in a somewhat slight oblivion until he caught us in his gaze. He noticed we were all laughing. He grinned and chuckled and gave us the thumbs-up sign, which became his legendary trademark when he couldn't readily think of something to say.

A while later, we sped around a bend in the lake, and from there, we could finally see Rupert's small, quiet community nearly a mile away. The three of us stood up, grasping the handrails as the boat smashed against the small waves as Bill steered the boat. Kit pointed his finger ahead at our destination. The three of us looked at each other and laughed, knowing what kind of reception we would receive. We prepared for the invasion. The closer we got, the clearer all the figures on the beach became. Young people and little children innocently played in the water. Older ones were strolling along in the grass or sitting in lawn chairs. We came in closer. Minute by minute, the people's curiosity began to grow. They began to take notice of what approached. Bill mashed on the accelerator. The engine belched louder. We made a large, sweeping turn in front of the dock. Uncle Rupert and his wife Margaret realized who we were when they saw the shark's teeth and eyeballs painted on the front of the boat. They collapsed back into their lawn chairs with disgust.

After the wide turn, Bill slowed Jaws down and idled up to the dock as the wake from our previous pass pounded the beach. Children ran down the dock, and all the adults backed off to the safety of the shore. A few feet from the first pylon, Bill put the boat in reverse and brought us to a dead stop just before he cut the engine. Although Kit jumped out onto the dock with a line, many of the kids reached out to grab Jaws by the chrome handrails. Bill saw this and went nuts. He began screaming, "*No, no, no! Get your dick skinners off my boat!*"

The children jumped back with hurt feelings and got out of the way. Maybe the parents didn't hear Bill or didn't understand the meaning of the word "dick skinner," because no one said anything to Bill about his outburst. Bill slowly climbed out of Jaws, trying not to drop his cigarette or spill his beer. Once upright on the dock, he lumbered up the ramp to where Rupert and Margaret sat in their lawn chairs. The scene in front of Rupert was always the same. Rupert offers Bill a beer. Bill talks louder and louder and begins to include more profanity as the conversation goes on. Margaret whispers into Rupert's ear, and then Rupert immediately asks Bill to leave. This time, it took less than five minutes before we were kicked off the property. That didn't bother Bill—it was mission accomplished once again!

Jaws never earned any awards for being reliable or maintenance free. Sometimes the engine would backfire, and the carburetor would catch on fire. While Kit dived for the fire extinguisher, Bill took the opportunity to light up another cigarette. As well as the engine problems, on several occasions, Jaws sank overnight just a few feet off the beach. Kit merely bailed her out the next morning with a mop bucket. After the dousing each time, he had to purge the engine cylinders of the lake water by removing the spark plugs and turning the starter over. The water would shoot out the holes like a surfacing whale. In no time at all, Kit had Jaws back in running order, and Bill was back to terrorizing the lake.

Some of us theorized that the beefed-up Corvette engine was taking its toll on the aluminum hull. We joked about how each time Bill stomped on the gas, more rivets would pop out. Actually, the rivets were coming loose on the keel, and Kit had to climb under the boat a couple of times and pound on them with a ball-peen hammer. Inside the boat, a trusted assistant held a steel wedge to ensure that the rivets flattened out correctly. That's the extent of any dry-docking that was performed, and that was usually in our driveway on Mission Avenue.

Jaws couldn't attract hot women, either, like the other jet boats on the lake that were manned by macho college kids—at least not attract them in a sexual sense. On one gorgeous afternoon, Kit, Pete, and Bill took a shortcut to the lake by launching Jaws in the Coeur d'Alene River at the historic Cataldo Mission (the oldest standing building in Idaho, built in 1847).

Bill had attended an outdoor Sunday Mass there once. He, being the card-carrying Catholic that he was, could act very devout at times, especially when the priest announced that the Knights of Columbus provided refreshments afterward (beer and wine). Bill sat patiently throughout one service, eying the large, silver beer keg sitting next to a picnic table in a bathtub full of ice. During the long, boring sermon, beads of sweat rolled down Bill's cheeks. He salivated. When the congregation was instructed by the priest to give each other the sign of peace (a loving handshake), a little old man turned to Bill and noticed the perspiration on his face. "It's quite hot out today, isn't it?" he whispered to Bill.

"Uh-huh!" Bill said, keeping one eye on the keg.

After the service ended and after a couple hours of "fellowshipping," Bill blessed everybody so intensely that he was asked to leave by his fellow knights.

The Cataldo Mission sat only yards away from the Coeur d'Alene River. The water snaked its way around the back side of the mission and meandered twenty miles further until it poured into the east side of the lake near Harrison. The river run was twenty miles by boat. The drive was thirty-five by truck and trailer. This sunny day, Bill and Kit opted to launch closer to home and make the longer boat ride to the lake, even if it meant dodging the shifting sandbars and deadheads that plagued the river.

Several smaller lakes lay next to the river and were inhabited by hundreds of vacationing families with boats, too. On one stretch of the river near Cave Lake, Bill sat behind the small, sun-faded Plexiglas windshield and held the wheel with one hand. He casually sucked on a can of Budweiser beer. Because of the wind, each time he tipped the beer back for a sip, he had to wipe the foam off his upper lip, and with each puff on his cigarette, he had to carefully lean forward to get out of the onrushing air. The inconveniences involved with drinking and boating didn't bother him at all; he kept it up all the time.

Kit and Pete each held a beer in their hands and had to shout to one another above the roar of the engine to keep their conversation going. Since there was no hurry to get anywhere, Bill kept quiet and was light on the throttle. Although they were only making a moderate speed of around thirty knots, the boat still shot the amazing forty-foot-long rooster tail of water off the back. The rooster tail itself created the look of real speed and performance. Without visibly seeing Jaws, it sounded even tougher as the exposed Chevy V-8 roared at deafening levels and spewed hot exhaust out the custom-made dump pipes.

Without anyone on board noticing, a low-profile, flashy red jet boat snuck up behind Jaws and slowly began to pass on the starboard side. At first, the occupants of the passing boat didn't notice what a sight Jaws was until they were side by side with it. Two young blonde girls with large, round breasts bulging from their skimpy bikinis sat on the deck of the boat and looked over at Jaws with a friendly glance. They instantly had to do a double take and reach up to hold their hair out of their eyes. Naturally, they glanced back a second time to see the shark's teeth and eyes on the bow. They began to point and laugh. Bill waved at them with a semisalute and grinned.

Since the girls kept pointing and smiling at Jaws, Kit and Pete's testosterone levels began to rise. They waved back at the girls and inconspicuously flexed their arm and chest muscles, trying to look as masculine as they could.

On board with the two bathing beauties were their male counterparts. They wore expensive sunglasses with the pink and yellow fluorescent lanyards that draped around the back of their necks. Their fancy, high-collared polo shirts read "University of something or something." When these two nitwits finally looked over at Jaws, incredible looks of disgust spread across their faces. To them, worse than the sight of Jaws was seeing their girlfriends giggling, smiling, and flirting with the crew of an enemy ship. The commanding university puke decided to handle the situation by pouring on the power and leaving Bill's garbage scowl far behind. They couldn't have their female quarry enticed by real men on a real boat.

The jet boat nosed ahead of Jaws.

Immediately, Bill increased the power and brought the two boats side by side once again. The faster the punks went, the faster Jaws went. The two college guys began to panic. They frantically looked back and forth between their throttle lever and Jaws. Fear came across their faces. There had to be more speed; they must get away from the menace that they were trying to pass. The two young women on deck were busy making eyes at Pete and Kit and couldn't care less who had the faster boat.

Just before tears began to stream down the college punks' cheeks, Bill romped on the accelerator, and Jaw's power plant roared. Bill looked over at them, held up his middle finger, and yelled above the noise, "Eat my dust, you sons of bitches!" Jaws sped away quickly, leaving the jet boat far behind.

Later that day, the two buddies on the jet boat reported the incident to their daddies and got immediately enrolled in a therapy session that taught them how to deal with their severe case of penis envy. Kit and Pete were much better sports. They only lost out on their fantasy of having two luscious blonde creatures fall into their arms, saying, "Who cares about money, summer cabins, or nice boats? We like you bums. And we like your piece of shit boat and that obnoxious drunk you call an uncle! Now kiss me, you fool."

During the hot summer of '79, every member of our family congregated at Bill's private beach reserve and made preparations for the Fourth of July festivities. Bill was in a good mood and showed up with Jaws that day with a well-stocked cooler of beer. Although Jaws was Bill's boat, Kit piloted the craft most of the time because at least he could stay sober long enough to handle it. Besides strutting Jaws's stuff around the lake, Kit enjoyed honing his skill at dragging our water-soaked carcasses behind the boat at high speed.

We tried a variety of objects to ride on. Water skis, at times, just weren't interesting enough. First in line after the skis, we tried the skidder inner tube inflated at forty psi. Sometimes we chose the fiberglass butt board, and other times we were simply barbaric. That's when Kit dragged us through the water as fast as he could until we could no longer take the hydrodynamic pressure up the nasal cavity and just had to let go.

Bill's lake property wasn't entirely private; he did have one neighbor who had a cabin a hundred yards down the beach from his place. The man was from California and was known to all of us as Perryman. I'm not even sure if that was his real name, but that's what we called him. Perryman could barely tolerate Bill. We only saw him on rare occasions, and this Fourth of July was one of them.

After Kit docked the boat that afternoon, we spent the rest of the day splashing in the water and eating chicken, hot dogs, and watermelon. Uncle Bill had been to a garage sale in Harrison earlier that day and was proud of the folding, metal-frame bed with the pee-stained mattress that he had purchased. He got a real steal on them—smallpox viruses by the dozen! Bill had great pride in his bargaining skills. He would have been proud to get a beggar to sell his lint ball for half price. Despite his great negotiating ability, all Bill ever brought back was junk, and this bed set was trash!

After Bill scarfed down a piece of chicken and some of Mom's potato salad (the kind with large chunks of pickles and boiled eggs), he decided to set up his prized bunk near the water's edge and take a short snooze. I thought he was trying to rest only. Actually, he was testing the bed's load limit, too. The frame bent under his weight, and the springs drooped close to the ground, but they somehow managed to hold.

Tim and I were all prepared to harass him. Although we were risking bodily harm, we decided to do it, anyway. As Bill lay on his side trying to catch a short nap, Tim and I devised a plan. Tim was to be my decoy. I had him walk over and sit down on the edge of the bunk next to Bill. Tim engaged in a simple, meaningless conversation with Bill by asking him really stupid questions like, "How come your tummy is so big, Uncle Bill?"

Bill could be tolerant only as long as he was sober. When he did get tired of being around kids, he would call us "peckerheads" and tell us to get lost. So far, we hadn't gotten on his nerves badly enough for him to say that. I sometimes called other little kids in the neighborhood "peckerheads." When my mom heard me say that, she would shriek and then cup her hands to her mouth, saying, "Don't say that. That is the same as calling them a … a penis-head." I laughed. I'm surprised she had the nerve to say "penis." Usually, it was "doozle."

Tim's inquisitiveness distracted Bill while I snuck up behind the bed and crawled underneath it, carrying with me a long, curved twig. From behind, without his shirt on, Bill looked like a large, pale, beached whale—a perfect target of opportunity. The only thing missing was his dorsal fin. Even though the bed sagged deeply in the middle, it looked like it was going to hold. If it didn't, I'd have to be rescued and end up looking like a steamroller had just gotten me.

Once I got in place, I reached the twig out, up, and over the edge of the bed and tapped Bill on the back. Immediately, as I pulled the twig back, I noticed the bed move as Bill rolled over to see who had just tapped on him.

Tim gave me hand signals like a catcher in a major league baseball game. One finger meant that Bill wasn't looking. Two meant that Bill was watching his back. After I tapped Bill the first time, Tim gave me the two-finger signal—Bill was looking. When he rolled back over, Tim gave me the one-finger, coast-is-clear signal. I reached out again with my twig and tapped Bill a second time. Immediately, he rolled over and saw no one there. Tim kept the hand signals going in proper order until after the fourth time. As Bill rolled back and forth in bewilderment, Tim gave me a one, so I began again. Suddenly, Tim gave me a two. Then I pulled back. Immediately, Tim gave me another one. Make up your damned mind, Tim!

I reached up to tap Bill the fourth time, and Tim's hand signals became erratic. Just as I tapped Bill, he grabbed the twig from my hand and began to scream and swear at me. Uh-oh! He called us peckerheads. I rolled out from underneath the sagging bed just like Dick Van Dyke on the fire prevention commercials. I scrambled to my feet and ran like hell. Bill was not a happy uncle. My mom looked up from her plate of food and gave me the evil eye but didn't bother saying anything yet.

A little while later, the temptation to bother Bill again became too great. From about twenty feet away, I began to throw little pebbles at him. When each pebble hit him in the back, he didn't move at all. He plainly said, "I'm going to choke the life out of you, you little shit!"

When Bill had just about enough, I threw a pinecone at him. It landed on the mattress only a few inches behind him. He felt the impact and had been coiled up and ready to spring on me. The only problem was that Bill was too big to move as fast as a snake. He did roll over quickly, and all three hundred pounds of blubber smashed the prickly pinecone. Bill screamed in pain as the barbs pierced the skin on his back. When he rolled back over and jumped up from his bunk, the pinecone clung to his skin for a moment. It finally disengaged itself and fell to the ground, leaving several red marks on Bill's back. He was hot and wanted to kill me but almost tripped and fell over the rocks on the portion of the beach that was not groomed. My mother finally looked up from her plate of picnic food and warned me to leave Bill alone.

Bill went on to nap for a bit after that, and then, after a few dreams of being attacked by peckerheads, he finally got up. He walked up the steep trail to where the cars were parked. He quietly drove off into the sunset in the Safari Wagon. We all knew that he was heading to the saloon. All that we kids could do was wait until after sunset when we could start our fireworks show.

Before darkness came, some of us began to light and throw firecrackers one by one. Steve was just getting the hang of it when a firecracker he lit burned halfway down the fuse and then stopped. He said, "Hey, Phil, here's one for you."

Phil thought it was such a nice gesture and thanked Steve for it. Just as Phil took Steve's firecracker into his hand, the fuse started up again and quickly burned down into the core. It instantly exploded between his pressed fingers. Phil jumped up and down, screaming and shaking his injured hand. He used a few of the same words Dad did when he got mad. Even though he didn't beat up Steve, he sure wanted to. However, once involved again in the fireworks display, he forgot all about the mishap.

After darkness settled in, we lit the majority of our stuff—the Roman candles, the bottle rockets, and even the ferocious M-80s. Over a half mile away, on the other side of the lake, the other vacationers were doing the same thing, but with a much smaller arsenal than ours. Even though we had plenty of fireworks, I grew bored quickly. How many times can you say "wow" or "ooie"? I felt bad that Uncle Bill wasn't around to experience the exhibition. Oh, well. He was probably seeing stars, anyway, on a bar stool in Harrison. If it wasn't from the booze, it was probably from somebody blindsiding him with a sucker punch to shut him up for a while. That had been known to happen.

There was a time a year or so earlier when Kit dropped Bill off at the Carlin Bay Resort and then came back an hour later in Jaws to pick him up. When Kit coasted into the restricted waters of the marina, he recognized Bill from quite a distance out. Bill was sitting on the end of the dock and holding his head low. The closer Kit came, the clearer it was—the red stains of blood on Bill's shirt. What had happened to Bill?

Uncle Bill explained that all he did was voice his opinion to a bunch of California bikers that he didn't like the Californicating of Idaho. After that statement, when Bill reached down to lay his quarter on the pool table, a size twelve, black leather riding boot kicked him square in the jaw. The next thing Bill remembered seeing was a Tweety Bird chirping around his head and Bugs Bunny holding a mallet, asking, "How many lumps do ya want?" Bill decided to leave the establishment peacefully without engaging in any belly bucking.

When I asked Bill in later years if he actually got thrown out the place, he replied, "No, sir. I didn't get thrown out. I left under my own power."

Later on during this Fourth of July night, once everyone had seen enough of our fireworks production, Mom packed up the goodies and loaded the car with my sisters and our other invited guests. Making sure Tim, my friend Dan, and I had our sleeping bags, she then climbed into the car and departed in the direction of Kellogg. The girls and guests went home as happy as could be expected after an afternoon of witnessing live bodies being dragged at high speed through the water by a shark-faced boat and after seeing a three-hundred-pound, flesh-toned whale disguised as our uncle impale himself on a pinecone and use extreme profanity. And, last but not least, they observed the meat almost blown off of Phil's fingers by a firecracker. The real trick would be if they listened, learned, and remembered, but I doubted if anyone would.

In the meantime, those of us who were tough were staying the night. That was none other than Dan, Tim, and I. We were going to sleep on the beach and ride back with Uncle Bill the next day (if he ever showed back up after driving into Harrison to celebrate).

When everyone fled the lake place, the water calmed down and appeared as clear as glass. As the stars came out, the beach grew extremely quiet. With nothing left to do, we dozed off in front of our campfire. The large chunks of sun-bleached driftwood that we piled on top of the fire began to burn down while we slept.

Later that night, at an undetermined hour, Bill returned in his typical form.

It was sometime after midnight when I was awakened by voices. At first, they seemed to be calm and normal, which made me wonder who in their right mind would be out for a stroll in the pitch-black night. But when the calmness turned into a lady gasping and hollering, I suspected that something was definitely wrong. These people weren't out for a stroll. They had come to see some fireworks. They had even said so. The lady's voice said, "I want to see these fireworks, Bill, but I think we're too late." Their tour guide was none other than Uncle Bill.

In a loud, disgusted voice, he reassured her that there *would* be fireworks. He said, "There *will* be fireworks, all right. My nephews have them all ready for us. Now do me a favor and shut the f—— up, you stupid mattress back. I've heard enough of your shit!" Bill then warned her husband Leroy about the barbed wire, but it was too late. Leroy lost his footing and went running straight into the barbed wire that ran along the beach line. I heard a few grunts and then the sound of tearing cloth. There went his shirt.

Their entire dialogue went on in complete darkness. I crawled out of my sleeping bag and threw a bunch of sticks on the fire. Within a minute, orange flames leaped out of our blazing fire pit and illuminated the barren beach. From the glow of the fire, I saw Bill lethargically leading a drunken old man back up the hillside, away from the barbed wire fence. Old Leroy took a step forward. He teetered back and forth for a moment and then fell backward onto his butt. Bill kept his grip on the man's hand as he fell to the ground and began to slide backward on his britches.

"Help me, dear! Help me, dear!" he cried to his wife.

I looked a little further up the hillside and spotted a lady limping down the trail with a cane. She had one leg in a cast, her other arm in a sling, and a white gauze patch over one eye. This scene of complete confusion baffled me. These idiots thought happy hour was still on down at Bill's beach property.

They eventually found the entrance in the barbed wire and made their way over to our fire. They sat themselves down in three folding lawn chairs that Mom left. The old lady grumbled about this and that. Her bitching was enough to drive anyone to drink. I didn't blame her, though—not in her condition. Besides being patched up from a recent automobile accident, she was an ugly old battle-axe on top of that. The severe wrinkles in her face lead me to believe that she was also a real boozer.

"Okay, boys, we want to see some fireworks!" Bill ordered. Dan and I had no problem accommodating him. Unfortunately, the first spinning buzz bomb that we lit spun through the air, sending a shower of sparks in all directions, and it headed right for the old bitch's head. She ducked just in time, and it missed her. Bill and Leroy burst out laughing. "Almost took out your other eye, there, Margaret!"

As Dan, Tim, and I lit the fireworks off one by one, their story began to unfold. Bill had been drinking and driving and had gotten into an accident with these two morons. Ole Margaret had just been in automobile accident two weeks earlier and broke her arm, leg, and injured one eye. Since Bill was drunk when he hit them earlier that night, he didn't want to involve the police. That was no problem because ole Leroy and Margaret were drunk, too. So Bill invited them into town for a drink to assess the damage. But which damage—the damage to their cars or to their brain cells?

Bill, Leroy, and Margaret whooped and hollered at our fireworks exposition and eventually waddled back up the hill, only to disappear into the same darkness from which they appeared.

Night slowly passed, and dawn arrived. The battle scene on Bill's beach was horrendous. Our sleeping bags were in disarray, and pop cans, watermelon rinds, and water flotation devices lay all over the beach. Even Pete's yellow rubber raft lay down the beach on a pile of rocks, almost completely deflated. Without any regard for the calm of the new day, I decided to wake up Tim and Dan by lighting off a couple of bottle rockets. They flew up and exploded in the sky. My two comrades soon joined me in shattering the morning silence that had filled the air for miles around the lake.

For fifteen minutes, we had a blast. That is, until a man came walking down the beach toward us. He stumbled over the coarse volcanic rocks that lined the shores of the lake. It was Perryman, and he didn't look happy. He stopped at the edge of our little campsite, next to the deflated rubber raft, about fifty feet from us. In his right hand, he held a revolver and let it hang limply, pointing it at the ground. His intentions weren't to point it at us but to simply make it clear that he had one.

Perryman spoke in a wavering, pleading voice. He was obviously very desperate, verging on being neurotic. He begged us, "Stop. Stop the fireworks. Damn it! It's seven o'clock in the morning, and you have woken up me and my family. Now stop it! Now!" He then turned and left as quickly as he came.

Just as Perryman disappeared around the corner, the deflated yellow rubber raft began to move. We thought an animal had gotten trapped in it. Suddenly, we saw an arm. The arm pushed back the yellow fabric, and a figure sat up. It was Uncle Bill. He turned and looked at us through his blurry, squinting eyes. "You sons of bitches almost got me shot. Now do like the man says and knock the shit off!" He laid back down to finish his snooze. I couldn't believe Bill was going to side with Perryman. I would have loved to have seen Bill punch him out like he did the other guys outside the bars in Seattle. But this time, I just wasn't lucky enough.

My older brother Pete told us of a time when Bill and one of his buddies had differences one night at Bill's trailer. Bill asked the guy to step outside, which he did. "Okay, Bucko!" Bill yelled at the guy. "Take your best shot!"

This guy was also over three hundred pounds. He was not quite as tall as Bill, but their blood alcohol levels were about the same, so it made it a fair fight. They stood several feet apart and began to take slow, arcing swings at each other. Their left and right arms swung in slow motion. They looked like two farmers' combines heading toward each other in an empty cornfield. With each swing, they took a step closer to each other. No punches connected. It was as if they were swinging at flies. The outcome would be determined by who connected first. Left swing … miss! Right swing … miss! Left swing—*Kablam!* Bill connected first! Bucko went flying and landed on his back. Down for the count! Bill and Pete went back into the trailer until the guy decided to wake up.

The only time I ever saw Bill punch someone was when he, my dad, and my Uncle Pete had all teamed up to help conquer a gallon of my dad's Paisano wine. They were all sitting in our living room one night, drinking and smoking up a storm. My dad smoked Tareyton cigarettes, and they smelled worse than burning horsehair. They successfully created their own inversion layer in the living room. We wouldn't clearly see the ceiling light until the low-pressure front moved in from the west.

With no apparent motive, Uncle Pete, who happened to be laying back in our reclining chair with one leg in a cast, began to mouth off to Bill. Bill threatened to punch him if he didn't shut up. Uncle Pete dared him to put his money where his mouth was. So Bill got to his feet and staggered over next to Uncle Pete. He reached his arm back and swung his fist down into the smiling face of his younger brother. *Kablam!* He let Uncle Pete have it right in the jaw. Bill, without much remorse, ambled away into the kitchen to get another glass of wine. My dad was too busy watching The Black Mask let loose of his opponent's neck and do an amazing Atomic Knee Drop on him in the middle of the ring. The TV audience cheered wildly in the background.

My dad loved championship wrestling. When we laughed and made fun of it and called it phony, my dad flipped out and yelled at us. He pointed fanatically at the TV and would almost fall out his chair. *"Look!* Look at that. That was real! I'm telling you, it's all real! You guys don't know how serious that is!" We let him believe what he wanted. Dad was the boss.

One night, Bill came into town, and my dad wasn't home. Ill-equipped for drinking without a trusted companion, Bill still made the rounds to his three favorite bars (later to be called the Drunken Triangle). After getting thrown out of a couple of them, he took the rejection personally. For Bill to take it personally was absolutely amazing. His whole intention was to be so obnoxious that he would be ousted. Being ordered to leave the bar was his primary objective. Each ban from a bar merely became as a feather in his cap. It gave him great contentment. However, something went awry this fateful night and set Bill into an emotional turmoil. He staggered out of the bar (under his own power, of course) and stumbled up the hill to my gramma's house near the nostalgic section of town known as Wardner.

Uncle Bob's quarters in the upstairs of my gramma's house resembled an armory. Since Bob never married, he resorted to having a lifelong love affair with guns and old cars. Whether Uncle Bob gave Bill any resistance to checking out a firearm is unknown to this day. What is known is that Bill hastily grabbed one of his favorite weapons—his World War II classic .30 Carbine. Not only did he secure the weapon itself, he thoughtfully stuffed a loaded, thirty-round magazine into it, grabbed his jug of whiskey, and headed back out the door. No one in the family really knew what was on Bill's mind at the time. One thing for sure was that Bill would never actually snap and go on a killing spree. Kellogg didn't have any clock towers or a McDonald's at the time, but it did have one post office. Lucky for those guys, Bill wasn't a postal worker.

Twenty minutes later, Bill arrived at our house, rapping furiously on the front door with his knuckles. My mother, donned in a nightgown, scrambled to the front door and let him in. She gasped at the sight of him toting a loaded weapon and a jug of whiskey. I heard the ruckus and sensed a state of emergency unfolding in our very own living room. I leaped out of bed and burst into the kitchen to witness the event myself.

Bill ripped a chair back from the kitchen table and sat down to pour himself a quick drink of whiskey, meanwhile clutching the .30 Carbine close to his side. He expertly threw the full slug of Black Velvet back into his mouth and swallowed with one big gulp. My mother pleaded with him to stay put for the night.

"No, Bill, no! Please just stay here!" she pleaded. Mom begged so sincerely that I thought she was going to cry.

But Bill was too irate for being kicked out. He was determined to "get 'em." Bill finally stood up, and with the semiautomatic rifle cradled in one arm and the jug of Canadian whiskey in the other, he headed right back out the front door. My mother ran outside after him and continued to petition for him to stay. All Bill kept growling over and over was, "I'm going to get 'em. I'm going to get 'em. If they want war, I will give them war!"

I stepped over and looked out our large kitchen window. There he was, slowly trudging under the streetlight and across the four-way stop, rifle and jug in hand.

A short while later, none of us heard any gunshots or police sirens wailing in the night. Fortunately, Bill had stopped only a few blocks down the road at Uncle Rupert's house. While he was indulging himself with one more drink, Rupert disarmed him and convinced him to accept a ride back up to Granny's house.

Bill had the uncanny ability to evade serious injury or trouble with the police, and for that, I was thankful. Uncle Bill inspired everyone in so many different ways. He taught us what improper etiquette was. He kept the bartenders on their toes. He gave periodic, unannounced drills for the local police. He challenged the circuit court judges to execute appropriate measures of justice. For example, the hundred-dollar fine he received for urinating in Yoke's Pak 'N' Save parking lot was fair and would keep law and order alive in Kellogg, Idaho.

As Uncle Bill's retirement date from United Airlines grew near, he sent ripples of sheer terror throughout the Silver Valley by announcing his intention to move back home to Kellogg to live out the rest of his days. My mom became emotionally distressed over that prospect in just the same way she did when she caught Bill and me drinking whiskey at the lake.

People weren't the only ones who felt great disdain for a drunken Uncle Bill. Another one not fond of Uncle Bill was our black alley cat named O'Malley. Bill caused a rift in their friendship when he apprehended the cat and poured a shot of whiskey down its mouth. O'Malley screamed and sunk his claws into Bill's hands.

After their toast together, Bill still held onto O'Malley and said, "Oh, you love me, baby. Don't you, O'Malley? You're such a nice kitty kitty!"

And just to prove it, Bill grabbed O'Malley by the head and pressed the cat's face up against the side of his. As Bill rubbed their two cheeks together, smashing the cat's whiskers, O'Malley found it to be a perfect opportunity to sink his sharp teeth right into the side of Bill's face. With one bite, their friendship ended right there.

Despite being bitten directly on the cheekbone, Bill felt no pain; he simply went to the kitchen and added a little bit of orange juice to his vodka drink.

Just as the famous Wizard of Oz said, "A heart is not judged by how much you love, but by how much you are loved by others." Bill was loved by all.

Chapter 10

The Summer of '80

For a typical June in Kellogg, the weather couldn't have been better than that summer of 1980. Not only was the weather the best, I would remember this summer as the best time of my life. I was seventeen years old and had never felt freer and knew that so much in life lay ahead of me. It wasn't that I did anything any more unusual than before. It was the fact that I had grown up now and stood on the precipice of manhood. I could drive, I could date, I could drink, I could work, or I could still act like a little kid and pull my childish pranks. I experienced a freedom that I would never feel again.

However, there was one major difference this year. As soon as the school year ended, we did not pack up and go to Canada for the summer like all my previous teenaged years. My father lived on the coast of British Columbia in a remote paradise, and we would spend our summers with him, only to come back to resume school in Kellogg. Few people in the town understood the true background of our family. My father was Canadian, and it happened to be a near-chance meeting when he hooked up with my mother while they visited a Jewish synagogue in Seattle. A mutual friend from Pasco, Washington, decided to play Cupid and arranged it.

After only two days together, my father proposed to my mother, and she accepted. Two months later, they were married at a small Catholic Church in New Westminster, British Columbia. After six years in Canada and after giving birth to my five older brothers and sisters, my mother encouraged my father to try a change in lifestyle and move back to her hometown of Kellogg. She resumed her teaching career, and my father launched his construction business. I was the first one born stateside with

Steve, Tim, and Allyson to follow. Often, it seemed like two families under one roof.

Throughout each school year, I longed so deeply to return to Canada. To me, our small, secluded place in a small bay seemed to be the place of dreams. At the end of every summer, I was reluctant to climb onto the small plane and return to civilization. For nine months, I planned and plotted all of my projects for the next summer—the new sailboat, the bigger tree house, the longer trails, and yes, to see the beautiful Leslie who worked at a nearby resort. This year, my father's negotiations with the mining company delayed our departure. He intensely fought over the terms of the sale of his gold claim to the largest mining company in Canada. One week of discussions led into another, and so I resigned myself to my fate of being stuck in Kellogg for the bulk of the summer.

Although I longed for the time that I'd spend in Canada, a deep sadness filled me every year as we departed our summer haven. Each year, the part of the family that went north grew smaller and smaller as we each graduated high school and went our own ways. I could tell that each year as one of us left and didn't return north, another piece of my father died. Not only was he dying spiritually, he was dying physically with a cancer growing inside him. It was something we didn't talk about within the family. We always seemed to know that when Dad's time was up, it was up.

To keep my thoughts off of my father and the trip to Canada, I took to the hills outside of Kellogg and camped out more than ever before. We figured Mom needed the break from us. The hot sunshine had actually caused all kinds of rare occurrences, such as the city opening the pool ahead of schedule and my sneaking off and drinking some forbidden beer with Dizzy Dan and—at other times—Josh Mueller.

I kept busy day in and day out climbing in the hills, and each week, my father called down from British Columbia on a radiophone. Over the crackling airwaves, he told us to wait just a little longer. We had spent the last four summers with him at the summer paradise, and this time, the holdup was torturing me. I had to stay busy. If I wasn't camping, I would then take to swimming at the city pool. While sunbathing on the hot cement and realizing all the free time that I had on my hands, I started to think of countless idiotic things to do.

Fate had lined up conditions perfectly. Both Josh and I didn't have jobs. It had been years since he had worked his paper route and a year since I worked at the local IGA grocery store. The lack of money became instrumental to our upcoming plans. Without the proper finances, we had to be extremely resourceful if we wanted to enjoy the movies at the local theater.

The formal name of the theater was the Rena, but we had our own name for the place. We had adopted it from an individual who showed definite signs of dyslexia. My brother Phil's friend Juan, the same one who waved the machete at the old lady across the alley, called the place "the Retina." So we followed suit.

Juan wasn't an optometrist and definitely not a rocket scientist, either. Juan couldn't even win a spelling bee. If he couldn't pronounce certain words, he simply used them the way he thought they might sound. During a visit to the dentist's office, he gazed up at the explicit, larger than life, colored posters of live cases of gum disease. That's where he spotted the word "gingivitis." The sight of the rotten chompers left an impression on Juan. There was no way he wanted to catch that rare ailment.

Juan went swimming with us once up the river that summer and saw a homely, pimply faced girl on the beach with a huge cold sore on her bottom lip. He brashly yelled out, "Ooooo, she's got chin-chivvies!"

Phil stopped for a second and asked Juan to repeat what he just said.

"Chin-chivvies!"

"What's chin-chivvies?" Phil asked.

"Just look at her face," he said as he pointed over at her. "She's got chin-chivvies!" After Juan's indelible experience at the dental office and his profound use of technical terms, we thought that chin-chivvies was some type of severe skin affliction like scabies. After spending weeks of accusing everyone of having chin-chivvies, we finally found out that it was Juan's pronunciation of the word gingivitis. He pronounced it as "chin-chivvies." In the same case of mispronunciation, Juan called the Rena Theater "the Retina."

After Josh and I cased the theater for several nights, we discovered that the Retina operated on a limited budget and limited staff. It was in that weakness that we found a loophole in their operation that would allow us in. After several reconnaissance missions, Josh pointed out to me that although the seven o'clock session was fully staffed for the show, the nine o'clock movie utilized only a limited staff and only kept the concessions stand open for a mere fifteen minutes. Get your grub now or go hungry! After that, it shut down, and most of the crew went home—all of them except one lady. When she got busy, the theater was left virtually unguarded. It was part of her routine to shut down the refreshment sales and then proceed upstairs to clean the bathrooms.

Josh tested out his limited-staff theory a couple of times by boldly walking through the front doors and seating himself in an empty chair. Unabated in his entry, he sat and enjoyed a free show. One day after swimming at the local pool and sunbathing on the hot cement, Josh devised the plan to get Tim and me into the movie that night with him.

When evening came, we positioned ourselves directly across the street from the Retina. We closely watched the standard operating procedures of the nine o'clock showing. Just as Josh had said, the concession stand lights went off after fifteen minutes, and two of the workers were dismissed for the night. The remaining lady abandoned the popcorn and candy and tromped up the spiral stairs. Our chance had come.

We bolted across the street and snuck up to the door. As gently as I could, I slowly opened it, and we tiptoed in. Finding clear passage, we went straight on through the curtains and entered the dark viewing room. It took a few moments for our eyes to adjust to the dim light. After a minute, we found an empty row of seats. It all seemed too easy, and to our benefit, the show turned out to be an X-rated feature called *Emanuela*. I have to admit that there were a few interesting scenes that I hadn't seen in *The Computer That Wore Tennis Shoes* or *The Swiss Family Robinson*.

After drooling over the fleshy adult entertainment and walking home with that on my mind, I decided to set my sleeping bag in the backyard again and sleep under the stars. Being outside would leave the opportunity for a beautiful Hollywood actress to find me … or, less desirably, an ax murderer free to slice my ass up. If nothing else, I always loved to hear the crickets at night and later the birds chirping in the twilight. The rising sun blazing across the morning sky always intrigued me. There was no better way to start a new day.

Each night just before I crawled inside my sleeping bag in the backyard, I routed an extension cord out of the bathroom window and connected it to a small radio that would keep me company. Right after I turned the radio on, I heard a slow, sad song. It was a big hit that had just been released. Bette Midler sang it and called the piece "The Rose." From that night on, I heard the song a million times more.

Several days after our free show, Josh mentioned going to the movies again. Ironically, he told me the current movie at the Retina was none other than *The Rose*, starring Bette Midler. I didn't care to see it, but a free movie was a free movie! This time, Josh puzzled me with what he carried to the theater. He packed a two-quart plastic pitcher with a brown paper lunch sack inside. I didn't even ask—I only waited to see. Just outside the Retina, we posted ourselves across the street in the same spot and timed the actions of the theater workers. They performed their minimum-wage routine just like clockwork. All was going according to plan.

Within fifteen minutes, the concession stand lights went out, and the lady ventured up the stairs to continue her duties. We dashed across the street and made our entrance. But this time, instead of immediately darting through the curtains, we stopped next to the stocked shelves of unguarded refreshments. Josh stepped behind the counter and opened up the brown paper lunch bag. He began to fill it with hot popcorn. Tim and I couldn't believe our eyes. We darted through the curtains and into the darkness. Finally, our eyes adjusted enough for us to find our seats. Meanwhile, Josh held the half-gallon Kool-Aid container up to the spigot and began to fill it with Pepsi.

The gurgling brown fluid flowed down and fizzed in the bottom of the plastic container while Josh casually and calmly took the lid off of the butter container with his other hand and gingerly used the ladle to pour the thick, hot, yellow liquid over the puffy kernels as if he were making a piece of art. Tim and I were inconspicuously sitting in our seats and wondering what was taking Josh so long. Had he been caught?

Armed with his snacks, he strutted down the aisle looking for us. As the scenes grew brighter and lit up the audience, some people looked over at us and noticed that something was peculiar about Josh and his pop and popcorn. One guy grumbled to his wife about wanting to get a supersized pop like Josh's. She elbowed him in the ribs. No one said anything directly to us. We simply sat back and enjoyed the free show and the complementary goodies.

A few days later, we tried again and arrived in front of the theater a couple minutes behind schedule. The concession stand had already been closed, and no one was in sight. Emboldened by the other successful entries, we opened the theater door and walked in. As the door shut behind us, a woman stepped out from behind a partition wall and said, "Oh, no, you don't!"

Josh, Tim, and I turned and ran back out the door and down the street toward our neighborhood. The woman attending the nine o'clock show had gotten wise to us and foiled our plans. She was bucking for that five-cent raise and probably got it. Although we were disappointed, we didn't make any plans to egg her car or anything like that. She was just doing her job. Besides, the few times that we did sneak in gave us enough to brag about.

Because of Kellogg's small population, the activities available to the youth were limited. The townspeople at times tried to drum up activity. When they did sponsor a noble public event, we made sure we disrupted it in one way or another. For example, one Halloween, the high school pep band transformed a condemned building into a haunted house. All they wanted to do was raise a little money and have a little fun doing it. The students elaborately created gruesome spectacles throughout the house and had gone as far as to have the sound effects down to a bone-chilling degree. In one room, a student stood over a bathtub of bloody internal organs (probably from a recently butchered cow). He stood in front of each passing group and started up a live chainsaw, laughing like a maniac.

One of the nights the haunted house operated, Roland Martell, Tim, and I paid our two cents' worth and toured their frightening exposition. It was a joke. After making it through the first time without falling prey to the devilish ghouls inside, we ran home, stole a few raw eggs out of the refrigerator, and, just for good measure, stuck some gravel in our pockets. During our second tour of the house, we splattered a few eggs on some of their satanic artwork. The fun part came when we chose live targets.

One room had a fireplace converted into a cage containing a wild creature (a dressed-up student) behind a safety net. When the spectators walked by, red lights flashed onto the creature as it roared, clawed, and lunged out at you. Being my second time around, I already knew the routine and was prepared for the timing of each event.

When we got to the scary-creature-sight, the red lights flashed on, and the creature leaped out. Roland screamed back at the animal. Tim jumped and yelled as if he was really scared, and I flung a piece of gravel in a powerful, underhanded throw. Just as the creature drew in a deep breath and jumped out toward us a second time, the gravel chunk hit him smack in the middle of the forehead. The poor band student fell backward, holding his head and writhing in pain. He didn't growl anymore. He just moaned.

Even though we laughed about it as we ran out of the house, I did feel bad about it afterward. (I often did after we did something rotten. For years and even decades later, my conscience reminded me of the things I've done.) Roland went against our recommendation and braved the house a third time, and like we expected, he was finally caught. A couple of clarinet players identified him as the main culprit when they viewed the vice principal's lineup of known troublemakers.

The city pool, just like the haunted house, became a target for us because it had attracted more swimmers this hot summer than I had ever seen. I would often go merely for the fun of swimming and sunbathing, but other times I went to flirt with the girls who showed up.

Ever since the theater incident, Josh searched for a little more excitement at night. When he didn't find it with me, he went with his other friends who drove cars—mainly with one of his good buddies who had a jeep. Josh went with those guys quite often, probably because they drank the beer, listened to the hard rock, and chased the girls more seriously than I did. It became obvious that summer that he was starting to outgrow my inventions and science projects.

One night, Josh's friends left him stranded at home, but even that setback wasn't going to hold him down. Around nine o'clock, just when I was about to head for the backyard and climb in my sleeping bag for the night, Josh knocked on our front door, accompanied by one of his friends who didn't have a car. With his typical devilish grin, he shared a great idea with me. "Hey, let's go swimming at the pool!"

"Swimming? That's a wonderful idea, except that the pool closed three hours ago," I said.

"No, listen. We can do it. All we have to do is climb over the fence. I did last week. It's so cool the way the steam rises off the water," Josh explained. "The water actually feels warmer because the air is cooler. Come on, let's do it, you weenie!"

With his awesome sales tactics, he talked me into it. That by itself elated Josh, but swimming by itself wasn't enough for him. He needed one more thing—beer. I chipped in a couple of dollars, and we marched off across town with our swimming suits sticking out of our back pockets.

His friend smiled at the thought of drinking beer. He should have smiled, because they had just put a new acne medicine on the market. I personally suggested a prescription of tetracycline for him (a double dose!). One of the pimples on his forehead was so large and sweltering that when I looked over at him, I thought the thing actually blinked. When I hypothesize about life, I consider all. There was the possibility that his true intentions were to get a free chlorine bath since Stridex medicated pads were too expensive. Regardless, we were all partners in crime this time around.

When we got to the front of the Circle K store, Josh ran over to a beat-up car that was just starting to back out. He slapped the back fender loud enough for the driver to stop. The guy rolled down the window and looked out at us. His long beard and black leather jacket shocked me. *Oh, shit, this guy's going to kick our butts!* I thought.

Josh turned on the charm one more time and coerced this man into buying us some beer. But there was one condition—we had to meet him on the dark street behind the store. Josh easily agreed to that and handed the man the money. From there, we ran around to the dark rendezvous point and waited for the delivery.

Minutes later, the car rumbled up to us, and the driver handed the brown paper bag out the window to Josh. Now only one other thing stood in our way—and that was the tall chain-link fence surrounding the pool. We scaled that easily and passed the beer over without a hitch. In the shadows by the locker room doors, we each cracked open a can of cold beer and slipped into our swimsuits. Cocktail hour at its finest!

We guzzled beer and waded around in the warm water. The steam rose off the water just like Josh said. He pretended he was a swamp thing crawling through the fog in a horror movie. "Rraarr!"

I felt the thrill of defiance once again in my bones. If we got caught, so what? If we didn't, better yet. Either way, we had a good time and also had something to talk about.

The empty beer cans soon stacked up by the edge of the pool. Also, my head began to spin from the alcohol. Since I never liked being in the water for very long, I got out and climbed up into the lifeguard's chair. I informed Josh that he was now kicked out of the pool for disorderly conduct. After that, I kicked his friend out for coming into the pool with open sores. Naturally, he flipped me the bird.

Okay, I had to kick myself out for impersonating a lifeguard. I jumped off the tall stand, back into the water. *Ka-splash!* Josh and I shrieked, hollered, and splashed loud enough to catch someone's attention. Lights in a nearby house came on. I knew we had been noticed, so I convinced Josh and his friend that it was time to go.

Our timing and precision turned out to be perfect. We left the beer cans where they were and climbed back over the fence. Just as we scrambled across the dark recess of the city park and headed up the side of the little hill, a patrol car turned into the pool's parking lot. The officer probed the pool building with the spotlight.

Finally, the uniformed patrolman climbed out of the car. After neatly tucking in his shirt and patting his large belly, he walked up to the fence. He looked around at the pool with his long, black flashlight. His beam searched the water and then the pavement. The spotlight finally rested upon several evaporating footprints next to a pile of empty beer cans. The three of us giggled in the bushes at the top of the embankment. "So long, sucker!" Josh whispered just loud enough for me to hear him. The cop had been a day late and a doughnut short.

As the officer climbed back into the car, he grabbed the microphone to his radio and made a call to headquarters. He urgently said, "Officer down! Officer down at the city pool! Thermos empty!" He gently put the microphone down and bit into a jelly doughnut. As he closed his eyes, he hummed to himself in sheer ecstasy and waited for the coffee to arrive. When he got off shift that night, he detailed in his report of how he chased off the bandits at the city pool and then performed mouth-to-doughnut resuscitation in the squad car until backup could arrive. It was a great night for everyone involved.

Sometimes, after so many close calls with trouble, I felt I needed a short break from all the sneaking around. My Uncle Bob hired me to help him build a fence uptown at my gramma's house. In exchange for my labor, he granted me an engine out of my cousin's old Honda Super 90 (which had been wrecked many years before). I had the perfect idea for the engine. It would be powering my first-ever homemade go-cart. Honestly, I didn't have the slightest clue how I was going to put it together, but I would find a way.

I knew that Kit had an arc welder that he used to build a few weird projects that he never finished. I figured he'd be more than happy to weld whatever I needed, especially since it would be a real live machine that he'd be part of.

I had one of Steve's friends who owned a truck take me to the dump to pick through the scrap iron pile. Black pipe, rusty pipe, galvanized pipe, it didn't matter. I would use anything that I could for this project. (I actually ripped out a couple of water pipes off a house that they were tearing down across town.)

The first day into the project, Kit welded two pipes for me. I watched very closely how he did it and caught a glimpse of the settings on the welder and also the type of rods he used. After welding only two pipes for me, he said he had to go on an errand out of town for a couple hours. That disappointed me. I wanted to get going on this thing now! Kit left, all right, and he didn't show back up in a couple hours like he said he would. I wasn't waiting anymore, so I arranged a couple more pieces of pipe and donned the welding mask. I went to work on it myself. The rod kept sticking, and the welder buzzed angrily while I frantically tried to break it loose. Finally, I got a few more pipes welded together and felt very proud about that.

Kit did come back the next day and saw my work. He displayed a touch of disgust in me for using his tools without permission, but I think my creation intrigued him because he gazed at my work and didn't say much more about it.

After putting together the basic framework, I soon ran out of welding rods. I happened to mention it in front of the Tobias brothers. They gladly borrowed a handful of them for me from the sawmill in which they worked. In addition to their contribution, Josh's dad, who worked as a blacksmith for the giant Bunker Hill Mine, snuck a few rods home in his lunch box for me, as well. Everybody began to pitch in. If they didn't have supplies to donate, they sure had the advice!

When the frame grew into the shape of a small vehicle, I had every kid in the neighborhood congregating in our driveway and drooling over the cart. In perfect adherence to an unspoken tradition, the same as always with everything I built, every bystander took turns telling me how I ought to do this and how I ought to do that. The unsolicited expertise began to get on my nerves. Not one of these people ever built a go-cart, and yet they were all experts. I got into such a big argument with Brad Curry over how I should do something that I ended up chasing him down the alley with a crescent wrench. At a full gallop, he yelled back over his shoulder, "Your piece of junk will never work!"

Several weeks into the project, I simply needed money to buy some of the required hardware. Kit knew some people at the new church he attended who needed a few strong hands to buck hay for a couple of days. Kit, Steve, and I volunteered. We left early one morning and arrived at a small parcel of land up the river. The large field had square bales already lined up at even distances. The older lady and her tomboy daughter were all ready for us to fill up the truck and waiting flatbed trailer.

We kept up such a good pace for the first twenty minutes that the girl yelled over to her mother, "Hey, Ma, these guys can really go! We've got some good ones this time."

Yes, but this bullshit job wasn't going to last long, I knew that. They were nuts. The bales weighed a ton, and worse yet, they were filled with fresh ash from the Mt. St. Helens eruption. The higher we had to lift the bales, the more the ash spilled down into our faces. At the end of the day, I took my $32.00 and ran. That money bought me a clutch lever and cable for my contraption. Even though the money helped, the project needed so much more.

Shortly after I gave up on it, Dad called down from Canada and gave us our orders; we could head north now since the gold claim deal went through. Unfortunately, the only ones who went north were my mom, Jeri-Anne, Allyson, and me. As we drove off into the sunset listening to "Looking for Love in All the Wrong Places" (the theme song from the movie *Urban Cowboy*), steam began to pour out from under the car hood. A radiator hose had burst, and when I had to crawl under the car, my head felt about to burst from the terrific hangover from drinking at the drive-in theater the night before. I had to take care of the car problems over the next two days as we trekked through Seattle, Vancouver, the ferry system, and the long drive up to the top of Vancouver Island.

The next few weeks with my father were so different from ever before. He had sold his gold claim and seemed to not have a worry in the world. We fished together, visited the watchmen at the logging camp across the inlet, and even drank moonshine that one of my dad's old friends had distilled at another logging camp in the bay. I had taken my sailboat out several times and sailed for hours thinking of life as the small ocean waves slapped up against the plywood hull. I loved the solitude and never wanted to leave that place.

After those few wonderful weeks with my father, August was nearly over. The morning that the plane landed on the water to pick us up, my father and I packed all of our bags down to the dock. Just as I climbed into the plane, I turned back to him.

"Okay, Dad, I'll be back in June," I told him.

He smiled with delight. "All right. I'll have everything ready for you."

Over the past week, we'd talked about my return after I graduated from high school. He planned to set me up with my own float cabin, my own chainsaw, my own boat motor, and all the tools I needed. I was going to take over the operation of his little cedar shake mill. We talked about writing novels and changing the world. My dad could talk so big and so convincingly that you'd think you were capable of anything. Now I looked out of the window of the small plane as the pilot pushed us away from the dock. My father waved good-bye to us. It was the last summer I would ever spend with him there. I never would return the following June.

On the drive back to the United States, we stopped at a huge Sears store in Seattle to shop for school supplies. I talked my mom into buying me some wheelbarrow tires for the go-cart. I couldn't care less about new school clothes. I wanted wheels, and wheels I got. (My Bazooka Joe bubble gum T-shirt was due any time, and that—along with my gray Kellogg High School Girls' Track Team sweatshirt—would do me just fine for new school attire.)

Once back home from Seattle, I went right back to welding on my little machine. A few weeks after school started, I took the go-cart for the first test ride. It had no brakes yet. (I was in a hurry.) However, I could almost stop it. I raced it to the end of the alley and downshifted hard, forcing the tiny Honda engine to bear the weight. My jamming it into first gear and dumping the clutch almost tore the 90cc engine up, but at least it would almost bring me to a stop.

One night, Josh and Tim stood on the side of the machine and held onto the high roll bar. They gripped the cold metal bars and hung on for their lives as they rode with me down the dark alleys. On our way down Mission Avenue, we screamed through the darkness, and an elderly couple who were out for walk turned to look at our approaching vehicle. They squinted and couldn't see what was nearing. That is, until we burst out from the blackness and came under a streetlight. The couple had to quickly step off the street as we whizzed past them.

We raced up the brushy trail to the high school parking lot, suffering a few minor scrapes from the bushes and tree branches. At the school, we did several large loops around the lot with the tires screeching. Tim and Josh yelled and screamed as if they were at the carnival. I should have charged them for the fun.

Suddenly, the axel broke, and that was the end of the ride. Although we were many blocks from home, we didn't have to push my buggy back. Lucky for us, the girls' basketball team had a game going that night. We easily hitched a ride back home with a lady who owned a truck. Josh asked her out, claiming he loved older women. She simply laughed. Josh was serious. I couldn't believe him.

Josh went on chasing girls while I indulged myself in more extracurricular scientific projects. Sadly, the go-cart wasn't one of them. After that night, the go-cart rested until spring, when I finally rebuilt it after I got kicked out of school for three days—all for spitting corn through a straw at my physics teacher. (He ran out of corn, and I kept shooting.)

Chapter 11
The Return of Roland Martell

Shortly after returning from Canada, I spent some time riding Phil's Kawasaki road bike between my sessions of working on the go-cart. I gave a few girls rides on it and purposely braked exceptionally hard at the stop signs so that their boobs would press against my back. I couldn't get slapped for that. It was only gravity. However, even though I thought that was a cute stunt, the pretty girls still scared the hell out of me, even at seventeen.

Despite my inner shyness, I had so many beautiful ones after me throughout my teenaged years. In junior high, the sexiest creature in the entire world, blonde with the most voluptuous figure imaginable, pinned me against the wall and wouldn't let me go until I kissed her. Sure, I wanted to kiss her, but not in front of the whole class—in my tree house, maybe, but not there.

The few rides that I gave to the girls could have gotten me dates, but I never bothered asking any of them out. I was faced with a dilemma that only the great Roland Martell could solve. What should I choose? In one hand, it was girls, and in the other, it was peashooters and whoopee cushions. Tough choice! Johnson Smith Company got my attention (and money) instead of the girls.

As I drove along the back roads during the warm afternoons on Phil's bike, I had plenty of time to spend in deep reflection. I kept wondering what life held in store for me after graduation. I promised my dad that I'd be back, and I still held the idea of building the big, ninety-nine-foot and three-quarter inch-long sailboat and sailing it to Australia for the annual Mad Max Convention. But I realized that there was still a big, huge world out there, and going back to Canada may not be in the cards.

Since I loved gallivanting around the countryside on the green machine so much, I put a lot of miles on it and felt obligated to give it a wash job. So, one afternoon, a few days after school started, I parked the bike on our sidewalk within mere spitting distance from the street. I stretched out our long garden hose and began to spray the bike down. (They didn't call me a hoser for nothing!)

Being the motorcycle enthusiast that I was, I immediately picked up on the sound of an approaching bike. It was a big-sized four cylinder. I turned and looked out at a passing Suzuki 850. Mounted upon it was a long-haired degenerate wearing a red bandanna, dark sunglasses, and a black leather jacket. The rider looked directly at me with a gruff expression on his face. I quickly looked away and didn't dare make further eye contact with this possible psycho.

The biker buzzed up the road at twice the posted speed limit and disappeared around the block. Less than a minute later, he returned back down the road. When I looked out at him a second time, he gave me the same threatening look. Oh, crap! Did I look at this guy the wrong way? Did he want to put on a set of brass knuckles and kick my ass?

Luckily, he passed by the house a third time and kept going—or so I thought. He immediately turned around in the middle of the street and came back in my direction. He let off the throttle and coasted the bike into our driveway right next to me. I gulped. It was going to be either fight or flight.

The tall monster of a man put the kickstand down on the bike, shut the engine off, and stepped off his machine. The stranger whipped off his sunglasses and moved slowly toward me. With each step he took, I heard the click of his boot heels as they hit the cement. I didn't want to be a weenie, so I stared right into his eyes and tried not to flinch. He stared back at me. This guy knew I was growing more apprehensive by the second, and so he decided to get right to the point by making the first gesture of goodwill.

A huge, toothy smile bloomed across his face, and his eyes glowed with excitement. With three words, he identified himself. He shrieked, "Current Events Time! Oh, it's Current Events Time!" It was Roland!

I burst out laughing and almost hugged the guy. (We did, however, shake hands.) Tim had been sitting on the couch the entire time, watching us through the window. He wasn't sure what was going on, but curiosity forced him to come and check out the mysterious visitor. A little reunion blossomed right there in our driveway.

Roland had some explaining to do. He didn't go into much detail, but he claimed that he had been sent to a juvenile detention center after his skirmish with Sheriff Crummly that fateful Halloween night four years earlier. Roland spent almost a year in the institution before being released to live with some relatives in California. Most of the details didn't come out because Roland was no good at the truth. His specialty was the big lies. In the middle of our reminiscing, we stumbled across the memories of the peashooting days. We couldn't just talk about it. We had to reenact it.

Tim and I invited Roland inside the house and surprised my mom with his presence. Roland told her that he had been a good boy for the past four years. She acted glad to see him but displayed a little skepticism, probably because of his outward appearance. Roland had grown so much that he now stood almost six foot three and weighed more than two hundred and fifty el-bees. Oops, I meant pounds, you sap!

We secured a few drinking straws from the cupboard, along with three huge handfuls of popping corn. Just as if someone yelled, "Last one outside is a rotten egg," we all ran for the door, stuffing our mouths full of kernels. A ferocious firefight quickly ensued. It consisted of nothing more than three peashootin' fools spitting at each other through drinking straws. Actually, it was corn shooting, but who gives a shit? A spit-covered kernel shot into your eye pisses a guy off just as badly as a dried pea.

In the middle of the battle, Roland announced his rapid-fire machine gun demonstration. Pshew! Pshew! Pshew! Pshew-pshew-pshew shew-shew-shew-shew! Tim buried his face in his arms to protect himself from Roland's onslaught of slimy corn.

At the peak of our fun, when we became desperate to pepper each other's faces, an elderly couple walked down our sidewalk arm-in-arm. After all those years, they were still in love. How wonderful! But would years of love prepare them for what they were about to see? Right when they were halfway down our sidewalk, Roland, unaware of the approaching pedestrians, jumped out from behind the hedge after bending over to shake the corn out of his hair. He reengaged in the fight with a beautifully synchronized barrage of corn.

The old couple turned both of their heads instantly at the sight of a tall, long-haired hippie leaping out of the bushes and blowing a peashooter at two helpless teenaged kids. They sped up their gait and almost broke into a panic-stricken dash to safety.

All the fun we had in the yard with the peashooters was only a prelude to what lay ahead. If we could revamp the corn-shooting that well, we could do the same with the other pranks that we used to pull. Our visit ended a while later, and Roland had to get back to other business after just arriving in town, but he did promise to stop by the next night.

When Roland showed back up the following evening, Tim joined in and helped us gather up a grocery bag of plums from the neighbor's yard. The plums proved to be great ammunition to use against moving cars. It was great fun all over again. Roland, being less agile than we, still couldn't get away from vengeful car drivers. Instead of running, he had to rely on camouflage. All Roland had to do was step into a dark shadow between two garages, and he couldn't be seen with the long, dark hair and black leather jacket.

After a few weeks of combing the neighborhood looking for trouble with Roland, October arrived with a chill. The plums were getting mushier than ever, which was both good and bad, depending on which end of the barrel you were on. To warm ourselves up after our plum-throwing sprees, I'd make us a pot of tea. Roland pretended that he was an English hippie and even held up his pinky when he took a sip out of his cup.

The three of us went as far as to sneak into Mom's stash of sugar cookies that she had been baking and freezing in advance for the holidays. Hopefully, she wouldn't get too upset with us. Instead of tea and cookies with Roland, we could be out freebasing cocaine or shooting up heroin and holding up 7-Eleven stores. So I thought she should let us slide on a couple of cookies.

The night to end all nights of plum-throwing came in mid-October. We searched for a new spot to throw from, one that would give us the advantage of cover, concealment, and duration of target exposure. The only place that fell within our strict parameters was the steep hillside five blocks down Mission Avenue toward the high school trail.

I carried a bag of soft plums with me in one hand as we marched down the dark alleys. The night air was rich, sweet, and very cool. The town was somewhat quiet this particular evening since it was still in the middle of the week. That didn't matter; we had enough staying power to wait around for some innocent person to drive by. I had given myself one big *A* for ambush after my years of hard experience. Besides, Roland had taught me of all his tricks, as well.

During "Career Week" at school, the only job I somewhat qualified for was the U.S. Army Green Berets, but that was out the question because I had a real problem with authority. In addition to that, I thought about being captured in combat behind enemy lines. I knew I wasn't going to be able to handle the vice grips on the balls or the bamboo shoots under the fingernails. So I kept experimenting to find out what my real life's calling was.

Roland, Tim, and I sat that night in the cold, shivering and hiding in a clump of bushes fifty feet up the side of the hill. Very little traffic came by. The few cars we did hit simply slowed down a little for a moment but then kept right on going. Kellogg was a very small town, and if I were to confront the people that I bombed face-to-face, I'd probably know half of them. Unfortunately, at night, it was even more difficult to identify the cars, let alone the drivers.

Finally, another car approached. I wanted to make this one count, so I lobbed three plums in a row. Tim and Roland let loose a couple themselves. The rotting plums rained down on the passing car. We heard multiple splats. In a flash, the driver slammed on the brakes, and the tires screeched against the pavement. He jumped out of the car, mad as ever, and looked up at the dark hillside where we were hiding. "Okay, you little shits. If I catch you, I'm going to kill you!" And he was serious.

I then realized who this guy was. He was the neighborhood psycho. His name was Elwood Canthrie. Kit called him "Can-three, Can-four, Can-five." It was wisest just to call this guy "Sir." That is, if you didn't want your windpipe ripped out for breathing on his car.

Elwood's car was his god. After twelve months of compulsively washing and waxing it on a daily basis, Elwood would then trade the black Pontiac Trans Am in for another new one, only to wash, wax, and chamois its paint job to a high gloss every single day of the year, as well. I had personally witnessed him with at least four new Trans Ams. There may have been more, but I wasn't his mother, so I didn't keep track.

This guy gave new meaning to the word *stress*. If you got short-changed one Egg McMuffin in a McDonald's drive-thru, you might reach about a five on the tension scale spanning from one to ten. If Elwood saw a mosquito land on his windshield without wiping its feet, he would hit about twenty-five and go into cardiac arrest. He was the only twenty-eight-year-old in Kellogg who had a heart attack from stressing out. This guy was severely unstable. A car of high school kids drove past Elwood's driveway once and made a smart remark. Elwood took off running, chasing the car down the road on foot. He wanted some butts!

Well, here we have it—the neighborhood psycho with several rotten plums splattered on the hood of his freshly waxed Trans Am. Elwood would settle for nothing less than us chained to a whipping post so he could tear us to shreds with his bare hands. Faced with this, I don't know what made me say it, but I blurted out the first thing that came to my mind. I yelled down to him, "F—— you!"

He jumped about a foot off the ground and swung his fists up in the air in our direction. He screamed out as if he were doing an Olympic dead lift. Elwood freaked out like a toddler whose dominoes kept falling over. He went into convulsions. I thought he was going to swallow his tongue. I almost laughed at his little temper tantrum. If he caught me, I probably wouldn't laugh. But we were safe because he didn't know where in the bushes we were. Ha, ha.

Finally, Elwood calmed down. He took a few deep, slow breaths and counted to ten just like he had learned on *Sesame Street*. Thank God! I didn't want to give him CPR. Within moments, he regained his composure and relaxed enough to jump back into his car and drive away. Roland and Tim sighed. I began to giggle. They were hesitant. How dare I tell the psycho on the street to f——off just after we degraded his pride and joy? We could be killed over this.

For a while after that, both Roland and Tim kept quiet while I gazed out at the lit-up city streets. They were watching the streets, too. Yeah, they were watching Elwood drive his car two blocks down the road, park it, and then come prancing back down the road on foot to come and get us. These two dipshits sitting in the bushes with me didn't say a thing to me about it. What? Were they so mesmerized at the sight of Elwood tromping down the road toward us that they couldn't inform me of it?

Instead of watching for Elwood, I sat back on my haunches, damned near whistling from the boredom, when Elwood darted into the bushes below us and started to climb up into our locale. The second I heard the footsteps crunching on the rocks only yards beneath us, I knew someone grew wise to our position. My adrenaline rose to new levels, and I immediately took flight and bolted up the side of the hill. The hill was so steep and rocky that my feet slipped, and I had to claw with my hands to keep going. I wasn't getting a clean getaway because Elwood immediately heard the ruckus and came running after me. He was one of Kellogg's biggest jogger nuts, and I knew he was in good shape. If he caught me, I'd fight just like a rat in a corner. He wasn't going to rip out my windpipe without me biting his nose off or something horrific like that.

Tim and Roland froze in place. Just when they believed that Elwood would fly right by them and head up the hill after me, he spotted Tim standing there in his light-colored ski jacket. Elwood came to a halt and walked toward Tim with his hands balled up into fists. As he stepped closer, he pointed at my defenseless little brother and said, "Oh, so you're the little shit who threw stuff at my car!"

Immediately, Roland jumped to his feet, startling Elwood by his size and posture. "No. He's the little shit!" Roland said as he pointed at me scrambling up the side of the hill. Elwood was baffled. Roland spelled it out for him in a very detailed story.

"It all started when Tim and I were walking down the road and met this dude. He says, 'Hey, do ya guys wanna drink?' 'Sure,' we said. Then he pulls out this bottle of Jack Daniels." Roland continued as if he had rehearsed the script many times. "So we were drinking along here in the bushes, and this guy just flips out and starts to throw things at cars. What was it that hit your car? A rock?"

Elwood suddenly butted in to correct Roland. "No, it was mushy plums!"

Roland gasped in total astonishment. "Guess some guys just can't handle their liquor," he added.

By this time, Elwood was totally sucked in by the tale. When asked to describe the guy, Roland said that I was very tall and skinny, with long, red hair, and I wore a stocking cap. At that point, Roland hushed his voice and cupped one of his hands up to his mouth and said, "I think he had a gun."

Elwood jumped back, and his eyes shot wide open. "A *gun?*" he gasped. "I used to carry a gun. But not anymore," he added.

Elwood began to wonder if there was anything he could do about the tall, skinny, red-haired menace with the stocking cap and gun scaling the hillside at eight o'clock on a mid-October night. He best go and wash the plums off his car. Elwood gratefully thanked Roland for all the useful information and trotted back down to the street. He was going to nail that son of a bitch in that stocking cap!

Within minutes, Roland and Tim were back at our kitchen table eating Mom's Christmas cookies and sipping on tea while I spent the next hour traversing the mountainside in darkness, trying to avoid a psycho with an attitude. That was probably the last time in my life that I ever threw plums or anything at moving vehicles. We had to think of something new, and just like that, something new popped up the very next day.

My sister Jeri-anne had recently graduated college and had moved back home while her application for flight training in the U.S. Air Force was being processed. She waited patiently for months while the military decided whether to accept her or not. In the end, she was denied. If she had any type of degree other than one in general education, they would have accepted her, but by this time, Jeri-anne was back to being her ole predictable self. Like always, she threw herself into the first creative project that came along. She found out that a big-shot play producer was in town, putting together a cast selected from the local populous to perform in his big hit. The play was called *Dancing on Silver*. I knew without a doubt that she'd get a role. Jeri-anne, being tall and slim with long, straight, dark hair, reminded me of the actress Tina Louise who had played the part of Ginger Grant on the television series *Gilligan's Island*. Jeri-anne, with all her looks and talent, easily secured one of the leading roles.

The producer, a Stephen Spielberg wannabe, had studied our local history and then based a comedy/musical on the historical details that he had dug out of the local archives. The play supposedly had something to do with the old mining days of the 1880s in North Idaho and our community's economic connection with Lake Coeur d' Alene. When I did eventually see the play, the only scene that stuck in my mind was this idiot riding a log down a flume and into the water. To each his own, I guess.

Roland happened to be over having tea and cookies with Tim and me one night when Jeri-anne burst through the door after coming home from one of her first rehearsals. Roland almost choked on a cookie when she mentioned that they were looking for help on the set. "Help?" Roland asked in feeble voice. It was too good to be true. "Why, hell, when I was in California, I spent a lot of time in Hollywood running the lights for a bunch of productions; I even did it for a few small bands like Van Halen. It's one of my specialties."

Jeri-anne paused and gave Roland a dubious look. Regardless, she ended up buying the story—and so did the sap in charge of the play. The next night, Roland was hired on as the official light man for the production. Roland—what a scammer!

The entire show was to be rehearsed and shown at the junior high school auditorium. Tim and I were saddened by the loss of mischief time with Roland since he was now preoccupied with his new job. Luckily, after a few nights, Roland met up with us before he had to be on the set and said he didn't have much to do but sit in the bleachers or wander around the school for two hours. Roland just slipped out the operative word: wander. He had nothing to do but "wander" around the school for two hours. Bingo! He promised to let us in the school through a side door so we could wander around, too—with our peashooters.

The next night, Roland let us slip in a side door by the gym. While the director barked out orders to the inexperienced actors, we snuck down the dark hallways and into one of the classrooms that Roland and I once sat in five years earlier. The corn fighting began immediately in the corner room where the two hallways met. The cinder block walls to the middle classrooms didn't go all the way to the ceiling. There were merely permanent partitions. Sound, light, gaseous odors—nothing was held out of the classroom. That openness became the key to our downfall.

We started blowing kernels of corn at each other in the dark. We laughed and then hollered when we got hit in the eye. I couldn't spit the kernels out fast enough, so I started to throw handfuls of corn at Tim and Roland somewhere out in the darkness. Many of the high-speed rounds they shot at me ricocheted off of the chalkboard. Actually, we were making quite a mess and a lot of noise. Suddenly, without warning, the bright fluorescent lights in the hallway came on. We had been caught.

Since Roland and Tim were on the side of the room by the door, they instantly escaped around the corner. I was on the far side of the room, and by the time I made it across the classroom and out into the hallway, the he-man woman janitor spotted me. Despite being seen by her, I was fast enough to run outside the building and loop around the back side of the school. The three of us came back into the safety of the gym.

After we calmed down and caught our breath while hiding under the bleachers, we then innocently walked down a short hall to the boys' bathroom. A large, collapsible gate had been stretched across the hallway just on the other side of the bathroom and locked. The janitor had just finished sealing off the area. We now felt safe. Tim, Roland, and I ducked into the bathroom and spent a couple of minutes giggling and relieving our bladders. (Oh, we were real hotshots!) Well, I walked my hotshot butt out the bathroom door and looked through the locked gate and into the eyes of an angry janitor.

She immediately identified me and stepped up to the gate with her keys still in hand and unlocked it. She pushed it aside, making a wide berth for me, and said, "You—yes, *you*. You're coming with me and cleaning up that mess." The old bag pointed right at me.

She caught me off guard because I was raised to respect the elders and other authority figures even though I didn't like to. I instinctively responded by taking a couple of steps toward the gate. Suddenly, rebellion filled my spirit. Once again, I blurted out the only two words that came to mind. "F—— you!" I said, and then I spun around and ran with Roland

and Tim trailing right behind me. For the second time, we found ourselves outside. Reality set in, and I embraced the fact that we couldn't go back into the school without facing immediate trouble. So Tim and I went home for tea and cookies and wished Roland the best of luck with the school janitor and the play's administration.

Unsurprisingly, Roland was fired from the set that night, and Jeri-anne took quite a bit of heat for recommending him as the light man. She was ashamed of Tim and me. I sometimes believed that my mother had planted a subconscious message in my mind, saying, "You should be ashamed of yourself," because I sure heard that a lot throughout my life. Hell, my whole life was about fun. Why should I be ashamed all the time, Mom?

The next day, Tim got called into the principal's office at the junior high and was verbally threatened, but luckily, he received no hack with the vice principal's paddle. My court-martial with the high school authorities was pending but never materialized.

Roland went on shortly afterward to create his own musical production. He formed a band named Rock Hard Cucumbers. Roland and his cohorts plastered hundreds of posters all over the valley announcing each of their scheduled performances. I heard them play once and had to plug my ears. Roland didn't have to do anything else to impress the world. His place in history had already been carved out. He just didn't know it.

Once I graduated from high school, I never saw Roland again. His memory lived on in my mind, stronger than with anyone I had ever met. I hope he faired well in the music industry.

Chapter 12

Animal House

It was a universally accepted fact that Tim and I had the propensity to find mischief anywhere we went. We found a new weekend haven in the beautiful (actually, duller than shit), historic city of Butte, Montana. Pete spearheaded the family's college efforts at the Montana School of Mines and spent his freshman year sampling the local living conditions by renting a modest room in a large house. His reports of college life were so positive and motivating that Phil returned to high school after a year absence while working in Canada for our dad. Phil chose to suck it up, make up for the lost time, and complete his senior year of high school a year late. He decided to pursue a college education just like Pete, Kit, and Jeri-anne had before him.

After Pete's first year was finally over, he and Phil teamed up in the fall to begin a new school season. They put their brains and money together and formed a joint tenancy by renting an old Victorian-style duplex on Granite Street just down the street from Montana Tech. By taking on a couple of roommates, they reduced their monthly expenses even more.

Their days in college were spent in the unique era of the late seventies. Certain technological advances were beginning to impact our society at the time. HBO had recently been introduced to the public and had become a powerful force in the world of television. One of our biggest thrills while visiting Pete and Phil for the weekend was watching cable TV. The programmers stocked the cable with all the new movies—movies like *Animal House* starring John Belushi.

Pete and Phil's place actually looked similar to the run-down frat house on the National Lampoon special. Just inside the front door of their place, a long set of steps ran directly up to the second-floor rooms. D-Day could have driven his motorcycle right up them just like in the movie.

In addition to the structural similarities, Pete and Phil's "Animal House" contained the same style décor and the same bacterial cultures in key areas (the refrigerator, the rotten garbage under the sink, and the month-old socks stuffed under their beds). Even the same class of people lived there as in the movie.

One of their roommates was a real sweat hog by the name of Mark Savage. "Savage" and "slob" were synonymous. In the dictionary next to the word "pig," the Webster company posted a picture of Savage armed with a leg of chicken in one hand and a frothy mug of beer in the other. He was named Savage because the staph bacteria waged a constant war for the surface of his body and were savagely destroying his epidermis. By the reek of his BO, I think they were winning.

Once, when I asked what Savage was studying to be, instead of immediately responding, he ignored me since I was only a little brother and didn't deserve any respect. Phil leaned over on the couch near the subject in question and brushed a paper towel across the slob's forehead. Savage squirmed and resisted without much success because he wouldn't dare let go of the slice of pizza that he was biting into. Phil showed me the sweat on the paper towel and said, "Savage here is studying petroleum engineering. He produces more crude oil than Exxon."

Savage swallowed what was in his mouth and made a feeble, boyish comeback. "Yeah, right. I got your petroleum hanging!"

Phil rolled his eyes and said, "I take it back. Savage is studying to be a dickhead. When he graduates, it'll be Mark Savage, DH—Bachelor of Dickhead." Savage ignored Phil. He was too busy ingesting his daily quota of pizza.

Savage never used the stove to cook on. He pledged allegiance to his trusty deep fryer. When other students donated blood to a blood bank, Savage was busy looking for a sweat bank to donate his sweat. Sometimes Savage would take off his glasses. When he did, two large smudges were visible on the top of each lens from the oils rubbing off of his forehead.

Savage made me feel good sometimes because I often felt sorry for having pimples. Savage grew them for a hobby. In fact, every time we went to Animal House to visit, Savage seemed to have the same prized zit on the side of his cheek. The sweltering, pus-filled organism actually dilated its pupil and looked around the room.

Savage wasn't the only character in the house. Pete and Phil had two more roommates. Bob Schmidt lived there, as well. He was in very sharp contrast to Savage because he was a very tall, thin, blond-haired gentleman.

Bob also wore a pair of wide-lens glasses and seemed to enjoy running with the Animal House gang as therapy to overcome his shyness. He loved the energy that he felt in the presence of Pete and Phil. Where they would go, he would follow. Bob even bought a motorcycle during his last days at Animal House. Then there was something almost taboo that Bob did once that Pete and Phil didn't—he had gotten himself a girlfriend. They were all too young to get hooked up.

To complete the wild group at their run-down fortress of studies, they took on one more roommate named Dave Weber. Dave was the cockiest of the bunch. He, too, was tall, but much thicker framed and more muscular than Bob. For an engineering student, he seemed to have more brawn than brains. If he couldn't argue his way out of a confrontation, he'd just threaten to pounce on you. With his large cheekbones and mandible, he had a slight resemblance to a young Arnold Schwarzenegger. In fact, Dave became one of the stars of the mining competition team that went to the national competition in Tucson, Arizona, and stole first place after having come in dead last the year before. My brother Pete heard of the previous year's defeat and took charge of the team, challenging Dave to show his stuff.

Most of the weekends that we younger brothers spent in Butte went pretty much according to routine. Pete and Phil felt obligated to take us out at least one time to Fairmont Hot Springs just a short drive west of Butte, and that was regardless of what time of the year it was. Since they were college students—studying instead of working—money was always tight. If we could sneak in without paying, we would, and we soon developed an effective system of getting past the attendant.

Phil would walk through the door leading to the series of indoor and outdoor pools and stop to chat with the lady in the booth. First off, he'd ask a couple of stupid questions. The trick was to ask her a stupid enough question that she had to turn and ask someone else working with her in the booth to help answer it. Something like, "Is this water rich with sulfur? I am allergic to sulfur."

While Phil distracted the lady, we got down on our hands and knees and crawled past the booth, enough to mingle with the rest of the paying customers. When we were in the clear, we'd get up and run for the locker room. It didn't always work, but getting caught was just as fun as getting by without paying. If Savage came with us to the hot springs, the management specifically frisked him for any contraband sandwiches. They strictly enforced the "No Eating in the Water" rule with him.

Sometimes we'd opt to go to the college pool just up the road from Animal House. That pool wasn't nearly as fun as Fairmont, but the last year Pete attended school in Butte, we pulled a few interesting stunts. Phil had met a girl named Molly, and yes, Phil had to eventually break down and admit that she was his girlfriend. The continual "just a buddy" reference didn't work for very long.

Molly was a very intelligent—but assertive—engineering student. Despite all her strong attributes, she had a serious vision problem. She didn't often wear her glasses because she preferred contacts. Despite the handicap, Molly still volunteered as a lifeguard at the college pool, but unfortunately, she couldn't wear contacts or glasses while she was on duty in one of the tall lifeguard towers.

With her vision as poor as it was, Molly couldn't readily identify each swimmer that came in to enjoy the chlorine-rich brine. Since we were aware of this, it led us to casually step incognito into the pool. Once in the water, we really caused a disturbance. Molly would yell at the top of her lungs for us to stop, and when we didn't, she would go nuts and threaten to have us thrown out and barred from the pool for life. Naturally, we laughed when we got out of the water and apologized with an oriental bow. Only then did she realize who we were. Sometimes we'd walk right past her with Phil, and she still didn't recognize us.

Phil, Kit, and I were blessed with terrific balance. We were able to stand on the diving board and then suddenly bend over and kick our legs into the air, walking on our hands to the end. We had once purposely caused a ruckus for Molly for an expressed purpose. This time, she squinted at us, not knowing who we were, and yelled warnings to us several times. Both Phil and I climbed up onto the diving board, walked on our hands all the way to the end, and then we dived in face-first. She shrieked from her realization of who we really were and felt as if she had been had by us. We were teasers.

No matter what we did during the day, we always returned to Animal House to begin our mandatory evening poker games. Phil was the self-proclaimed poker king and also the biggest cheater. Although we had fun playing with him, we often did wonder why we never won. We had been cheated by him time and time again.

The Tobias brothers often drove to Butte and let us ride with them. Because of Phil, they loved poker as much as we did. Even though they were Phil's guests, they still tried to cheat because they knew he was. We couldn't often catch Phil playing underhandedly, but when he caught Tom and Greg, he bashed them in the chests with his fist and then grabbed up a handful of their shirts.

"Okay, f——r! Ante up. Pay the pot a dollar for cheating!" he screamed at them in between licks on his ever-present Popsicle.

They'd have to throw in a dollar to keep playing. It was usually Greg who cheated because Tom was too busy eternally pondering the answer to the ultimate question: "Why is there air?" Phil once told Tom the answer. "To fill a balloon!" But Tom always forgot.

As kids, we often invented our own terminology for things in our world. One in particular was our keyword for candy, potato chips, or Twinkies. We referred to any type of junk food as "grits."

"Hey, here's five bucks. Go buy me some grits," Phil always instructed us.

I used that term until my army days. I had to eventually give it up because all the southerners kept thinking I wanted some of that hot, steamy breakfast mix.

We ate all kinds of grits, but Phil's favorite was the Popsicle with the double wooden sticks. Sometimes we sat for hours playing poker. Phil would slurp on these Popsicles the entire time we played. He was the toughest Popsicle-eating hombre in the West. To this day, we have home movies showing us gathered around the table with the Tobias brothers, with Phil eating Popsicles and playing poker.

Animal House wasn't necessarily known to us younger brothers for any super-wild times. It was just another place to get away from my mother's watchful eyes. We just knew it as a unique hangout where Mom couldn't tell us when to go to bed or what dirty movies we couldn't watch.

There was a time when things got a little hairy and even dangerous for us at Animal House. I was a senior in high school while Pete was a senior in college. Since he had left his big Ford four-wheel drive truck in Kellogg, he asked Mom if she would let me take a Friday off from school and drive it over to Butte for him. It was a great opportunity, and Tim even got to come with me to keep me company on the road.

I drove Pete's big 4x4 truck to school that morning, showing it off as I coasted through the parking lot, smoking a big cigar and hoping that the vice principal wouldn't see me. At lunch, I drove down to the junior high and picked up Tim. Our only other stop was to fuel up at the gas station. From there, we headed east on the interstate. Tim and I were quite excited that sunny spring afternoon. Besides the free rein of Pete's truck for the three-and-a-half-hour drive, we took advantage of his unlimited supply of 8-track tapes and listened to them all the way over. There is nothing like listening to the Fleetwood Mac album *Rumors* over and over on an 8-track.

Once Interstate 90 shoots over Lookout Pass and into Montana, the countryside next to it levels out into beautiful, green pastures with endless, fenced-off ranches. Train tracks run next to the highway for miles and miles. Tim and I tried counting the cars on some of the longer trains but quickly gave up. There were just too many of them.

Boredom almost set in until Tim began telling me of a really neat movie he watched the last time he was over at Animal House. The movie was called *Phantasm*. His favorite part of the movie was when the guy in the Good Humor truck got attacked by the floating steel ball with the spinning drill protruding from it. The movie sounded so wild that I figured Tim must have been making it up.

Near the end of Tim's movie review, we came around a long turn in the highway. On the other side of the hill, a long train with a humungous string of cars sat idle. Why was it not running? There weren't any facilities out here in the middle of nowhere for it to stop. I got it—Phantasm got the conductor! Tim burst out laughing, and that kept us going until we reached a sign pointing toward an exit. It read Phosphate. I didn't see any sign of a town, and I sure didn't see any big piles of phosphate. So we went back to cracking jokes about the conductor and the phantasm for the next fifty miles. For some reason—maybe because I was a senior in high school this time, I'm not sure—I felt that we may be in for an exciting weekend unlike the ones in the past. Only time would tell.

After three and half hours of driving, we finally arrived on Granite Street with Pete's truck. I parked it right in front of Animal House and felt proud that we delivered it without incident.

The weekend seemed to go according to routine—that is, until Sunday afternoon when we were left alone in the house with no one else but that fat slob Savage.

Savage didn't like us younger brothers very much. He thought we all sounded like clones, so he called each of us TR1, TR2, and TR3. "TR" meant tape recorder. Tape recorder one, tape recorder two, and tape recorder three. We found it hard to offend Savage, even as hard as we tried to insult him back. He simply didn't have the brain capacity to know when we were denigrating him. However, there was one way to set him off like a keg of powder—and that was to mess with his food. He'd kill if you touched his Banquet frozen chicken.

On this uneventful, quiet Sunday morning, Pete and Phil bid Tim and me farewell as they both headed off to church. My mother had raised them to be devout Catholics. They attended Mass no matter where they were on a Sunday morning. It was as good as punching a time clock for God. Tim and I were only going to be around long enough to finish breakfast before we headed back to Kellogg, this time driving what used to be Jeri-anne's little white Ford Pinto. She had graduated from college in Pocatello the summer before and had sold the car to Phil's girlfriend. Since his girlfriend carpooled with friends back to Spokane, we got the job of returning it to her, and this was all before the days of Drive America.

I wasn't in a really big rush, even though we acted like it. I just wanted to skip the morning church service. With that out of the way, I figured that Tim and I had enough time to engage in one last game of pool. The pool table sat in the middle of the living room adjacent to the base of the stairs as it always had for the past four years.

We tried our trick shots and goofed off, not even trying to play an actual game. We were just being stupid. Soon after we sank a few balls, an upstairs door creaked open. Since the house was old and probably haunted, we didn't think much of it.

A few seconds later, I head a tiny *plunk* and looked down on the floor. Just a few feet away, a small, black firecracker rolled around with the fuse burning. Ka-*blam*! My ears hurt from the explosion. It was our old friend Savage lobbing them down from the top of the stairs. Did that bastard want a war? Well, he got one. It was no secret that Pete and Phil kept firecrackers all over the house. They were part of the college student supply kit.

Tim ran into the kitchen and snatched a pack of matches off of the counter while I unwound a hundred-pack of Black Cat firecrackers that I had been eyeballing all weekend. Tim lit the match and stuck it up against the thin, gray fuse of a single cracker that I was holding. It sparked to life. I then ran to the bottom of the stairs and threw the tiny explosive up at Savage. It blew up immediately, sending tiny shreds of paper flying into the air. By the time I could get another one ready to light, Savage had already tossed another one down the stairs at me. This time, it landed on top of the pool table and exploded on the faded green felt. So much for respecting your possessions, Savage. We will show you that war is hell!

We went back and forth for a while, throwing the firecrackers at each other. I frantically tried rushing closer and closer up the stairs to that fat bastard. Chickenshit that he was, he stayed up at the top of the stairs in a much safer place while Tim and I faced the bombs that came raining down on us.

I finally had enough of the bombardment, and so I threw an entire pack of Black Cats up at our rival. The series of sporadic explosions that followed sounded like the beaches of Iwo Jima. The whole house filled with bluish gray smoke and smelled like sulfur and gunpowder.

That final offensive led to an instant cease-fire. Savage stepped halfway down the stairs and started yelling at us for making a mess.

"Look at what you little shits did! Your brother is going to kick your asses!" he screamed.

"Ah, stuff you, you fat-assed son of a bitch. You started it!" I yelled back.

"Now clean it up, you peckerheads!" he ordered Tim and me.

I told him to get stuffed as Tim and I hastily grabbed our bags and fled out the front door. We jumped into the small white Pinto and pulled away. Within minutes, we were on the highway heading for Kellogg.

Long before we even hit the Idaho border, Pete arrived back at Animal House and heard Savage's tainted side of the story. Oh, crap. Papa Peter had to immediately call Mom with a full report. And so, since she had been briefed beforehand, she had the leg irons waiting for us by the time we pulled up to our house on Mission Avenue. It seemed like I always got into trouble no matter where I had been—summer camp, Boy Scouts, Animal House, wrestling practice, and even youth activities with the local church. It's like I fought the law, and the law always won. (Not the real law, that is.)

Later on that evening, Pete sat down in his room at Animal House and penned a harsh letter reprimanding me for my irresponsible actions while I was in Butte. He titled the letter "Dear Idiot." How could I be so heartless as to disturb the peace-loving Savage as he studied the Bible in the privacy of his upstairs room? When I received that letter, I was even more adamant about doing the opposite of whatever Pete suggested that I do.

Pete, Phil, and all their friends eventually graduated from Butte and went on to fine careers. According to Pete's proposed plan for me, I was supposed to apply for acceptance into the electrical engineering program at Montana Tech the following school year. But like always, I did exactly the opposite of what he ever advised me to do. I joined the army instead and never again had the pleasure of visiting Animal House.

Chapter 13

Barfsville

Despite the fun we had at Camp Easton, I finally realized that summer camp, the YMCA, and the Boy Scouts were designed for sissies. It didn't make any sense for me to advance my membership in any of those conventional organizations. Who needed that crap when the hillside lay only a hundred yards away from our house on Mission Avenue? We did all the camping we wanted and didn't have to take orders from anyone or follow any rules.

It didn't take us much time to develop our own style of camping. Camp cooking was a cinch. All we knew about it was to plop an open can of chili in the fire and stir it with a stick. And for hygiene, just don't crap too close to camp—and you'd better bury it!

While most people look for a campsite in a readily accessible area, we always ventured off the beaten path and found a place that was wild, overgrown, and needed chopping out; that made us feel like real pioneers. I regret to say that in our later years, with the use of our motorcycles, we did get a little lazy. We didn't like to hike so far, so we just drove off the road, through the bushes, and as far off the beaten path that the foliage would allow us. That was where we would set up camp, in virgin territory.

During the infamous summer of '80, I stumbled across a unique campsite right off the dirt road near the top of the ridge above Swinnerton Gulch. The road itself ended only a short distance further, so we knew that there wouldn't be much traffic. Also, based on the geography, we felt that we were far enough away from civilization to feel comfortable. The neatest feature of all with this location was that a forest service trail lay at the end of this dirt road, and it led either back down to Kellogg or further up the mountains to Graham Peak. I had often hiked directly to this camping spot, starting from the bottom of the hill near our front yard. Meanwhile,

Tim and the rest of the gang drove up the Montgomery Gulch way on their motorcycles and into Swinnerton. They'd usually meet me there an hour later after I had humped up the mountains all by myself with a heavy pack stuffed with cans of Western Family chili and a package of chocolate Twizzler licorice. When it came time for hastily planned campouts, this site was ideal. This little hidden plot, just yards up the bank from the main road, would always do just fine.

After camping at this location a few times, we began to implement a few good ecological practices. It was in the way that we cleaned up after ourselves like good little citizens. The fire became our biggest friend. It burned up all our paper, plastic, butt-wipe, and even our tin cans, whether we had opened them up or not. The exploding cans were always the last items on the fire because when they blew, there wasn't even a fire left behind for us to put out. Also, we didn't have to pack all that useless weight back into town. It had been consumed by fire, or at least rushed into deterioration by the searing heat.

Tim had gotten stuck with a stubborn can of corn once. He didn't want to pack it into town or even eat it, so he saved it for the last thing to be incinerated. The can sat on the fire for quite a while, swelling under the heat and pressure that caused the ends of it to bulge out. Expecting an explosion, we hid behind the trees and our backpacks. We waited and waited. The can swelled all that it could. It should have burst by then. This can instead formed a tiny hole in its seam that spewed out high-pressure steam.

Tim was mad. He demanded a bona fide detonation. Like a mongoose sneaking up on a cobra, Tim crouched down and cautiously stepped closer to the fire with a rock in his hand. He intended to smash the can with the rock and make it explode.

Just as Tim flung the rock into the fire, Josh Mueller threw another one—but faster, just like a baseball. It hit the can before Tim's did, catching him off guard. There was a tremendous eruption. The shock wave of steam, corn, smoke, and ashes flew into Tim's face, causing him to do the best backflip I had ever seen by an amateur. He lay on the ground motionless for a few seconds. I seriously thought that Tim might have been injured. Josh and I rushed over to him and helped him to his feet. Tim turned and looked right at me with a dazed look on his face. I started to laugh hysterically. There was no blood on his face or clothes—just hundreds of yellow corn chunks splattered all over him. Fifty feet away from the fire, we found the flat, rectangular piece of tin that used to be a can of Del Monte whole kernel corn. The immense pressure flattened it right out.

Although this particular site provided us with many nights of camping pleasure over the previous year, we were eventually forced into naming it "Barfsville" after a ghastly maneuver known only to drunks or sick people. This defining campout came in the early spring of 1981. Actually, spring hadn't arrived yet. The snow had barely melted off the ground, but that didn't stop us from getting away for the weekend. My mother had bitched enough at Tim, Steve, and me, and she was really getting on my nerves. I hated it when she continually asked if I needed my head examined. She had no real appreciation for all of my projects. She never got to see my nine-foot hot air balloon, the "Hindenburg," only the ashes that were left on the back porch when it accidentally burned up. She complained about all the strips of wood strewn around the backyard after I crashed my hang glider jumping off the garage roof. And this time, it was all the metal pipes and chunks of welding rods left over from the rebuild of my go-cart. I *had* to call this campout to order. The other neighborhood kids seemed to be as anxious as I was. They constantly drilled me every day that week. "Are we going? Are we going?"

I caved in under the pressure and announced that this one was to be exclusively a motorcycle jaunt. Ironically, I didn't have a motorcycle at the time. My go-cart had been running recently, and the idea of taking it on the trek would be a historic first for our gang of hellions.

On Saturday morning, the members of our group began to arrive in the alley behind our house. Brad Curry came with his pristine Yamaha 100. Tim had his lime green Kawasaki KX80 racer. I had my homemade dune buggy-style go-cart ready to go, and Dan had just pulled up in his old—but proud—blue and white 1966 Ford pickup. In the back of it stood his trashed-out Kawasaki 175.

The Cooper brothers were waiting for us outside of town at their house at the bottom of Montgomery Gulch. They had two small, red, matching Honda XR80s all fueled up. Last of all, the Kerrigan brothers had come over from Elizabeth Park on their blue Yamaha 175 and were waiting for us at the Coopers'. Since everyone knew that Dan was the only one of age to buy alcoholic beverages, they planned well in advance and had already provided the money for him to buy their choice of booze.

With the arrival of Dan, the last of the preparations included me strapping several backpacks and sleeping bags to the roll bar on my go-cart. I wore a pair of logging boots, black work pants with suspenders, and my usual JCPenney's red plaid shirt. With all of us in place, the alley behind our house looked like the starting line for the Baja 500 desert race.

I had just turned eighteen. Tim, Max Cooper, and the Kerrigan brothers were all about fifteen. My brother Steve and Brad Curry were only sixteen. Drinking was supposed to be forbidden for minors, but since we weren't in the Boy Scouts, YMCA summer camp, or girls' basketball, anyone who didn't like it could smooch my big white butt. We didn't often bring alcohol on our campouts, so this once shouldn't hurt anything. I had to justify it somehow because, in a sense, I was responsible for the lives of everyone in the group since I was the oldest, not counting Dan. I did wonder for a second if I could have been making a mistake. Regardless, it was time for us to pull out before I heard any more complaining from my mom. She couldn't stand it when we decided to go camping. She complained about how long it took for us to get our stuff together and get out of town. We rummaged around for a couple hours at times, hunting down all the neat stuff we wanted to take. Preparing this time was no different. We had already gone through her cupboards several times. Not only that, our motorcycles began to congest the alleyway, and too many nosy neighbors were peering at us. The moment to blast off finally came. My mom came out onto the back porch and with almost tears in her eyes and with a painful look on her face, pleading with me, "My God, when are you guys going to leave? Can't you just finally go now? You are driving me crazy!"

That was definitely our cue.

Tim headed off first with his little green Kawasaki buzzing like a mad hornet. Brad followed on his Yamaha, trying to keep up with Tim, and I sped behind them in the go-cart. With every puddle the front tires cut through, muddy water splashed into my face and drenched my legs. I realized it was going to be a brutal ride for me. At the end of our alley, Dan pulled out onto one of the side streets and went his own way with Steve in the truck with him. The plan was for him to meet us at the base of Swinnerton where the locked gate would prevent him from going any further in his Ford.

Tim led the way down each alley and stopped at the end of each block, looking from side to side for any lingering police cars. Each time the coast was clear, he signaled with his hand for us to continue on to the next segment of alley.

After several blocks without being detected, we made it to the edge of town by the building with the helmet-shaped roof known as the Miner's

Hat. While it originally started out as a drive-in hamburger place in the early '50s, it went on to become a real estate office for decades after that. After cautiously passing that cute little structure, we pulled out onto the old highway. I shifted through the gears on my galvanized pipe-framed contraption and built up some real speed. I was probably making about forty miles an hour down the straights because I was clocked one time on the same stretch of road during the previous summer before I had rebuilt the machine.

We flew down the old highway, pointing and laughing at each other. Since I didn't wear a helmet, the wind whipped into my face and eyes while small rocks pelted my body everywhere. The small Honda engine screamed behind me just inches away, deafening me. The entire metal frame of the cart vibrated. Even the small, rusty steering wheel pulsated in my hands, numbing my fingers. None of this mattered because the adrenaline coursed through my body like it always did during the peak of an adventure. The excitement and thrill of what we were doing was almost too much. But once again, with the escapade came the fear of being caught. We were still in great danger of being intercepted by a Shoshone County deputy or even a state trooper. For some reason, we never looked down upon the county or state law enforcement. They just seemed to be a group of professionals doing their jobs, but there was something different about the Kellogg police. They were definitely of a different breed. They seem to waste so much time quelling the fun of the local youth. It's like they had nothing better to do. Uncle Bill always called them "the town clowns," and from all of the years of experience with them, every time we saw one of the local patrols, we couldn't help but think of them as clowns. Here we were now out of the Kellogg city limits, out of their jurisdiction. I cruised down the old highway being escorted illegally in my funky little cart down a main county road. We looked like a pack of dogs running with a big tomcat in the middle of the cluster. Luckily, there were no police to be seen during our dash to the base of Montgomery Gulch. Safety lay only minutes away.

We joined the Coopers and the Kerrigans and formed even a larger procession with the additional motorcycles. As we left the Coopers' driveway and raced up the gulch in a big pack, old ladies tooling in their yards stopped in the midst of their gardening and stared at us in the strangest way. It was as if they were cave people seeing fire for the first time. A couple of vicious dogs ran out in the road but got kicked in the teeth by a couple of our riders.

Just at the base of Swinnerton Gulch, we encountered a much muddier road, which incessantly splashed me with mud and left me severely drenched, dirty, and freezing. I began to think that this go-cart idea wasn't so practical, after all. Fortunately, the sleeping bags that were strapped to my roll bar were all wrapped in plastic garbage bags. Not far up this road, we encountered a heavy wire mesh gate that had been recently installed by a logging company. Dan and Steve arrived minutes before we did and were in the process of unloading their gear. Since he wasn't going to be able to make it through the gate in his truck, Dan had parked it on the side of the road and was planning to take his Kawasaki the rest of the way.

Besides the task of unloading Dan's bike, we had to drag my go-cart up the embankment and around the gate and get it back down onto the road. Once we were all past the gate and lined up once again, we pulled away in an every-man-for-himself race to the top of the mountain.

However, I began encountering engine problems. Less than a quarter mile further along, the engine on my go-cart died and wouldn't start again. Damn! We still had several miles to go. No one wanted to wait for me, and I was packing too much stuff to ride on the back of someone else's bike. Once someone pointed out the fact that I had fallen far behind, Dan sent Steve back down the road on his bike to find me. I climbed out of my go-cart and kick-started the engine over and over, but it kept sputtering to life for a moment only to quickly die on me again. There was only one solution. Steve had to latch on to my cart with a rope and tow me with Dan's 175 several miles up the mountain to our campsite.

Once the tow began, Steve fought hard to keep the bike from being pulled over by the deadweight of my machine. I sat behind the wheel and once again found myself with mud and rocks being shot into my face by the spinning back tire of Dan's bike. It was harder than we imagined, but I stayed behind the bike and ate his mud for the remaining two miles of road. When everyone else at our camp heard the howling of Dan's motorcycle straining to pull me up the final stretch of road, they all came running out of the bushes and cheered as Steve and I shuddered to a halt in a snow-covered patch of road just below our secret haven.

Even though our campsite was tucked in the bushes on top of a ten-foot-high bank, we still managed to drag the dead go-cart up it and into the safety of our camp. We had all finally arrived. Luckily, no one had asked Dan about the booze, and so it wasn't taken out immediately; there was too much work to do. Even before setting up the tents, tarps, and makeshift lean-tos, we first had to go out into the woods and drag back as much dry firewood as we could find.

If retrieving wood by hand proved to be unfruitful, as an emergency measure, Tim had brought along his trusty little chainsaw as a backup. Tim was the only nine-year-old that I had ever known to get a chainsaw for Christmas. My mom bought him his first one years earlier—a teeny, tiny green Poulan. He thought it was so neat that he wanted to get another one to match it and then make a set of holsters so he could pack them around like matching six-shooters. Tim didn't have a gun to bring into the woods to protect himself from wild animals. He instead simulated to me on many occasions how he would saw a bear's nose off with the little Poulan if it tried anything funny.

Usually when we camped, the only protection from the elements that we ever used was a large, rectangular tarp. We cleverly propped it up in front of the fire as one huge lean-to. To my dismay, the other campers had somehow been properly indoctrinated by the Pussy Scouts. (Oops! I mean the Boy Scouts.) Or they were taught camping etiquette by their fathers, because they all had tents and other useful accessories. That was okay, because our father taught us some stuff, too.

Dad caught me once trying to make a fire on the back porch with a bow and wooden rod. I had seen it illustrated in some of my survival books but never could make it work. Instead of spanking me for trying to create fire, Dad grabbed the pieces out of my hands and barged his way through the house and into the living room. He became very serious in an instant. "Now watch this," he ordered. Dad coiled the loose rope from the bow several times around the middle of the wooden dowel I was using. Then he braced the top of the dowel with a wooden block that I had carved a notch in. He then stuck the other end of the dowel into the block of wood on the floor. Slowly at first, he began to push and pull on the bow from side to side, and the dowel began to spin inside the coils of rope. Faster and faster, Dad began to drive the bow back and forth until the dowel spun wildly. Smoke began rising from the small chunk of wood on the floor. The living room began to fill up with a blue haze. Red-hot cinders rolled out onto our dark blue rug. Dad stomped them out and finally gave up. He asked if I got the idea. I sure did.

That wasn't the only thing Dad taught me. He taught Dan and me how to sharpen a knife. For my birthday one year, I got an authentic-looking Commando knife with a sheath and sharpening stone included. Once again, Dad caught me red-handed playing with a knife (and he had no idea where I'd gotten it). He grabbed the knife and sharpening stone out of my hand. In an instant, he was once again transformed into a serious expert and began to clash the stone and blade together in quick *slish-slash, slish-slash* motions. All he needed was a hot grill and some Teriyaki sauce, and he could have passed for a Ukrainian jinsu.

He paused for a second, and by the expression on his face, I knew that something wasn't working like it should have been. Without any warning, my dad took in a quick breath, hocked up some spit, and blew a loogie onto the sharpening stone. "Hock-tooey!" Splat!

Dan and I laughed.

Dad, immediately annoyed at our nonserious attitude, yelled, "*This is survival I'm showing you, and it's not funny!*"

Okay, then, we'll just laugh our asses off in private for the next six months, or maybe we'll put it into a book someday for everyone to laugh at. I knew how to turn a situation around! Dad was classic—one in a trillion.

While we set up our camp, each of us relied on our own experiences to guide us through the process. For example, I improvised somewhat by using the Sunday paper and some gasoline to start the fire, and instead of hocking a loogie on the blade of my knife to sharpen it, I just used the fancy kitchen gadget that Mom ordered off one of those TV commercials. Thanks, anyway, Dad, for the knife-sharpening exhibition!

But when I saw a new kid that came along with the Kerrigan brothers hanging a sign on a nearby tree that read Latrine, I lost my cool. I shrieked as if I were having a seizure and then ran up to it. I yanked it off the tree and spun around in few wild circles like a discus thrower. I heaved that sign as far down the hillside as I could. When Tim's friend looked at me with that dazed expression and asked why I did that, I spread my arms out as if ready to conduct an orchestra and screamed at the top of my lungs, "The whole damned mountainside's the shitter! Just don't crap near the camp!"

Immediately, everyone in camp started laughing. This guy was a newcomer, and the latrine sign must have been some nasty habit that he picked up in Boy Scouts. "What are you going to do next? Hire a butler to come up here and tuck you in tonight?" After that comment, I thought the kid was going to cry. I slapped him on the back and broke the tension with a little chuckle.

Later on, just before dark, we all took turns opening the lids on our chili cans and sticking them in the fire to cook. We then took turns describing the pranks that we had recently pulled off at school and talked about all the school bullies we wanted to beat up. In the midst of all the small talk and the winding down to feast on our snacks, Dan pulled the tequila and whiskey bottles out of his backpack. With a devilish smile on his face, he laid them on the ground next to a large rock. He knew the outcome of this scenario.

Soon enough, our younger campers stopped talking and started drinking. They begged Dan to show them how to do the salt, lime, and tequila shot in proper order. As soon as they got the hang of it, Dan and I left camp. We casually walked up the road, trudging through the melting snow patches and on to the top of the ridge. I wanted to see the final moments of daylight turn into a beautiful pink sunset and then watch the stars come out.

We climbed up the small forest service trail to the top of the ridge and looked down at the lights of Kellogg that began to illuminate the valley down below. Kellogg seemed like a tiny patch of civilization that had cropped up in a desolate mountain valley. Over a matter of minutes, the western horizon slowly turned from bright yellow to darkly orangish red. The sun had already disappeared before we arrived. Venus twinkled low in the sky above the dying twilight. I made a wish on her as the first star that I had seen that night. In adherence to my strict camping tradition, I pulled out a cheap cigar and lit it up. I was eighteen, and since having smoked these dog turds since I was twelve, I was now an expert. Ted Mulligan had taught me well.

More than anything, I loved to be in the mountains. The woods gave me a sense of security and peace I could find nowhere else. I could actually think without any distractions, even dream my dreams without anyone nearby to say, "Oh, you can't do that!" Although I wished I could live alone in the wilds, I looked out at the horizon and said to Dan, "There's a real big world out there, and after graduation, I'm going to check it out!"

Naturally, Dan, being two years older than I and supposedly more experienced, agreed with me. *Oh, yeah,* I thought. All Dan could tell me was about the time he hitchhiked to California with a couple of hippies and how they became "one with the universe." I think that was the only place Dan ever went in his whole life, but I wasn't going to cause a confrontation on a mountain ridge and burst his bubble. If Dan could snatch the pebble from my hand, he'd be qualified to tell me anything.

After standing there talking with Dan for thirty minutes and noticing that all the stars were out and shining brilliantly, we walked back down to our humble camp only to find a totally dysfunctional group of guests. Both bottles of alcohol were empty and sitting on top of the blazing campfire. Steve sat behind the wheel of my dead go-cart with a drunken grin on his face while his head weaved from side to side. In one hand, he held a plastic cup that he randomly sipped from. When he noticed Dan and me looking at him, he fluttered his lips and made an engine sound as he spun the steering wheel from side to side. He was in an imaginary race, and he was loving it.

Brad Curry sat on an overturned bucket next to the campfire. He was catatonic. His eyes were fixated on the leaping flames that danced on the burning sticks in front of him. Obviously, he had consumed too much of the evil liquid. On the far side of the camp, Max and Andy Cooper were swearing at each other. "I'm the bigger brother, and you'll do as I say!" Max slurred at his younger—but larger—brother Andy.

Andy stood holding a folding shovel, poised to smash his brother's face in. "I'll kick your butt. You know I can! Now give me my drink!"

"No! You've had too much, and this is all that's left," Max said. He then held a canteen cup up to his lips and took several desperate gulps. Andy reached out and tore the cup away from Max, spilling some of the contents. Andy barely got it to his lips when Max tackled him. A brotherly fight ensued. They rolled around on the ground, screaming, yelling, and grunting.

Tim and Myron Kerrigan sat on a couple of unrolled sleeping bags next to the fire and giggled fiendishly at their own little tales of mischief. "So I told that Post Falls cheerleader that she gave me a 'Blue Veiner.' It took her a minute to figure out what it meant. Then she hit me!" They giggled childishly and both ended up wiping the slobber from their mouths.

Dan and I shook our heads in disgust. The only person unaccounted for was Walley Kerrigan, Myron's fraternal twin. Just then, we heard crashing in the bushes on the north side of camp. It grew louder and louder. Was it a bear? Finally, a human figure appeared. It came running toward camp. It was Walley. He held a long stick with both hands. I could hear him mumble something. He didn't stop running when he got to the edge of camp. Instead, he leaped over the fire and yelled, "I'm going to catch me a widdle wabbit! Kill the wabbit! Kill the wabbit!" He bumped into Brad, knocking him to the ground, and continued running right through camp, disappearing back into the woods once again. His voice trailed off behind him, "Gonna get me that wabbit …"

It was all Dan's fault. He had bought the alcohol for them. I hoped he was proud of himself. Dan and I were adults now, and these punks were in our charge. We let them convince us that they were experts at drinking. Actually, we weren't convinced. We had just made an exception this time. But what were the parents going to think? Well, Mr. Cooper already called us Major brothers assholes on other occasions. He'll do it again this time—that one was a given.

Although we had brought beer along on a few previous campouts, these young followers of mine had their own tricks to pull. Their favorite trick of all was the hyperventilation gag. It took two people to pull this stunt. The volunteer would breathe in and out in very deep breaths and then pause for a moment as he exhaled all that he could. Meanwhile, the other participant would bear hug him from behind. Somehow, the subject's oxygen supply would get cut off, and they would collapse and pass out for a brief moment. Their limp bodies would come back to life in a few seconds, and they always asked, "How long was I out?" When I witnessed that for the first time, it scared the hell out of me. Maybe just plain alcohol was better.

By the time Dan and I settled down in camp, the sky was completely black. The stars were no longer visible because the inclement weather was due to overtake us at any time. The clouds had already moved in.

I stacked a bunch of wood on the fire and sat back to chat with Tim and Myron. They tried to act more serious while talking to me, attempting to show me how well they could handle a drink. As we talked, I started to hear a gurgling sound. Across the fire from us, the once catatonic Brad now had a long stream of clear saliva oozing past his hand (the one that he had stuck into his mouth). It oozed straight to the ground in one large string. He was trying to stick his fingers down his throat so that he could cause himself to vomit and get the inevitable over with. He gagged and gagged with his wet fingers sticking deep inside his mouth.

Steve finally got tired of sitting in the go-cart and came over to the front of his tent. Just before he crawled inside, he noticed an opened can of sliced peaches. He reached into the can with his bare hands and began to eat them like a cannibal would eat a medium-rare cerebellum. Steve finished and then burped rudely as he went into his and Brad's tent. He was turning in for the night—or so he had hoped.

The Cooper brothers stopped their fighting when Andy gave up and retired to his sleeping bag. Max wasn't so lucky. He lost his balance and fell backward onto a log directly across from us. He held his two hands up to his forehead and moaned. He'd had too much to drink. The longer I sat talking to Tim, the louder and longer Max moaned. Soon he laid himself facedown on the log and hugged it so close that he was cheek to cheek with a big knot.

Walley Kerrigan made a couple more loops around camp looking for the little bunny rabbit before he stopped, panted, and fell over head-first into the lean-to that he and Myron had made earlier that day out of pine boughs. One by one, the teenaged punks were dropping around us. The sooner they went down, the sooner I could get some sleep, but I knew it wouldn't be that simple.

Finally, Tim tucked himself into his sleeping bag under our large, raised tarp, and Myron took up a sleeping position next to his brother Walley in their shelter. Tim and Myron spoke back and forth for a few minutes. Their speech grew slower and slower as they began to pass out. At the last minute, Tim got up and staggered to the edge of camp to relieve himself. As soon as he got done, he bent over then coughed for a second. Suddenly, a spray of vomit shot from his mouth. He heaved a second and then a third time before wiping his mouth off with the back of his hand and casually walking over to his spot next to us.

"What was that all about?" I asked him.

He looked at me with a drunken smile and said, "I figured it would be better to do it now than later." Soon, he and Myron were passed out. All that was left alive in camp was Dan and me. Max continued to moan to himself until he just couldn't take the pain any longer. He had to summon a higher power. He finally began to pray out loud. "Oh, God!" he cried out. "God, help me! Help me, God!" It was those same four words repeated over and over. "Oh, God! Help me, God! Help meeeee aaaaaahg-rrrrralph!" There went his dinner, chunks dropping to the ground from his mouth.

Things around camp were all wound down now (that is, regarding motor activity). The digestive system actions were just beginning. Brad couldn't make himself barf nor swallow his own fingers, so he crawled into the tent with Steve. A minute later, their tent rattled and shook, and it didn't even closely resemble the scene from the movie *Brokeback Mountain*. Steve poked his head out through the flap and heaved. His vomit, rich with yellow chunks of peaches, splattered on the top of Brad's boots. Bear grease and bile—what a mix! Steve returned to the tent only to roll back over and poke his head out one more time. He was handing out seconds.

Dan and I kept talking for a while until we felt sorry enough for the dying Max Cooper to simply cover him up on the log with his own sleeping bag. He sporadically cried out to God, but to no avail. He had committed his sin.

When I returned to my seat, Steve's tent shook again, and he roared but didn't waste his time coming to the door of the tent. He barfed inside next to his own pillow (or maybe on Brad's pillow). Every ten minutes or so thereafter, Steve rolled over inside the tent and puked up again. Must have been some good peaches. Brad was out of it and totally oblivious to Steve's gut-wrenching hurls. He was condemned to breathing in putrid vapors all night.

Just after I got inside my sleeping bag and closed my eyes, I heard someone else hacking up dinner. It was Walley Kerrigan. I knew that because Myron woke up and started yelling at him. "Walley! You're puking in our hooch!"

"I am not!" Walley yelled back. He wasn't, huh? Then where did he think he was barfing?

After several hours of sleep, I woke up from a dream and wondered where I was. A few moments went by until I opened my eyes and focused them on our dying fire. The flames were nearly gone. Most of what remained was nothing but fading red coals. The outside temperature had dropped drastically. I could tell by the smell of the air that it would probably snow soon. I wasn't going to freeze my butt off, so I rolled out of my sleeping bag and stuck my boots on. I put the rest of our wood onto the fire and realized it would not be nearly enough to last until morning.

Most of our wood came from large clumps of thin trees. These clumps were more like humungous bushes—half of the small trunks were dead, and half of them were alive, coexisting. The real trick was getting the dead ones out. At three o'clock in the morning, I didn't feel like messing around fighting to extract fifteen-foot-long, awkward sticks from its tangled clump.

When I grabbed the first one and it didn't budge, I got mad and immediately altered my plan. I walked over to Tim's pile of stuff and grabbed his little green chainsaw. Although I was shivering with huge goose bumps all over my naked legs, I primed the chainsaw and pulled and pulled until it screamed to life. I stuck the whizzing chain into the clump of trees and let it rip. The deafening, high-pitched scream of the 2-stroke engine startled everyone in camp. Tim looked up from his sleeping bag and saw me standing there exposed to the elements in my undershorts, wearing a pair of unlaced boots and wielding an angry chainsaw while tiny, white snowflakes drifted down around me. It was a sight he'll never forget. I'd have liked to have thought of myself as a magnificent Greek god saving the day, but in reality, I probably fell a little short, especially in my shorts.

Within five minutes of cutting, dragging, and stacking, I managed to get enough wood to keep the fire blazing until morning.

By sunup, the hungover campers stirred to life but were reluctant to get out of their sleeping bags. They lay still for as long as they could until their bladders nearly burst. Even the thought of any kind of breakfast didn't appeal to them. We all just wanted to pack up and go home.

Our campsite became a place of moaning and gnashing of teeth. When a slight breeze blew through camp, it carried the stench of human vomit with it. From that day forward, the place would forever be known as Barfsville, a site where a battle between man and bottle took place. Long live the stupid!

Chapter 14

Jonesy and the Death Machine

Despite the intriguing oddities and the freaks in our neighborhood that really deserved harassment, we also had some very nice, loving, giving people nearby who helped keep the community in balance. Once such family living on Mission Avenue was the Jones family. Mr. and Mrs. Jones were a humble couple. They minded their own business. They lived within their means (which was equivalent to the standard of living in the rural parts of Ethiopia). And they just did the best they could. Academically, they blew the bell curve and got group discounts on annual IQ tests. At mealtimes, their kids skipped four of the food groups and stuck to their favorite group—junk. The chocolate-smeared faces were a dead giveaway that they'd just finished a recent feeding frenzy.

Because of their affable nature, they suffered none of the wrath of our youth. After witnessing the conditions they were up against, I declared a clemency for them. For example, their house was somewhat cramped. For years, Mr. and Mrs. Jones slept on a hide-a-bed couch in their living room just a few feet away from their front door. If a visitor came by a little too early in the morning, that didn't matter. They were invited right in. "Come on in!" Yeah, come on into the pigpen, all right. "Oops! Don't trip over that stack of poopy diapers! Oh, would you like a cup of coffee? I can't reach it from my bed here."

Other than keeping a messy house and displaying remnants of a year-round yard sale, they were all right people. They just smelled a little on the mildewy side.

Nobody called Mr. Jones by his first name. Everyone in town simply referred to him as "Jonesy." Jonesy loved any and every type of sport—professional or amateur, national or local. He'd certainly let you know

189

about it, too. It was quite difficult to sneak down our sidewalk without him broadcasting his views regarding the previous night's game.

"Howdja like the game last night?" was his usual greeting, which he shouted from across the street.

Each time that I arrived at our house, he accosted me long distance with his unexpected yell. I had to pause and point at my own chest. Who, me? I had to think really fast of how I was going to respond. What game? What kind of game? Which game? Where was the game? I didn't give a damn about any game. I hated football, I hated basketball, and I didn't give a rat's ass about baseball, either.

So, out of sheer politeness, I yelled back the most ambiguous remark I could think of. "Oh, yeah, what a real cincher!" or "Kept me on the edge of my seat!" The only thing that kept me on the edge of my seat was when I had to lift one cheek to pass some gas. I didn't want to hurt his feelings, so I merely humored the guy since he was so nice and likeable.

Another interesting fact about ole Jonesy was that he had a couple of daughters that we had dubbed the "watermelon and pumpkin sisters." (They did have a little toddler brother that we resorted to calling "raisin" just to keep the nicknames in order.) The watermelon and pumpkin sisters, if one could ascertain by their nicknames, were somewhat obese.

People always try to be polite and say that an overweight person has a gland problem. However, after my own personal experiences of horking down the grub next to many a lard-ass, I had to agree with the findings of one world-renown doctor. He plainly stated that, after examining hefty people for so many years, the only real problem 99 percent of them had was a spoon, knife, and fork problem. Maybe these chubby kids across the street were just a product of too much silverware lying around and not enough sports. I left it at that and kept humoring ole Jonesy about his football games.

Jonesy kept a vigil on his front porch in a very similar way to Rod Thompson, except Jonesy was there for relaxation. Rod scanned the perimeter from his front steps in an attempt to seek out and destroy trouble. All that fat bastard needed was a cape and he would have been right up there with Batman.

Another difference between the two of them was that Jonesy cleverly posted himself in an old reclining chair that was long overdue for the dump. The chair became a crucial part in his quest to save the expenditure of extra calories. Also, it made it easier for him to reach his potato chips. Jonesy had set himself up perfectly on his comfy little throne of Salvation

Army land. His front porch turned out to be just the perfect spot for him. Actually, it turned out to be perfect for us; we could keep an eye on him and knew if he was watching.

Since Jonesy never caused any problems for the neighborhood (or us), we left him alone. In fact, he liked us so much that he gave us gifts on occasion. I once found a twenty-dollar bill that he had lost at the supermarket. Upon returning the lost money to him, he gave me five dollars as a reward, and I thought that was great. However, the greatest gift he could bestow on us came after I left home for the army.

After I had been away for over a year, I came home on vacation one sunny June afternoon. Upon my arrival at the house in my full dress uniform, I realized that all the neighbors would take notice of my homecoming. Sure enough, there sat Jonesy on his front porch. I felt the presence of a stupid-ass rhetorical question being brewed up just for me as he saw me get out of the car. I bolted toward the front gate as if I were dashing between the hedgerows at Normandy trying to avoid Nazi soldiers.

Oh, shit! The gate latch was stuck, and while I fumbled with it in growing desperation, he blurted out a typical greeting. "Hey! Watcha think of the game last night?"

By this time, I had rehearsed the drill for so many years that I instantly went straight for my backup plan. I then feigned a coughing spell, pointed at my throat, and had to wave him off and run inside before I became hoarse from yelling across the street. I was glad to know that Mission Avenue hadn't changed that much during my absence.

Months later, as summer turned into fall and fall turned into winter, it was then that he bestowed the greatest gift of all on my younger brothers Tim and Steve.

Our neighbor Jonesy not only loved his old, beat-up reclining chairs, he loved trashed-out, secondhand cars. Actually, they were secondhand when he first got them, and then severely trashed-out after he got done with them. Maintenance wasn't one of his strong points. He thought an oil change meant bathing and washing his hair. When people remarked to him about how we were now living in a disposable society, he thought that they were talking about cars, too. He claimed he was no mechanic, but I believed by the way he bent over to pick up the daily newspaper that he must have had visions of being a plumber by the horrific sight of his butt crack.

This enviable gift was none other than one of his disposable cars. The automobile in question was a pale, aquamarine-colored, very early

'60s-model Plymouth. Tim described it in great deal in a handwritten letter that was sent straight to my army unit with the Eighty-Second Airborne Division.

Oh, he and Steve were so excited—not because they now had a car, because they already had their own cars. Tim had 1968 Ford GT Torino Fastback, and Steve had a 1970 Ford Mach I Mustang. They were so excited about this particular Plymouth because this jalopy actually ran … kind of. And the car had a special personality all of its own. Their greatest aspiration was to keep it running long enough to find a cliff to drive it off. The car was dangerous. It was a death trap, but it was a machine all right—a death machine.

Until the impending death and burial of the car was planned and arranged, Steve and Tim invited their friends over to assist in some of the special modifications. The modifications would have made Carroll Shelby at the Ford factory extremely jealous. Instead of treating the car as a real vehicle, they made it into the equivalent of the elephant man from the circus. I'm sure the car's spirit cried out, "I am not animal! I am a car!"

Naturally, this old Plymouth had its share of dents and cosmetic deficiencies, but my brothers decided to make lemonade out of this lemon. With their friends in eager compliance, they spent an afternoon giving the car body a whaling that it would never forget. Armed with clubs, baseball bats, axes, and sledge hammers, the juveniles reenacted the scene from the movie *Grease* when they added their finishing touches to "Greased Jalopy." As Tim and Steve took turns beating on the car body, they giggled themselves silly. Mitchy Mueller was immediately alerted about the action and ran through a neighbor's yard to our place—only he had to pay a dollar to use a bat. Some of the elderly neighbors heard the racket and stared out their windows in awe at the sight of the advanced bodywork being performed right in broad daylight. One of the old ladies looked through her picture-paned window and reached for her chest.

After working up a good sweat, both Steve and Tim unanimously agreed that the dents simply weren't enough. The car needed just a little more personality. Next came the spray paint. They laughed and giggled some more, so hard that the neighbors were sure that they were on drugs or maybe sniffing the paint. My two brothers painted slogans all over the car in various colors of paint. Politically correct they were not. The slogans read: Eat Me! Kilroy Was Here. The Love Machine. Kill Castro! Other symbols were the middle finger and a couple of red swastikas.

After watching *Animal House* again for the fiftieth time and becoming so inspired, Tim took a pair of tin snips, cut a hatch in the roof of the car, and installed a set of hinges on it so that they could exit from the top like a light-armored vehicle.

Once they were satisfied with their work, they started up the loud, mufflerless beast and drove down Mission Avenue, terrorizing anything that they came across. Both Steve and Tim took their turns driving so that the other one could poke his head out of the roof hatch and wave a machete at people walking down the sidewalk. There was never a time in all their lives that Tim and Steve got along so well together. However, this was not to last long, because one had to remember that this car was disposable, and the duty of disposing of it was not far away. But they never gave it a thought. The thrill of the present moment was too great.

The dark alleys proved to be the most rewarding grounds of all. Steve and Tim "doored" garbage cans, chased stray cats, and drove through some of the yards that had no fences. Steve once opened the passenger door at high speed and let it hit a telephone pole. In a debriefing after that particular test ride, he claimed that the door had never shut so fast. Luckily, his arm was out of the way. Naturally, the driver's door was marred for life like the rest of the car. Soon enough, Steve and Tim realized the danger of driving the beast in public, so they adopted a very crucial strategy—they only went out in the machine after dark.

After phoning home a few times from Fort Bragg, I had heard enough about their new toy. I had to see this Death Machine in person, but I had used up all of my accrued leave time. Like always, after I had joined the military, I felt like I was missing out on something back home.

Sadly enough, on a Friday night during a bitter cold February, I received a very disturbing phone call at the barracks. It was my mother. From the outset of the call, she sobbed but quickly addressed the issue. My father was dying. I knew that the day would come just like a thief in the night, and I was actually more prepared for it that I'd thought. By Monday morning, I was on a plane flying across the United States to get home to see my father before he took his last breath.

The flight from Bragg always took an entire day. I had several different flights to catch with several different, lengthy layovers. One flight was canceled, which left me bumped to a later flight that would put me into Spokane well after midnight.

By the time I called home to Kellogg from a Spokane airport pay phone, the only person willing and able to make the hour-long drive to pick me up was Tim. Along with him came his good friend Greenie, whom I had met the previous summer during a wild night where I had crashed the ensuing senior prom for the class of 1982. Greenie thought I was the closest thing to a Greek god. Ever since our camping days, I seemed to have developed a following that mainly consisted of my younger brothers's friends. At that point in my life, being in the Airborne and having won a few more fistfights, I could do no wrong in Tim's eyes, and he let all his friends—boys and girls alike—know about it.

However, not only was I about to see my father for the last time, it would also be the last time that I would ever saw Greenie alive, as well. On this memorable night, I let him wear my beret all the way home from Spokane and will never forget the glowing smile on his face in the darkness as it was vaguely lit up by the dash lights on Tim's Torino.

Greenie's real name was Roy Blake. He was such a faithful friend to Tim, but tragedy ended Roy's life a short time later when a drunk driver careened into him as he walked the river road home one spring night. For years, Tim kept a black-and-white photo of Roy in a wooden frame on a shelf in one of the bedrooms at home on Mission Avenue. For decades, every time I'd pulled my old maroon beret out of my box of treasures, I'd think of Greenie and the night he wore it.

Tim, Greenie, and I arrived in our driveway in Kellogg after two o'clock in the morning, and the first thing Tim had to do was to give me a walk-around of the tattered car parked in the driveway. I just wanted to crawl into bed, but Tim had to relate more amorous feats performed by Steve in the vehicle.

Apparently, Steve had been out practicing a stunt. (In later years, Steve perfected it in a different vehicle. The stunt consisted of one part Crown Royal, one part Ford Taurus, and one part snowbank). With the Death Machine, Steve found it very exciting to ram the mountainside just up the road from our house. Coming down from the top of Vergobbi Gulch, each time he stomped on the accelerator, the ill-running, eight-cylinder engine lurched the car forward with what power it could muster. As he approached the rockslide that spilled into the roadway just below the small cliff, Steve flung the steering wheel over and mowed the side of the hill with the front bumper of the car. The rocks, dirt, and sparks that showered the roadway were more than Steve could handle.

There was a night that he performed this type of maneuver that nearly put an end to the short-lived Death Machine. After one extreme bash against the dirt-and-rock mountainside, while Steve laughed himself into convulsions, the engine sputtered and backfired, causing a small gasoline fire around the carburetor.

As he coasted a block further down the road, Steve sensed something was wrong under the hood and stopped in front of house with an unlit porch. He quickly jumped out of the car and popped the hood up. He gasped at the sight of the hellish, orange flames leaping off the top of the engine and the black smoke that curled into the night sky. With no time to lose, he quickly took off his jacket and beat wildly on the bare, burning carburetor.

Less than a minute after Steve began battling the fire—inadvertently fanning the flames—an elderly man who lived in the house turned on his outside porch light to investigate. The aging gentleman peered out from the curtains, but then, only a moment later, he felt brave enough to step out onto his porch.

Steve glanced over at the man and presented a pleading look. Instead of the man extending sympathies to Steve, he bore a large grin on his face as devilish as the Grinch himself. Why wasn't the man offering assistance? Steve was desperate here, risking an outright explosion. Instead of assisting Steve, the man chuckled out loud and with great audacity laughed and said, "Ha, ha, ha! I just called the police. Ha, ha, ha!"

Panic then overtook Steve, and pure adrenaline coursed through his veins. In one violent exhibition, Steve beat at the top of the engine so hard that he finally extinguished the flames. With the police supposedly on their way, he slammed down the hood, and in sheer desperation, he raced a half a block home on foot. Fortunately, he solicited Tim's immediate help, and within seconds, they flew out the door and fired up Tim's '68 Torino.

Tim squealed the tires as he pulled out of the driveway and tore off down the street, ignoring the four-way stop. He made a quick loop behind the Death Machine, and with Steve out of the car and matching up the bumpers, the sirens from the emergency vehicles grew nearer and nearer. By this time, the old man had retired into the safety of his house, leaving Steve to deal with the wrath of the local police.

With bumper against bumper, Tim pushed the dead hulk down Hill Street with the Torino while Steve dead-sticked the Plymouth. Just past Mission Avenue, they swerved directly into the dark alleyway. As they reached the safety of the unlit alley, the fire truck and police car raced down Mission Avenue and came to a screeching halt at the four-way stop just before turning the corner to where the burning Death Machine once lay.

Steve and Tim were saved by only seconds.

The fire truck and patrol car whizzed up to the reported locale of the burning car. However, there was no car—just a chuckling old man peering out his window and taking a swig off his bottle of Geritol. It was time for him to change his Depends. And damn! The local police were fooled again.

After escaping a certain run-in with the cops, Tim and Steve ditched the car in a small space across the alley behind our house. Without letting Mom know a thing about the incident, they stole a large tarp off of her woodpile and covered up the Death Machine with it instead. Although it was safely resting in the alley, it had to be covered up because any passing patrol car that may have ventured down the alley would have recognized the car's cosmetics instantly. Even today, this episode is remembered as the most successful joint rescue effort ever experienced between the two brothers.

Later that evening, Steve and Tim seated themselves in front of the TV, munching on potato chips and watching the sequel to *Mad Max*—the movie *The Road Warrior* starring Mel Gibson. (And people wonder where the Major brothers got all their ideas.) Those two shows happened to be ones that Tim watched hundreds of times. Tim could recite any bit of dialogue in any part of either movie with complete accuracy. The skeptics that say Hollywood doesn't influence people are full of shit. Anyone who has seen these particular movies would easily see striking similarities between it and real life with the Death Machine. The only exception in this case was that no one got killed in Kellogg, and gasoline was in abundant supply.

After arriving so late from Fort Bragg and listening to Tim tell me of the recent mishap with the car, I fell asleep very quickly, and morning came just as quickly. The realities that I had to face were all too real. I had a dying father to deal with on one hand and a whacked-out automobile story on the other. I hurt deeply inside over my father's condition but found solace with my zest for life and adventure.

Luckily, when I awoke, I realized that Tim was already off at school, which gave me a chance to go back to sleep for a while. At noon, I climbed out of bed and was right in the middle of heating up a can of my favorite Snow's clam chowder when Tim promptly came home during his school lunch hour. It was then that he proudly gave me a demonstration of the Death Machine's unique features.

Tim could have started an awesome career as a Plymouth salesman. "Step right up, ladies and gentleman, and notice the ease of opening up this escape hatch. Even a child could do it." He probably wouldn't have done very well with Chevy or Ford, but the walk-around that he gave me on the Death Machine would have gotten him an instant job at Dave Smith Motors just a few blocks away.

With a hot bowl of chowder in my hand and my green army jacket zipped up tight, I stood in the driveway watching Tim systematically lift the hood of the car and point down at the engine exactly like Vanna White does on *The Wheel of Fortune* television game show. The exposed greasy blob that lay stuck between the two fender walls was barely recognizable as a power plant. There was no air cleaner. It had probably been lost years ago. But what difference would it make, anyway? Any clean air that got within ten feet of that engine would only get filthy itself.

After the initial walk-around, and in between my slurps of chowder, Tim climbed inside the car and sat behind the wheel. He pumped the accelerator several times before turning the key. The engine shook and rattled and finally roared to life. The cooling fan blew noxious vapors up and into my face, but worst of all was the distinct sound of a knocking connecting rod. I knew enough about engines to know that that wasn't good.

"Watch this!" Tim yelled above the noise of the engine. "We've got water injection."

He revved up the engine and turned on the windshield wiper spray. Instead of the water spraying onto the windshield, it sprayed through its tiny hose stuck directly into the throat of the carburetor. The engine immediately bogged down and gurgled. Tim responded by stomping on the gas. The engine subsequently roared with agony, choking on the water. Huge plumes of black smoke followed by clouds of water vapor poured out of the exhaust pipe and filled our entire driveway. Meanwhile, the knocking sound in the engine grew louder and more violent.

With the engine now cleansed internally with windshield wiper cleaner fluid, Tim shut off the water injection and revved the motor up higher than ever. Knock, knock, knock, knock, knock, knock, knock, knock, knock, knock, *ka-blam!*

Silence ensued as the dying echo of the once-speeding engine faded into the ethers. The engine had thrown a rod and burst a cavity out of the side of the engine block. The engine had stopped cold. Both Tim and I stared down at the engine compartment in total amazement. As the chowder dripped off my trembling spoon, Tim now gazed at me through the dust-laden windshield as if to ask, "What now?" He climbed out of the car and came over next to me. We looked down reverently at the mechanical wonder and put our hands over our hearts to honor our dead. We both knew that the car would never run again, ever.

Tim took the loss like a real man. "Oh, well. We knew it would happen sooner or later," he admitted.

"I'm surprised that it lasted this long sounding like that. How long did it knock like that?" I asked.

"Oh, it always made that sound," he replied. "Too bad I couldn't have taken you out for a ride in her."

Actually, I wouldn't have wanted to be caught dead in the thing. I spent my time in the Safari Wagon and risked my life and my driving record. I was nearly twenty years old now. He was the one still in high school and had to return before his lunch break was over. At least he had his beloved '68 Torino GT Fastback to drive away in.

Getting rid of the rotting carcass of the Death Machine became a little more complex than it should have been. First, Steve and Tim decide to part it out. Unfortunately, they had different ideas of what "half-ownership" meant. That became apparent a few days after the engine-blowing session. Steve had found a buyer for the battery and eagerly sold it for ten dollars. News of the transaction got around the high school community quickly, and Tim eventually found out about it secondhand. He raced home for lunch and confronted Steve in the kitchen.

At this time, I was busy pouring myself a bowl of chicken noodle soup when they both met in front of the kitchen sink.

"Okay, Steve, I heard that you sold the battery for ten bucks. I want five of that," Tim demanded.

Steve stood next to the kitchen counter and choked for a few seconds after taking a huge bite of his peanut butter sandwich. His eyes displayed bewilderment as the thoughts stirred in his mind. He finally swallowed the rest of his bite and found enough room in his mouth to speak.

"What? Are you crazy?" he asked.

"Give me five bucks!" Tim yelled.

"I'm not giving you shit! I'm the one who sold the battery."

Tim nervously rocked back and forth on the balls of his feet, ready to fight for what he felt was rightfully his. He made another attempt to reason with Steve. "Give me the five bucks. The car was half mine."

Steve kept as calm as he could and explained his philosophy. "Oh, no, that's not how it works. I sold the battery. You go sell the radiator. Whatever you sell, you keep."

"No way, man. Listen, you sucker! I want my five bucks now!" Tim pressed on.

I knew then that the tension between the two of them was mounting, so I stepped between them and ordered them to break it up. Maybe I shouldn't have done that, because I may have been the one responsible for making a fight out of it. Tim lunged at Steve, and I pushed him back.

"Let me at him! Let me at him!" Tim begged.

"Yeah, let him at me," Steve said as tossed the rest of his sandwich on the counter and stood back into a fighting stance.

I spent the next few moments attempting to be the peacemaker—that is, until Tim's temper didn't allow him to use logic any further. Steve had already graduated from high school and had gained a lot of weight, while Tim was still a scrawny little junior. I knew by his size and boxing experience that Steve could easily mutilate little Tim. That's exactly what he did the moment I relented and let Tim at him.

Tim dove in and gave a wild swing up toward his older brother's head, which missed. Steve threw several consecutive punches that all connected with Tim's face in rapid succession. *Crack, crack, crack!*

Tim absorbed all of the blows and fell backward onto the floor. He held his face with his hands and touched his mouth for a second with his index finger. After noticing the blood, he became filled with an uncontrollable rage. He climbed to his feet, preparing for another attack on Steve. I once again stepped between the two of them in an attempt to keep the peace. It was a no-win situation for Tim. Steve was just too big for him.

Just like before, Tim begged for a fight. "Let me at him! Let me at him!"

So I did.

Crack, crack, crack! Steve whaled on him again with the same eye-blackening and lip-busting results. Tim fell back for a second time, reaching for his face again. I personally winced, imagining the pain of a punched-in face. Instead of going for round three, Tim got to his feet and quickly retreated out the back door, slamming it behind him and almost breaking the glass. Steve looked at me soberly and simply shrugged his shoulders as he reached down to pick up his half-eaten peanut butter sandwich.

I was glad to have the violence stopped. Over the years, every one of us brothers had gone through the same thing. Steve versus me. Kit versus

Pete. Phil versus Kit. At this point, I felt relieved enough to sit back down at the kitchen table and finish my lunch; the fight was over.

Just as I started to slurp up the rest of my soup, I heard a couple of loud thuds followed by a few other crashing sounds. I ran over to the kitchen window next to Steve and looked outside. There stood Tim, in front of the Death Machine like a strong man at the carnival, swinging an eight-pound chopping maul at the engine helplessly sitting under the hood.

Steve followed me out the back door and stood on the patio with me as we watched the destruction. Tim knocked the carburetor off the engine, bashed the radiator a few times, and then mangled the alternator. After a few more blows, he then threw down the maul and barged rudely past Steve and I and into the house. I guess he didn't like an audience when he did his handiwork.

I was curious as to what Tim was planning next, but just as I entered the house through the back door, Tim rushed through the kitchen and exited out through the front door. I rushed to the living room window and witnessed a bloody-lipped and black-eyed Tim jumping into his Torino and heading back to school.

Although the Death Machine was quite dead, it now became time for someone to dispose of the body. The two fighting brothers had to share the responsibility of getting rid of it.

A day later, Tim, Allyson, my mother, and I drove over four hundred miles to Vancouver, British Columbia, to visit my dying father in a cancer ward at a Burnaby hospital. It didn't take me long to forget about the mischief my brothers were involved with back home.

On the night we arrived at my aunt's house in New Westminster (a suburb of Vancouver), I took a hot shower, shaved, and put on my freshly ironed dress uniform. From there, we drove to the hospital and parked the car. Once I stepped out of the elevator with Tim, Allyson, and my mother following me, I walked down the long hospital corridor sporting my maroon paratrooper's beret, my shiny jump wings, and the assortment of colorful decorations on my chest.

I had recently taken my jump boots to the cobbler in downtown Fayetteville to have metal taps installed on the heels. With my mother and youngest brother and sister in tow, I heard the metallic clicks of my heels echoing down the hallway with every step I took. The place smelled as cold and clinical as any hospital that I had ever been in.

The nurse led us into the room where my father lay. We stood next to his bed, and as my mother picked up his limp hand, he slowly opened his eyes, and they sparkled with excitement. It took him a moment to recognize me in uniform. Once he did, he glowed with pride over me. It was then that I resented the military because I chose it over my father and his dream for me to return to the beautiful British Columbian coast. For an hour we sat on the bed next to him making small talk, laughing and joking using humor to keep the atmosphere positive and upbeat. My father embraced his cancer with courage. He wasn't afraid or rattled in any way. I had never seen a person be more accepting of their fate than him. My mother held onto his hand and would from time to time stroke his hair as she kept the tears from dropping from her eyes. She was as tough as he was.

After that night, we only saw him a couple more times over that weekend until I had to return for duty at Fort Bragg. We all knew that he was a goner. But I never cried, although the pain was like a knife stuck in my heart. We were taught to shed no tears.

Two months later, my unit was to be deployed for our annual live-fire exercise at McGregor Range near White Sands, New Mexico. After showing up with all our equipment to board the planes at Pope Air Force Base, we were ordered to stand down for eighteen hours while a freak snowstorm battered the southern Texas area. In fact, the storm was so severe that an F-4 Phantom fighter jet had crashed during an emergency landing at El Paso International Airport. Since we were slated to jump, the weather conditions needed to be optimal. Back at my barracks, I waited in my room hour after hour with my thoughts more focused on the fate of my father than on the pending drop into New Mexico.

After a sleepless night listening to my roommate snore on the top bunk, we finally got the word to move out. A procession of trucks took us back to the air force base to a departure point known as Green Ramp. Typically, on local parachute drops we'd don our parachutes and sit on long benches waiting for our planes to taxi over. This time, since we were both way behind schedule and also making a long distance jump, the engines on the five camouflage-painted C-130 Hercules aircraft were already fired up. The props were spinning and the tailgates had been lowered down to the tarmac. As I ran up the aluminum ramp into the back of the plane dragging my full field pack and my M-16, the hot jet exhaust from the whining turbines blew into my face like a warm topical breeze. It smelled like burned kerosene—a scent that I'd never forget.

Hours later, while we were cruising at thirty thousand feet, I stood near the tail ramp of the plane putting on my parachute. As the plane descended, it buffeted, causing me to nearly fall while strapping on my reserve chute and attaching my rucksack below it. All of our drops were low level at a mere eight hundred feet and the pilot was slowly taking us down to that altitude. By the time we were all hooked up and near the drop zone, the two side doors of the plane creaked open as the hydraulic arms pushed them out of the way. The deafening roar of the high wind and four whining, turbo-prop engines blasted inside. Since I was the number two man in the stick (a single row of troops poised for a jump), I was close to the door and looked out only to see the cloud cover a few feet from the top of the plane. It was as if I could reach up and touch it with my own hands.

Now, the tricky part of making the final plunge out the door is to conquer your own fear, and you have to focus—and I mean *really* focus. We were all heavily laden with our main chute, reserve, and all of our combat gear. Not only were we nearly immobilized with the equipment, we had to mentally rehearse the emergency procedures over and over and over. At an altitude of sometimes less than eight hundred feet and with seventy-six feet of static line, parachute canopy, and suspension lines, you actually had only about seven hundred feet to react to a malfunction— mere seconds—or you were dead. It was only the intense focus on these procedures that kept my fear at bay.

The green light on the warning panel eventually flashed on and the jumpmaster, seeing that, immediately stepped back and yelled, "Go!" In a split second the guy in front of me disappeared. Since I was next, I instinctively lurched forward and pushed my static line and metal hook down the overhead steel cable toward the jumpmaster. I then turned and grabbed the sides of the opened door as I jumped up and out. With my chin tucked into my chest and my hands gripping the sides of my reserve, I felt the sudden drop. The violent wind whipped my face and body as I tumbled down into a very short free-fall. With my eyes wide open I saw the ground flash below me past the tips of my boots, then as I continued to roll I saw the tail of the plane streaming away from me, then it was the mountains off in the horizon. Finally, I caught another glimpse of the sky and the blossoming olive green parachutes. All of this flashed visually before me in seemingly slow motion. After a brief moment of suspense I felt a slight tugging on my shoulder harness like a fish nibbling on a hook. Suddenly with one hefty jerk my parachute opened and I found myself drifting along in an eerie silence. The roar of the plane was gone. I was relieved when I looked up and saw that my parachute had indeed fully opened. Then, just a few seconds later, the silence was broken as another C-130 screamed overhead with jumpers bailing out each of the side doors.

Looking down I realized that the ground was growing closer and closer with each second. I braced for impact as the earth raced up to me. Watching the ground approach so quickly was like suddenly pushing the fast forward button on a video recording. The right side of my body crashed into the ground and I rolled half way over in a sideways somersault before coming to a stop. I had made it. I breathed out with a huge sigh of relief knowing that I had touched down without breaking any bones. Next to me the parachute canopy, no longer having any weight to carry, drifted lazily down the ground just feet away.

It was a good jump. However, instead of landing in white sand like I thought I had seen from the door of the plane, I landed in four inches of freshly fallen snow. Unfortunately, I had left my field jacket back at Fort Bragg thinking that it would be hot in New Mexico. Silly me. Luckily, once we got assembled and situated at nearby McGregor Range, our commander kept us busy enough hour after hour, and day after day, setting up the equipment on the firing line for our unit's annual qualification. The continuous activity kept me plenty warm without my jacket. The snow soon melted and the blazing sun reclaimed its rightful position in the clear skies. As beautiful as it was it still wasn't enough to keep my thoughts away from my dying father. My soul ached endlessly wondering if I would ever see him again and if I would ever return to Canada if he died.

After two weeks on the range watching the live-fire of the 20mm Vulcan anti-aircraft gun, I wandered into the mess hall for dinner but found myself at great unrest. For some reason, I didn't even feel like eating. One of my friends, a tall, lanky Cajun from New Orleans, tried to cheer me up by pulling a small prank on me, which set me off instead. I lashed back and knocked his glass of milk over into his lap just before I dashed across the mess hall and out to the front steps. There, I was jumped by a lieutenant who caught me from running from the scene of trouble. Stopped dead in my tracks I couldn't even speak. No words would come out of my mouth.

"What's wrong, soldier?" he asked as if he realized something grave was wrong with me.

Still I could not speak.

"Let me take you to see the commander," he told me, and I nodded in agreement.

Somehow, my sixth sense alerted to me that something was wrong. When I was ushered into our captain's office, I simply reminded him that my father was dying, and I just didn't feel good about the whole thing. Instead of letting me fly out from El Paso the next morning, he promised to let me return home on leave as soon as we got back to Fort Bragg on Friday. I just had to do my job the best I could for the next three days.

Friday afternoon, after a four-hour flight home to North Carolina, the C-130 Hercules that carried me back came in low and slow over Normandy drop zone. This time, they had switched me to the number one man to lead the stick out the door because one of the new guys in front of me had pulled out a rosary and trembled with fear. It was one of his first jumps with the unit, and the jumpmaster feared that he might freeze up at a critical time during the drop. Since I had over eighteen months on jump status, they put me at the head of the stick. No problem.

After the green light flashed on and the jumpmaster yelled, "Go," I bailed out of the plane just as I had done three weeks earlier over the desert. This time, after my parachute opened, I found myself drifting head-on into another jumper. We both slipped hard to our right, and we brushed each other in the air only a few hundred feet above the ground. A collision like that killed PFC Clemens from Charlie Battery (and a new guy fresh out of jump school) just a year earlier when both parachutes collapsed. I was lucky this time.

Once on the ground and waiting to be bussed back to our barracks, the suspense was killing me. I simply wanted to call home. Instead, we had to wait for a half an hour while the same planes that had dropped us made a return pass just a few feet above the ground, "LAPESing" (Low Altitude Parachute Extraction System) our equipment down the tailgate and out the rear of the plane. The small drone chute blossomed behind the tail of the plane and dragged out one of our vehicles strapped to a large pallet. As the plane sped away, the package skidded through the dirt, violently bouncing along before it came to an abrupt halt in a cloud of dust and sand.

In the small bleachers at the edge of the drop zone were the top brass from Fort Bragg with some military dignitaries from Pakistan. They had come out to watch our arrival and were obviously impressed by the activity so far—clapping and then turning to each other to shake hands. Meanwhile, my friend Hausworth from Cincinnati had located his petite girlfriend and was busy hugging and kissing her almost squishing her with each embrace. She had driven thirty miles down from the small town of Sanford, a place where we would often get drunk and go dancing trying to forget that we were paratroopers for at least one night. Here I stood alone while the entire world was going on all around me. I was in sheer agony. I just wanted to call home.

Eventually we boarded a group of busses and headed back into base. Two hours later, after sitting around the barracks and having cleaned my M-16 and returned it to the arms room, I ran to the nearest pay phone just outside a small PX (post exchange—a small, military-run store). I called home collect, and Tim was the one who answered and accepted the charges.

"Hey, Tim. I just got back to Bragg!"

He paused for a moment and simply said, "Hey, man. Dad died on Tuesday."

When I asked what time, it immediately dawned on me that while sitting in that mess hall in that New Mexico desert a few days earlier, I did indeed know the very hour that he had died. I slumped but then leaned my head back to draw in a deep breath of air, attempting to maintain my composure. My vision began to blur as my eyes filled with water.

"We're going tomorrow morning to Vancouver for his funeral with the Canadian relatives, but then there's another service for him in Kellogg on Wednesday," he said.

"Shit. There's no way I can make it to Vancouver by tomorrow. But I'll definitely be home on Wednesday," I told him. Without much more to say, we both hung up and knew that our family had just witnessed an end of an era.

My life away in the military reminded me of Tristan's in the movie *Legends of the Fall*. He traveled the world, leaving behind the things so precious to him. In comparison, I had laughed and joked so much in my life about flirting with girls but never committing to any of them. But now, while away in the army, I had severely fallen for a girl back home, a beautiful strawberry blonde with deep, brown eyes, and the distance away from her tore my heart to pieces. I had left her as well as my dream of being in Canada behind, and all because of my uncontrollable lust of adventure. I had lost them both and had then come to realize that maybe there was a flaw in my philosophy, the unwritten rule that I had always lived by: be audacious—and if audacity gets you into trouble, even more audacity will get you out. However, sometimes it just doesn't work out that way, which I often found out.

The Death Machine lay motionless for quite some time in my mother's driveway after its death, as well as my father's. My mother finally pressured Steve and Tim to do something with the terrible eyesore. Thank goodness that blood is thicker than water, because my two feuding brothers eventually made up after their fight and worked once again on the car, this time to dispose of it.

With great pride, Steve and a friend of his friend acted as honorary pallbearers and towed the Death Machine to a stretch of dirt road a few miles outside of the city limits to a place called Gold Run. It was a spot where most of the local gun owners did their target practice, just past the community of Elizabeth Park.

Up a small gulch just above Gold Run lay a small wrecking yard called Gold Rush Auto Wrecking. When Steve and his friend arrived at the gate with the Death Machine in tow, the first question the owner asked was, "Do you have the title for the car?"

"No. This car was just given to us, and we never licensed it," Steve told him.

The guy scratched his chin and then shook his head and said, "I'm sorry, boys. I can't take the car without the title."

"Ah, come on. Can't you just use it for parts?" Steve asked.

"Nope. If you don't have the title, I can't take the car," the man insisted.

Left with two choices—take that car back home or abandon it—Steve chose to abandon it outside of the city limits. Why not? He wasn't the legal owner of the car, and this was rural Idaho. What's one little ole abandoned car going to hurt?

Less than a quarter mile away from the bottom of the gulch, Steve found a nice, deep, wide ravine to push the car into. Steve and his friend abandoned it in place and threw a symbolic handful of dirt onto it. Steve gave a eulogy that would have made any sensitive person cry. "God, we give you the Death Machine. In life, he loved little kitty cats, he loved garbage cans, and he especially loved telephone poles. You created the Death Machine as a very special car. We now return him to you. Hope he has fun in that big demolition derby in the sky."

Steve and his friend abandoned the car where he lay. After a few passing days of silence, Steve and Tim felt somewhat confident that the chapter of the Death Machine was truly over. Nothing could be further from the truth.

Although Gold Run is known for its target shooting, it is also known as a nice place to ride motorcycles. Andy Cooper found his way out there one day, racing around the dirt piles and climbing up the side of the hill on his motorcycle when he accidentally came across the lifeless Death Machine sitting lonely in a ditch. It was like the scene from the children's book *Are You My Mother?* when the little bird looks up to the abandoned car and asks that proverbial question. Sometimes Andy didn't act any smarter than that little bird.

Over the years of camping with him, Andy proved time and time again that he wasn't the brightest one in our gang. His ideas were usually a lot dumber than ours. (He was *so* dumb that it took him two hours to watch *60 Minutes!*). When he saw the wreck, he instantly thought of a way to liven things up a little at Gold Run. Somewhere out of the blue, the idea flashed into his brain that fire could somehow bring him satisfaction from his little outing.

Andy anxiously pulled the rubber fuel line off of his motorcycle's carburetor and drained some gasoline out of the tank and into an old plastic jug. He dumped the flammable liquid onto the seats and fabric inside the body of the lifeless Death Machine. A couple of matches later, it burst into a flaming mess. The car burned for a while and sent clouds of black smoke into the sky as Andy sped away on his little Honda, leaving nothing but a dust trail behind him and a blazing inferno onsite at Gold Run.

Soon enough, the Kellogg police, as well as the Shoshone County Sheriff's office, were notified. When they arrived on the scene, one of the local patrol officers from Kellogg instantly recognized the hulk as the one Steve and Tim had at our house on Mission Avenue.

After the fire was completely put out by the fire department, the police made a special trip to the Major residence and informed our mother that the car must be properly disposed of. Actually, it didn't even legally belong to Steve, but the pressure was on because ownership was nine-tenths of the law, and it had been in his possession. Besides, Jonesy was the nicest guy in town and shouldn't be bothered to deal with such trivial matters.

Fortunately, after being asked for the title, Jonesy searched and searched until he finally found it under a heap of garbage. This time when Steve towed the charred hulk back up the hill to Gold Rush Auto Wrecking, the owner of the junkyard got a lot less than if he would have just taken it the first time. After looking at the blackened mess and scratching his chin and shaking his head just like the time before, the owner reluctantly took the decimated remains of the old green Plymouth. It was there that the Death Machine final met his maker.

Epilogue

I ended up reenlisting in the army since I no longer had a place to return to in Canada. I spent nearly seven years in the military, and each time I returned home on leave, I watched the once-vibrant Kellogg continually fade into oblivion as the economy sank deeper and deeper with each mining company that went out of business. I will forever tell the true stories of what transpired there during my youth, for I believe that it has always been my mission.

As the rest of my siblings became of age and left home, my mother inspired all nine of us to go onto college and receive higher educations since she had been a teacher her entire career and wholeheartedly believed in it. More than her coaching, it was my oldest brother, Pete, who, after having been so inspired by my father's thirst for greatness, pushed each of us siblings to try to reach our true potential. It was I, Anthony, who always resisted any direction. I had my own path to follow.

During my lifelong search for my own personal holy grail (the one that would give my life meaning), I have always remembered the words of a sixth-century Chinese poet. I had actually quoted this poem during my graduation speech in 2002 at Grays Harbor College when I was the student president addressing my class in the midst of the commencement ceremony:

> *The great way has no gate. There are a thousand paths leading to it. But pass through the barrier and you walk the universe alone.*

> —Wu Men

My philosophy is that you go out and you find your own wind. You damn the torpedoes. You overcome whatever obstacle is holding you back, and then you go forth courageously. Then you will truly walk the universe alone.

Although the events of my life have baffled some people, intrigued others, and confused many more, I still have never wavered from my deepest desire to simply let others know that the greatest gift that each of us can bestow upon the world is ourselves. So go forward and fear nothing.

Remember, life is nothing but a story.

My siblings and I attended the following colleges:

Peter
- Montana Tech School of Mines, Butte, Montana AAS (Engineering)
- Montana Tech School of Mines, Butte, Montana BS (Engineering)
- Cape Town University, Cape Town, South Africa MBA (Business Administration)

Kit
- North Idaho College, Coeur d' Alene, Idaho (Diesel Mechanics)
- Montana Tech School of Mines, Butte, Montana (Engineering)
- University of Idaho, Moscow, Idaho BS (Engineering)
- Idaho State University, Pocatello, Idaho MBA (Business Administration)

Jeri-anne
- Idaho State University, Pocatello, Idaho BA (Education)
- University of Montana, Missoula, Montana MA (Education)

Philip
- Montana Tech School of Mines, Butte, Montana BS (Engineering)

Kimmerly
- North Idaho College, Couer d' Alene, Idaho (Nursing)
- Whitworth College, Spokane, Washington (Paralegal)

Anthony (Okay, so I got around.)
- Fayetteville State University, Fayetteville, North Carolina (Literature)
- Grays Harbor College, Aberdeen, Washington AA (Business Administration)
- Saint Martin's University, Lacey, Washington (Finance)

- Washington State University, Pullman, Washington (Finance)
- University of Idaho, Moscow, Idaho (Psychology)

Stephen
- Boise State University, Boise, Idaho BA (Political Science)
- Eastern Washington University, Cheney, Washington (International Relations)

Timothy
- University of Witwatersrand, Johannesburg, South Africa BS (Business Administration)

Allyson
- North Idaho College, Coeur d' Alene, Idaho (English and Music)
- University of Witwatersrand, Johannesburg, South Africa (English)